WATCHING THE TRAFFIC GO BY

WATCHING THE TRAFFIC GO BY

Transportation and Isolation in Urban America

PAUL MASON FOTSCH

UNIVERSITY OF TEXAS PRESS, AUSTIN

Requests for permission to reproduce material from this work
should be sent to: Permissions, University of Texas Press,
P.O. Box 7819, Austin, TX 78713-7819
www.utexas.edu/utpress/about/bpermission.html

♾ The paper used in this book meets the minimum requirements of
ANSI/NISO Z39.48-1992 (R1997) (Permanence of Paper).

LIBRARY OF CONGRESS CATALOGING-IN-PUBLICATION DATA

Fotsch, Paul Mason, 1965–
    Watching the traffic go by : transportation and isolation in urban America /
Paul Mason Fotsch. — 1st ed.
        p.   cm.
    Includes bibliographical references and index.
    ISBN-13: 978-0-292-71425-0 (cloth : alk. paper)
    ISBN-10: 0-292-71425-4 (cloth : alk. paper)
    ISBN-13: 978-0-292-71426-7 (pbk. : alk. paper)
    ISBN-10: 0-292-71426-2 (pbk. : alk. paper)
        1. Transportation engineering—United States.   2. City and town life—
United States.   3. Popular culture—United States.   I. Title.
    TA1023.F68   2006
    388.40973—dc22
                                                                                          2006008602

DEDICATED TO THE BUS RIDERS OF URBAN AMERICA

CONTENTS

ACKNOWLEDGMENTS

Individual responsibility is a powerful myth, but most of us recognize that individuals are a product of community. This project was fifteen years in the making, and I thank the thousands who have contributed to my understanding of urban space. Here I will name but a few.

Great teachers are often underrecognized among academics, and I have had many. They include Michael Forster, Marshall Sahlins, George Steinmetz, Marilyn Ivy, Dan Schiller, Herb Schiller, Andrew Goodwin, Val Hartouni, Tom Long, John Caldwell, and especially Moishe Postone, who taught me most of what little I know about the Frankfurt School. The University of California at San Diego provided a diverse community of activists and intellectuals. Groundwork Bookstore and the Communication Department had their share of both. Friends and colleagues from my time at UCSD who carried me through the bogs include Sharla Blank, Jackie Romo, Mary Garbesi, Rick Bonus, Sarah Banet-Weiser, Mari Castañeda Peredes, Dee Dee Halleck, Keith Pezzoli, Michael Schudson, David Ryfe, and Susan Sterne. Suzanne Thomas, Corynne McSherry, Tamera Marko, and Marita Sturken generously commented on various chapter drafts.

While I was at Arizona State University, my friends in the Bachelor of Interdisciplinary Studies program helped keep me cool. At California State University, Monterey Bay, I benefited from a uniquely engaged campus. Within the Division of Humanities and Communication, I drew encouragement especially from Josina Makau, Debian Marty, and Renee Curry, while Elizabeth Ross and Gabe Brahm introduced me to Monterey Bay's quirky community. One could not ask for better colleagues than are found in the California State University, Northridge Communication Studies Department, and I want to thank especially Peter Nwosu, Ben Attias, Tony Perucci, and our extraordinary office manager, Yoly Avila. Of the numerous librarians I have relied upon, special thanks go to Antonio Calvo and Jacqueline Solis.

I often learn as much from my students as they learn from me, and the CSU system attracts some of the best. Jessica Sanchez, Melissa Reyes, Greg Grio, Lee Stokes, Bonnie Rodezno, Derek Still, Carrie Iino, Nareg Bardakjian, Dewi Villasenor, and Maggie Rojas are just a few who have shared their truths with me. I also benefited from the research of graduate students who include Claudia Franco, Melanie Hillard, and Sachi Sekimoto. The assistance of Chun-Lan Hsu made final revisions pure joy.

A few close friends were always there when I needed their expertise. Alexander Juutilainen was a technological wizard and Frankfurt School authority; Tamara Falicov helped me through the publishing process; Jeffrey Bass gave me the social anthropologist's viewpoint; Chloe Burke was my source for all things U.S. history; Steve Dubb wrote detailed comments on nearly every chapter. My heroes are friends who combine warmth with a deep commitment to social justice. Joel Woller acts locally and thinks globally; Rekha Banerjee keeps me rooted in the feminist ground; James Warden is my bodhisattva; Ben Evans fights for U.S. political prisoners; Lara Vinnard defends the reviled. The creativity and productivity of Samantha Barbas and filmmaker/executive/social worker Julia D'Amico motivated and inspired me. The Reverends Peter Boehlke, Nancy Landauer, and Kay Barré gave me spiritual sustenance.

Having a network of friends native to Los Angeles and New York helped guide me through these cities' intricacies. From Los Angeles, I thank Corina Kellner, Mary Romo, Rachel Mayeri, and especially Fazila Bhimji, whose knowledge is rooted in more than a decade of urban activism. Those who helped make New York a second home include Chris Pearson; Sikay Tang; Andrea, Linda, and Jeff Stewart; Stuart Rockefeller; Anjali Grant; Gregg Miller; and above all, Scott Wilhelme and Lynn Underwood, who let me stay with them countless times. Words cannot express all that Lynn has given me, but a pug named Wassily is a start.

Members of my dissertation committee gave trenchant criticisms of my work. They include Robert Horwitz, Susan Davis, and Jim Holston. Vince Rafael, my chair, continually pushed me to rethink key concepts and retain a critical tension throughout the study. At the same time, he was always there for encouragement as I moved toward publication. George Lipsitz is the quintessential generous scholar. So many times when I was ready to abandon this project, it was George who gave me the confidence to continue. Additional people who have incisively commented on the manuscript in part or in whole include Norman Denzin, Robert D'Amico, Alex Marshall, E. C. Barksdale, and João Vargas, whose knowledge of the history, theory, and politics of cities is encyclopedic. Needless to say, all errors of fact or interpretation are my responsibility.

I owe my love of the city and dislike of suburbia to my parents. My mother, Marcia, sent me to St. Paul's diverse public schools and introduced me to the music of Billie Holiday. My father, Harold, lived a few stops down on the Selby-Lake bus line and stayed there for thirty years in part due to my late stepmother, Judie, a city girl who was born among southern European immigrants in St. Paul's floodplains. I am also blessed by a crazy bunch of loving siblings. Tom White taught me more than he knows about city life. Chris and Dori Fotsch hosted me in Thousand Oaks whenever I visited L.A. I also thank Jim, Margaret, Lisa, Jen, Steve, Dave, Heike, Tony, Eric, Christine, Mark, Lori, and too many nieces and nephews to list. Thanks also to St. Paul natives Joe and Shirley Ferraro and my stepmother Donna Harrington.

Finally, I must acknowledge my editors at University of Texas Press. Alex Barron first took interest in the manuscript and carried it through initial reviews. Jim Burr confidently took over in midstream. Both made the process of publishing a first book transparent and as painless as possible.

Many thanks go to the following for permission to use previously published materials.

An earlier version of Chapter 3 was published in *Cultural Critique* 48 (spring 2001). Reprinted by permission of the University of Minnesota Press.

Portions of Chapter 4 were published as "Film Noir and Automotive Isolation in Los Angeles" in *Cultural Studies – Critical Methodologies* 5, no. 1 (February 2005). Reprinted by permission of Sage Publications.

Portions of Chapter 6 were published as "Contesting Urban Freeway Stories: Racial Politics and the O. J. Chase," *Cultural Studies* 13, no. 1 (January 1999). Reprinted by permission of Taylor and Francis, www.tandf.co.uk.

Excerpt from Nathanael West, *Miss Lonelyhearts & The Day of the Locust,* copyright 1939 by Estate of Nathanael West. Reprinted by permission of New Directions Publishing Corp.

Excerpt from Pearl E. Levinson, "World of Tomorrow," printed in *The Official Poem of The New York World's Fair, 1939.* Reprinted by permission of the Academy of American Poets.

WATCHING THE TRAFFIC GO BY

INTRODUCTION: STABILIZING MOBILITY

In the fall of 1991 I moved from Hyde Park, a neighborhood on the south side of Chicago, to University City on the northern edge of San Diego. In Hyde Park, where the University of Chicago is located, many people walk to campus, local coffee shops, or grocery stores. In University City, adjacent to the University of California, San Diego, people largely travel by automobile, even when going shopping at stores only a few—albeit long—blocks from home. University City is a classic example of what Joel Garreau (1992) calls an "Edge City": it contains central elements of a city—shopping centers, office buildings, and homes—but is at the periphery of an older city. These new cities are designed to accommodate the automobile with wide roads and large parking lots, and this accommodation can make walking inconvenient, even hazardous. A large number of Americans live in neighborhoods of this sort, and a large majority rely on the automobile as their form of transportation.[1] For me, the landscape felt sterile and, without a car, isolating. It seemed odd to me that people would choose to spend so much time in their vehicles.

During my first spring in San Diego I watched television when every news station in Los Angeles and San Diego broadcast via helicopters an uprising that followed the acquittal of police officers who had brutally beaten an African American motorist. During this uprising, certain exits of the Harbor Freeway were closed to shield drivers from the violence erupting in surrounding neighborhoods. This event revealed a link between the individual isolation provided by a transportation form and the isolation of a group. On the one hand, the attack on Rodney King indicated a penalty for African Americans who travel outside predominantly black neighborhoods. On the other, the closing of the freeway evoked the separation of these neighborhoods from drivers passing through Los Angeles, and the broadcast of the Reginald Denny beating warned whites of what could happen if they failed to bypass these neighborhoods.

Like the individual isolation of the automobile, the social isolation of low-income African Americans and Latinos/as has become naturalized for a large part of America. The idea that one segment of the population has rates of unemployment and poverty significantly higher than average is a distant problem for most of the United States—a problem that briefly became salient in the aftermath of the uprising (Williams 1993).[2] These disparities are tolerated because they are seen as unconnected to the lives of those who inhabit the "edge cities" or suburbs of the United States. Narratives that promote a reliance on the automobile support this disconnection.

This study focuses on the narratives that built and continue to sustain support for the automobile-centered city in the United States. I answer the question of why it was popular to allow freeways to restructure cities, while allowing mass transit to decline, by considering examples of popular culture—from turn-of-the-century magazines to contemporary television—that reveal the dominant attitude toward developments in urban transportation. By "dominant" I do not simply mean the attitude held by most city residents; the key is that this attitude was held among those who had the most power to implement changes in a city's infrastructure. This group varied in its size and composition over time, and the struggle to construct and maintain these changes varied in its difficulty. The political and economic history of urban transportation is central to understanding which discourses surrounding urban transportation had the most power, and I draw extensively on many excellent histories of the automobile's rise.[3] However, my question is not primarily who bought the cars and how they built the roads, but why these choices were appealing.

The answer to this question begins by recognizing the historical and geographical context out of which new transportation forms arose. Since the end of the nineteenth century, the American city has been a place of dramatic change for longtime residents and new arrivals. These changes have been enabled in part by innovations in transportation and communication that evolved with each other's aid. The telegraph increased the efficiency of the railroad by allowing rapid notification of trains or other problems down the track (Carey 1989: 215). The railroad in turn provided the right of way for construction of telegraph lines. Trains also dramatically increased distribution efficiency, making large-scale factory production more economical (Trachtenberg 1982: 59). This accelerated the demand for industrial laborers, and the establishment of steamship service across the Atlantic meant that a large number of these laborers could be brought from Europe (Daniels 1990: 185–186).

Economic growth had physical and social impacts on the industrial city. Pollution and overcrowding strained municipal resources. Established residents of the city were forced to confront a large foreign-born population speaking different languages and following different traditions. Immigrants not only encountered a foreign language but also a strange environment and new daily demands. Those coming from rural backgrounds were now required to work according to the factory clock rather than the demands of the agricultural season. Moreover, frequent downturns in the industrial economy led to periods of unemployment (Trachtenberg 1982: 90–91).

For both new and longtime residents of the city, the modern economy's transformation of consumption could also be disorienting. The new ready-made form that commodities took in the nineteenth century proved mysterious for urban residents familiar with purchasing goods directly from producers (ibid.: 122). When the railroad carried commodities to the city, it concealed the locale and conditions under which the commodity was produced (Schivelbusch 1986: 40). In addition, the telegraph conveyed information on the quantity and price of a commodity independently of its arrival, so the cost of an item became separated from the wage of the laborer who produced it. The near-simultaneous communication between cities along with the rapid distribution of goods by the railroad permitted the development of a national trade in commodities. As James Carey (1989) points out, the decontextualization of markets from space allowed by the telegraph is a primary element in what Karl Marx called "commodity fetishism." For the urban consumer, this meant goods were dramatically severed from their conditions of production, adding to the unfamiliar nature of the nineteenth-century city.

Industrial capitalism also brought tremendous disparities in wealth that marked themselves upon the city. They could be seen in the difference between the overcrowded and poorly maintained tenements near the factories and the fashionable apartment buildings at a distance from the noise and smoke of industry. As Gunther Barth (1980: 20–21) notes, the city provided a place for those who had become rich in the new economy to display their newfound wealth, and stories of how people suddenly became rich fueled the poor's belief that social mobility was possible. At the same time, the disparity in wealth along with poor working conditions inspired frequent social unrest among the working class, and strikes often led to violence.[4]

After such discord peaked at the turn of the twentieth century, the modern city remained a place of rapid change. National policy dramatically limited immigration in 1924, but cities continued to grow from internal migration, especially by southern blacks escaping the violence of Jim Crow and searching for economic opportunity. Industrial cities faced economic decline during the Great Depression from which they never really recovered. With the economic boom sparked by World War II, industry began to locate primarily on the urban periphery, and many middle- and working-class whites moved along with it. Excluded from the suburbs, people of color remained in central cities, which continued to decline and became associated with crime and hopelessness (Beauregard 2003; Sugrue 1996). Since the 1980s, cities have gone through yet another major transformation: improved transportation and communication have allowed the global decentralization of production and centralization of business services in a few large cities such as Chicago and New York. The growth in both high- and low-skilled service jobs has attracted the greatest immigration wave since the turn of the century (Sassen 1991).

In all these transformations of the modern city, mobility has played an important role. Immigration and improved distribution fed the industrial city's growth, and the relocation of industry to the suburbs led to its decline. The globalization of production fostered the increased diversity of urban populations as well as the inequalities among these populations. Urban planning emerged in the late nineteenth century in response to the physical and social problems this mobility created for cities. Transportation's concrete connection to daily life made it one element of planning that was easy to grasp. Thus, new transportation forms became popular because many viewed them as helping to calm the instabilities of the modern city. In this narrative, *as a form of mobility, transportation could help stabilize the turbulence of modern mobility.*

As will become clear, the narrative resolutions found in these transportation plans affirmed inequalities of race, class, and gender, and the implementation of these plans helped sustain these inequalities. In the most striking example, freeways became part of federally subsidized postwar suburbanization that drained central city resources while largely excluding people of color and isolating women. Yet it is important to emphasize that transportation forms did not by themselves have specific impacts. Rather, it was the way these forms were used, symbolically and physically, that encouraged particular social consequences. It is the malleability of technology—the fact that its impact is not predetermined—that makes the discourses surrounding it important.

No claim is made that the texts studied here manipulated the public and policy makers into transforming the urban landscape. However, it is assumed that changes in the social world cannot be understood apart from discursive struggles. Ernesto Laclau and Chantal Mouffe (1989) still provide one of the best elucidations of this view. They argue that elements of the social cannot be predefined or given a specific causal effect because they do not exist outside the symbolic. Being part of the symbolic means that elements of the social "lack an ultimate literality which would reduce them to necessary moments of an immanent law" (98). Since social elements are also symbolic elements, there is no separation between the discursive and the material realm: "Every object is constituted as an object of discourse, insofar as no object is given outside every discursive condition of emergence" (107).

For example, in the view of a traffic engineer, a behavioral law can be formed through observation that determines when the installation of a traffic signal will improve the flow of automobile traffic through an intersection. The argument is not that the traffic engineer lacks predictive capacity but that the logic behind a signal's installation relies upon discursive elements. The engineer views one of these elements, the intersection, as a space to speed cars through. But it could also be viewed as a place to speed bicyclists and pedestrians through or as a meeting place for individuals, as in William Foote Whyte's *Street Corner Society* (1981). The street intersection—a material part of the built environment—is a part of multiple contested discourses. Thus, the logic of the traffic engineer rests upon meanings that are unstable and contested.

The value of studying cultural forms is found in their ability to provide a window into how some people make sense of the world. At the same time, to the extent the ideals presented in these texts correspond to how the city is constructed, they also reveal how its construction is legitimized. The texts studied here were chosen in large part for their consistency with how urban transportation evolved. Especially in the early chapters, the focus is on popular representations of urban transportation. These representations resemble closely—even predict—major elements of transportation design. For the later chapters, the focus is less on the representation of transportation as imagined than on transportation as built, and the texts studied make salient an element of urban life that has become naturalized, taken for granted—in other words, hegemonic.

These hegemonic narratives are also unstable, and the meanings that are linked to urban plans and urban forms are continually being contested. In part this is because a discourse can never be complete; there will always be gaps between narrative constructions of the world and the world as experienced, leaving open the possibility for struggle. In his essay on "Walking in the City," Michel de Certeau (1984) notes a gap between urban space as designed and as used. Within this gap can be found the failures of strategies constructed by professional planners and politicians to resolve the problems of the city and a space for resistance to the hierarchy inscribed in these strategies. For example, in an attempt to attract middle-class riders back to the New York subway, the Metropolitan Transit Authority instituted policies to eliminate the "chaos" of panhandlers and graffiti writers; but the homeless continued to find spaces to sleep in subway tunnels, and graffiti writers began scratching their tags into fiberglass windows instead of using felt-tipped pens. Struggles over the use of urban space impact the narratives constructed around cities, just as the narratives inspired the strategies used to control urban space: graffiti came to epitomize the subway's decline, which inspired an obsession with its elimination.

This study explores the evolution of urban transportation through the interaction between the discursive and the material. As suggested by de Certeau, what makes the study of discourses surrounding urban forms fascinating is their material embodiment in the city. Walking, driving, or taking a train through the city becomes like reading a book. The form of transportation does not dictate its use or how it is understood, just as the words of a text do not dictate their interpretation. However, one can argue that particular uses and interpretations are encouraged.[5]

Challenges to transportation systems may appear in clearly linguistic forms such as in films or books, but they also may take place through practices that are equally symbolic, such as gathering a crowd on a freeway or spitting gum on the floor of a subway car, which in itself can be linked to political change. The hope is that the wide-angle perspective taken here encourages others to pursue what might be called an urban dialectic. This is an approach to the study of the city that telescopes from the micropractices of surviving in the city to the macropolitics of national policy—a telescoping enabled by their commensurability as symbolic actions stabilizing or destabilizing urban narratives.

While my intention is to infuse urban space with political and cultural meaning, in this project I do not attempt to analyze space at the subtle and complex level imagined by Lefebvre in his influential *The Production of Space* (1991). At the same time, like Lefebvre, I emphasize how the built environment is simultaneously symbolic and material. Furthermore, following Lefebvre I argue that the symbolic and material construction of space is a product of and a response to particular histories—in this case, the histories of U.S. industrial cities. Lefebvre suggests that space includes the interaction of the perceived, "spatial practice"; the conceived, "representations of space"; and the lived, "representational spaces." By this he means first, that space plays functional roles, which members of society *perceive* and negotiate. Second, professionals or others seeking to legitimate the dominant social order *conceive* the rationale for particular spatial developments. Finally, people create ways of *living* in space that may or may not conform to the way space is perceived or conceived (38–39).

While these three elements are always simultaneously interacting with one another, the present study focuses primarily on two dynamics. First, I consider how representations of space, the dominant conceptions of how transportation should serve the modern city, are translated into spatial practices, the roads and transit systems that become part of the everyday operation of U.S. cities. Second, representational spaces, the activity of artists, writers, and residents, are examined as a response to the conceived ideals, the representations of space, and the material workings, the spatial practices, of urban transportation.

To put it in slightly different terms, the organization of this study follows loosely the evolution from the revising of ideal models to the resistance against built environments. The chapters are grouped into three parts corresponding to three historical time frames and, more importantly, different moments in this process of revision and resistance. Part I concerns the period of the automobile's initial rise to prominence at the turn of the twentieth century. Models are first being conceived of how new forms of transportation will benefit the twentieth-century city. The automobile emerged at the same time that trolley lines were being constructed throughout American cities. In Chapter 1 I argue that the popularity of both the trolley and the automobile must be understood in the context of their appearance in the late nineteenth century, at a time of rapid industrialization, urbanization, and immigration. These factors led to suburbanization and its potential restorative aspects; transportation developments succeeded for parallel reasons. By looking at magazine articles from the turn of the century I find the eagerness to ride on the trolley and drive an automobile was about not just a desire to travel from city to country but also to control an increasingly mechanized world. Ultimately, the choice of the car over the trolley better served to stifle the radicalism provoked by this world.

When automobiles surpassed trolleys as a form of transportation, traffic congestion became a problem that new plans for the city had to address. In Chapter 2 I look closely at Benton MacKaye and Lewis Mumford's (1931) description of "townless highways" and its embodiment in Radburn, New Jersey. This description and this town influenced the way automobiles would be incorporated into future suburbs. Although Lewis Mumford is best known as a critic of the automobile, some of his early writings show a desire to have it resolve urban problems that he, like other supporters of decentralization, saw as the root of American cultural decline. Ironically, MacKaye and Mumford's design inspired suburbs that developed in a manner antithetical to their garden city ideals. Furthermore, the influence of their plans possibly hindered the type of democratic participation they hoped to encourage.

Part II follows the entrenchment of the urban highway at midcentury accompanied by artifacts of the highway's popularization and a few voices of dissent. Chapter 3 looks at Futurama, an exhibit at the 1939 World's Fair sponsored by General Motors and designed by Norman Bel Geddes. The Futurama exhibit, perhaps more than any other promotional event, helped to popularize the concept of an interstate highway system that was realized with the passage of the 1956 Interstate Highway Act. An exploration of the exhibit finds not only resonance with the earlier narratives about escaping signs of the modern city but an attempt to address increased fears of social and economic instability. The context of greater government intervention in the economy and the rise of European fascism provide part of the logic behind applying the pessimistic cultural analysis of Max Horkheimer and Theodor Adorno (1944/1989) to GM's Futurama exhibit. Equally important, GM's utopian exhibit epitomized what Horkheimer and Adorno considered the dangerous parallels between the methods of U.S. capitalism and fascism.

Chapter 4 follows the critical theory of Horkheimer and Adorno from the freeway vision of the Futurama to the freeway reality of Los Angeles. While GM exhibited a plan for a future designed around the automobile, this future was already taking place to a large extent in Southern California. Since the automobile-designed city was to become the standard, it is interesting to look at its prototype in 1940s Los Angeles. Horkheimer and Adorno wrote *Dialectic of Enlightenment* after shifting their exile from New York to Los Angeles, and I argue that their book's pessimism has parallels to the pessimism found in two examples of *film noir* directed by Billy Wilder, a pessimism that can be read in the rise of the automobile's dominance in Los Angeles.

Part III concludes with two studies of the dominant transportation form's contemporary legacy and moments of resistance to this legacy. Chapter 5 turns back from Los Angeles to New York to find the history of U.S. abandonment of public transportation—and by implication of central cities— marked on the New York subway system. Yet in the 1990s, the subway became one element in a story of New York's revitalization. The revitalization took place in the context of an increasingly global economy; thus New York's subways can also be read as a reflection of the economy's impact on urban space. The politics of New York's transformation have entailed new forms of erasure and repression but also new forms of resistance and gaps for expression. I will look at the renovation of the New York subways both as embodying the urban politics that helped form what has been called a "dual city" and as a project where older forms of public interaction and public discourse have the potential to take place.

Los Angeles is an appropriate setting for the concluding chapter because it contains the quintessential U.S. urban transportation landscape. Moreover, by focusing on the freeway chase of O. J. Simpson in the summer of 1995, I show how the interaction between the dominant urban transportation system—the freeway—and the dominant medium for public discourse—the television—helps to articulate the deeply racialized politics that exist in the United States today. These politics are exemplified by the success of large capital interests in aligning themselves with the white working and middle class to form what Edsall and Edsall (1991) call a "top down coalition," or what might be seen in Gramscian terms as a hegemonic bloc. Significant to enabling this coalition was the postwar subsidization of the suburban white lifestyle, including the construction of interstate freeways. Thus I return to the themes that began this introduction to show that the naturalization of the automobile might be linked to the naturalization of racial privilege.

PART 1

TRANSPORTATION AS ANTIDOTE
TO MODERN CITY

■ ■

CHAPTER 1

THE TROLLEY, THE AUTOMOBILE, AND AUTONOMY

We have endured two generations of racket. We have driven progress at high pressure. Professor Orton some time ago suggested that as steam power went out we should pass into a period of more quiet and peace—a period of progress of a more equable sort. The indications are all that way.

THE INDEPENDENT 1903B: 1048

The Independent has chronicled with great pleasure the remarkable revolution in social affairs achieved by the rural telephones, by rural free mail delivery, and by the electric trolley. We believe that in the automobile we have the beginning of a revolution which will surpass all the rest.   *THE INDEPENDENT* 1903A: 1162

The above quotes from a popular American religious magazine celebrate the arrival of the trolley and automobile to urban America at the turn of the century. On one level this celebration is based on the hope that these new forms of transportation will benefit the physical environment of the city. In contrast to the steam railroad, electric rail is quiet and smooth; it lacks the soot and smoke of the steam engine. "The trolley comes without noise: it is a still force, an expression of immense power, without the boastfulness of steam. This will count greatly in the coming age, when the high-strung nerves of the American people will demand a chance to react and gather tone" (*The Independent* 1903b: 1048). The trolley seems to be the antidote to the "racket" of the industrial city. The automobile likewise brings environmental and public health benefits to urban residents. It would lead to "the entire banishment of the horse from city streets—a measure much to be hoped for on the score of cleanliness and health" (*The Independent* 1903a: 1163).

On another level, the praise these articles give to the trolley and auto-mobile comes from a belief in their positive social impact. The editors of *The Independent* use the language of revolution to describe this impact. The trolley is viewed as signaling the beginning of a new age, "a period of more quiet and peace," and bringing "progress of a more equable sort." The auto-mobile is described as part of a "revolution in social affairs" that other tech-nologies, including the trolley, have aided in creating. Moreover, the auto-mobile would, according to *The Independent*, even surpass the trolley in its revolutionary effect.

It is no surprise that *The Independent* uses an emancipatory tone to dis-cuss the trolley and automobile. Founded in 1848 by Congregationalists to fight slavery, under the editorship of Henry Ward Beecher it had pressured President Lincoln to issue the Emancipation Proclamation during the Civil War (Tebbel 1969). But the attitude expressed by *The Independent* was also in concert with most magazines emerging in the late 1890s and first decade of the twentieth century. As Matthew Schneirov (1994) notes, during this period before the emergence of the radio, magazines reached their peak as the first nationally distributed form of mass communication. The titles that rose to prominence in this era—*McClure's*, *Cosmopolitan*, and *Munsey's*— became famous for their social crusades and their promotion of new techno-logical developments. Both of these elements are reflected in the articles on transportation from *The Independent*. Moreover, the popularity of the new "ten cent magazines" even inspired periodicals such as *Atlantic Monthly* and *Harper's*, which usually kept to "serious" literature, to take on social issues and popularize new technologies.

The prevalence of these topics corresponded to an increasing interest on the part of middle-class reformers in addressing problems of the city. Rapid industrialization had dramatically impacted the environmental and social conditions of the late-nineteenth-century city. New industries brought noise, smoke, and soot to the city, and the rapid increase in laborers required by these industries strained material resources. New migrants faced inadequate housing, poor sanitation facilities, and a lack of open space. At the same time, economic downturns, like the depression of 1893, led to periods of wide-spread unemployment and poverty, while industrialists like John D. Rocke-feller used ruthless tactics to acquire fortunes. It is in this context that middle-class readers of popular magazines supported various urban reforms, such as the expansion of new forms of transportation.[1]

Many writers viewed improved transportation as helping to restore a Jeffersonian ideal of democracy to the city. According to this ideal, the small farmer's ability to work on land he owned taught him to think independently

and enabled him to participate in a representative government.[2] Urban reformers saw the physical and social conditions of the city as a threat to this
ideal. Significantly, while both the trolley and the automobile were viewed as
helping to reconstruct rural values that the city discouraged, ultimately the
automobile was described as more effective in this reconstruction. Narratives
surrounding the automobile went further than those surrounding the trolley
in addressing problems of the industrial city. A key part of the automobile's
superior attraction was its ability to displace the problems of economic inequality with problems of individual responsibility. While the trolley revealed
class conflict within its space and in the struggle over its ownership, the automobile placed responsibility on the individual for geographical and social
mobility away from city slums.

ELECTRICITY CALMS STEAM

Not a little emphasis is to be placed on the fact that electric trolley cars
are dissociated from the noise of the steam car. As a matter of health,
especially brain health, this is quite as important for the residents along
the route as for the passengers. How we have endured the brain racking
rout of steam is difficult to understand. It has much to do with nervous
exhaustion and insanity. In all ways the trolley is to be welcomed as
associated with an age of peace and order. Steam has performed mir-
acles: it has much yet to do: yet electricity presents itself to us as a
moral and intellectual potency as well as physically the superior force.
(*The Independent* 1901: 1996)

Before it was compared with the automobile, the trolley was compared with
the steam engine. The railroad began being used for commuting to the rural
outskirts of the city in the mid-nineteenth century. The attraction, as Peter
Schmitt (1990) makes clear, was an idealized image of rural living. The atmosphere of the country and the pleasures provided by its beauty were separated from the labor of working on a farm and the additional inconven-
iences the lack of plumbing and heating created.[3] In fact, on average the
comforts and conveniences of the suburban home surpassed those found
in the city, since new building standards required features that urban structures, most obviously tenement houses, lacked.

   In other words, the countryside had to be manipulated in a way that
would make suburban space livable for the middle class. As Kenneth Jackson puts it, "The theory that early suburbs just grew, with owners 'turning

cowpaths and natural avenues of traffic into streets,' is erroneous" (1985: 135). Housing plots were subdivided and promoted for sale by speculative developers, and in order to sell them, many services first had to be established: sewer and water lines were developed, local roads and streetlights were built, and rail lines were provided that linked the homes to urban centers (ibid.: 131).

Escape from the city was only partial. Dolores Hayden (2003: 24) emphasizes that while nineteenth-century residents of the "borderlands" enjoyed their pastoral setting, they also valued access to urban life. Equally important, suburbs were economically dependent on the city. Robert Fishman writes, "If suburbia was the bourgeois utopia, it existed in inevitable tension with the bourgeois hell—the teeming world of the urban slum—from which suburbia could never wholly escape because the crowded city was the source of its prosperity" (1987: 135). The wealth that eased the middle class move to the suburbs was created by the modern industrialization that also gave the city its unappealing characteristics. "Places like Lake Forest, Bronxville, and Brookline enabled the select few—and their supporting minions—to enjoy the benefits of American production and resources without bearing the burden of living near noxious fumes, deafening noises, and poor people who made the prosperity possible in the first place" (Jackson 1985: 102).

Although the steam railroad brought escape from the city, it also carried the smog, smell, and noise of the city to the country; the trolley allowed the experience of the country without these industrial distractions. This contrast is made evident when *The Independent* allays fears that the trolley will bring to suburban residents the problems of the steam train: "The progress of the trolley has led to some expressed misgivings as to the effect it will have on secluded natural resorts—places where we may have been able to hide ourselves for a time from the buzz and corrosion of work. The steam car certainly did a great deal to spoil the woodland and break the heart of the Fairy Queene" (1902b: 1379). But, the editors write, "the trolley is more quiet than a carriage and cleaner than a cart. It fits easily into rustic life. Wherever it goes, the farmers come down from the hills as if it were an old friend. Its mechanism is out of sight: it has nothing to alarm the timid" (ibid.). The trolley appeared to be less "imposing" on nature than the railroad and thus better allowed those living in the suburbs to maintain a shield from city life.

Yet, from the perspective of urban reformers, more important than eliminating industrial signs of the city was the trolley's capacity to give groups previously excluded from country pleasures access to its imagined benefits. "[The solitudes] are no longer left for the enjoyment of those only who can afford to patronize costly hotel resorts; or to the very few who can stroll through the wilderness with guide and gun. Hereafter the city crowd can get into the remote districts, the glens and the woods; they can find the lakes and the trout streams" (*The Independent* 1902b: 1380). For the progressives of *The Independent*, the trolley was a way to counter the immorality of tremendous social inequalities. "It is a new age. The revolution is centered in the trolley, and in the telephone, and other agencies that make us all akin. There will still remain rocky wildernesses and the mountain resorts, the great forests for the hotel proprietor and his moneyed patrons. These the trolley will rarely meddle with. It belongs to the common people" (ibid.).

The attitude of *The Independent* is shared with writers such as Edward Bellamy, whose widely read *Looking Backward* portrays American capitalism as steeped in depravity. It was published in 1888, when trolleys were first being introduced, and in it the conscience of the wealthy gets revenge: "The squalor and malodorousness of the town struck me, from the moment I stood upon the street, as facts I had never before observed. But yesterday, moreover, it had seemed quite a matter of course that some of my fellow citizens should wear silks, and other rags, that some should look well fed, and others hungry" (Bellamy 1888/1996: 206). At a time when the gap between rich and poor was very evident, the idea that technologies such as the trolley would "make us all akin" had much appeal.

Significantly, a large source of the wealth that formed this inequality was embodied in the railroad trusts. According to Alan Trachtenberg (1982: 57), "Not only did the railroad system make modern technology visible, intruding it as a physical presence in daily life, but it also offered means of exercising unexampled ruthlessness of economic power." Thus the trolley's distinction from the railroad came not just from its silence and gentle treatment of the environment, but its separation—at least initially—from the conceit of the wealthy railroad executives. "[The trolley] grows rich off the crumbs of business that a steam road would despise" (*The Independent* 1903b: 1048). The steam railroad's arrogance toward lower-class customers was paralleled by its disruption of the typically poor and working-class neighborhoods through which it noisily passed. The small and amiable trolley appeared to be the antithesis of the locomotive's imperiousness. This partially explains the delight expressed in the title of an article from *McClure's* describing the potential replacement of steam by electricity: "The War on the Locomotive: The Marvelous Development of the Trolley Car System" (Moffet 1903).

Displacing the image of arrogant wealth associated with railroads might also calm fears of continuing labor strife. Bellamy's *Looking Backward* sharply describes the concern over the unpredictability of labor struggles in the late nineteenth century: "It was agreed that affairs were going from bad to worse very fast, and that there was no telling what we should come to soon. 'The worst of it,' I remember Mrs. Bartlett saying, 'is that the working classes all over the world seem to be going crazy at once'" (Bellamy 1888/ 1996: 33). This fear helps make sense of the hope for a more "equable" progress. Similarly, the desire for "peace" and even more telling "order" can be understood not just in terms of peace from the noise of manufacturing and industry but also from the noise of laborers in the streets and their disruption of daily life. "It is not, however, with speed and comfortable traveling that we concern ourselves so much as with greater results in the way of social revolution" (*The Independent* 1903b: 1048). The technical revolution of the trolley here displaces a violent revolution of the working class.

Thus, while the rise of the trolley may address the immorality of economic inequality associated with railroads, the most pronounced element in this discourse of reform comes in the trolley's ability to regenerate the morals of those who reside in the slums. Joel Tarr (1996) notes that in the 1870s, Congregationalist minister Charles Loring Brace warned in his book *The Dangerous Classes of New York* of the deleterious effect of overcrowding on public morals and advocated the dispersal of population from city slums. Specifically, Brace recommended building a subway or an elevated railway with cheap fares to enable workers to settle in "pleasant and healthy little suburban villages" (Tarr 1996: 315).

In this view, the trolley, by providing access to the country, would improve the morale of the working class as the suburbs had for the middle class, but it would also improve the morality of this class. "Those who have all their lives been huddled into tenements or twenty foot fronts are finding the sunny slopes, the glens and the brook sides and are getting a new meaning to life" (*The Independent* 1903b: 1048).

The trolley is given a more explicit role in transforming the urban population in an article from the San Francisco–based *Overland Monthly:*

> To consider the inter-urban road as a moral agent is not new. The reason of it all is very clear. The rearing of children on city streets is not calculated to produce a creditable type of manhood or of womanhood. Cheap and frequent trolley transportation service to the adjacent country gives to the man of moderate means that which has hitherto been the exclusive property of the rich—namely—an opportunity to quit the congested and more or less vicious sections of the city and rear his family in surroundings pure and sweet, both morally and climatically. (Ford 1903: 381)

The article continues on the need to escape the city and concludes with a re-mark by a visitor to San Francisco who declares, "You would have a health-ier, happier and a more contented people if you had more homes, more gar-dens and more elbow room" (ibid.). In this view the city is irredeemable. The country is "pure and sweet, both morally and climatically," while the city is "vicious."

For some, the country could also help resolve the problems of frequent economic downturns in the city. Again *The Independent* leads in its opti-mism by claiming, "The trolley will tend to dissolve the rapidly forming masses and distribute them where work is always abundant" (1903b: 1048). This quote reveals a fear of the "rapidly forming masses" that are behind strikes and other protests in the city, and it recognizes that a lack of em-ployment may inspire these actions. However, the solution to this lack—jobs working in the country—precisely misses the dramatic transformation of the economy, which forced a migration of people from the country to the city.[4]

The notion that people would find job security in the country came from an attachment to the republican ideal, but this ideal depended on abundance of land. Frederick Jackson Turner emphasized in his 1893 essay *The Signi-ficance of the Frontier in American History* that the lack of "free" land at the end of the nineteenth century required a shift in the American charac-ter on which the nation was established. According to Turner, individualism fostered by "open" land led to the intelligent and independent-thinking cit-izen who created American democracy. Of course, what Turner describes as "free" and "open" land was in fact occupied by native peoples who were con-sidered incapable of being citizens; thus, white male citizenship depended on the removal of Native Americans.[5]

The ideal of individualism adds a deeper understanding to the romance of the country embodied in the discussions of the trolley. While the hope that city residents would find work in the country was unrealistic, the country-side was associated with an independent lifestyle, and thus access to it sym-bolized access to citizenship. "The average citizen of moderate means, can now, on any day, take down his rod and reel, and say: 'I go a fishing.' A few hours will take him out among the hills and the brooks and he will come back refreshed. The country is at his door. He has no cause for marring na-ture, nor for destroying the beautiful" (*The Independent* 1902b: 1379). Ulti-mately these sentiments reflect the belief that citizenship in the United States is based on the independence and common-sense survival skills of rural life. Of course, this was a type of citizenship only available to white men. The irony here is that while the trolley signified a new acceptance and enjoyment of technology, it also signified an ability to maintain a preindustrial knowledge.

Not all members of the middle class expressed comfort with the idea of laborers frequenting the countryside. An article in *Atlantic Monthly* is more ambivalent about the increased access to the country by the laboring classes. At first, a description of the conditions the trolley helps create reaffirms its moral benefits:

> Of these conditions, or elements in a condition, that is happiest which tends to deplete the city and persuade the people into roomier healthier districts where factories and slums are not: where flowers and trees are many. And, lacking the power to remove the city folk for good and all, it does a lesser, yet a kindly service, by taking them out for an occasional summer day, at least. (Skinner 1902: 799)

But the author also lists among negative consequences of greater access to the country "an increase in the size and number of melancholy institutions called pleasure resorts, within reach of the cities; therefore, the vexation of hitherto tranquil regions by rowdies and picnic parties" (ibid.). While access to the country and suburban fringe could improve the moral character of the urban working class and new immigrants, it likewise could bring the degraded moral character of these groups to areas where the middle class lived and played. This fear emerged among middle- and upper-class New Yorkers when rail service increased access to Central Park and Coney Island. Residents who lived near Central Park became concerned when members of the working class began using the park for sports such as baseball, a trend that increased as trolleys began to link lower Manhattan to the park (Rosenzweig and Blackmar 1992). And the access rapid transit provided to Coney Island helped transform the formerly exclusive beach into a commercial recreation center for the working class (Kasson 1978).

Even greater potential for social mixing existed within the space of the trolley. While the trolley might create elbow room by dispersing the urban population, it could also increase crowding—in particular the uncomfortable crowding of disparate classes—for those who were forced to ride in the same packed railcar. The potential for class tension is both evoked and contained in the 1902 *Atlantic Monthly* article by Skinner. Initially the author claims the trolley corrupts manners: "Such manners as people used to have in American towns hardly survive the scramble in the rush hours. Women were treated with consideration, even in New York, once. Now, when they ride they may cling to a strap, and the burly fellow who has pushed his way past them and taken a seat will be seemingly indifferent to their presence" (808). The description of the offender as "burly" seems to indicate his class status as a manual laborer. Yet, in the same paragraph the writer points out that "gentlemen" who offer their seats to women "are as often in overalls as in broadcloth. To them the women need never look in appeal, and indeed she often looks in sympathy, for when they have done a day's work in a foundry or a shipyard, while she has been making calls or attending a concert, she appreciates their right to rest" (ibid.). Not only is the threat of social mixing neutralized, the author reaffirms the trolley's role in resolving the problems of social inequalities. By forcing people of different classes to intermingle, an imagined sympathy will develop to mend social conflict. Furthermore, in apparent contradiction to the earlier statement fearing the decline of morals due to trolleys, the article reveals that although women may not always be offered a seat, "The crippled, the suffering, the aged, and the woman with a child in her arms may always command a seat, no matter how many and rough the passengers. It is a better world than it used to be" (ibid.).

The Spectator column in another religiously oriented magazine, *The Outlook*, resolves the potential social conflict in a different manner. The interaction among groups of different social classes is seen as a source of entertainment: "Oh yes! The vulgar and the commonplace intermingle with the distinguished, but they add to the interest by the contrast they bring into the life of the moment" (Spectator 1903: 109). The humorous descriptions of the wife of a working man with her family, the fashionable woman, and the young lovers also show an appreciation for the equalizing aspects of the trolley. "It is the trolley-car that is the authorized spirit of democracy, treating with equal familiarity in its approach the stately mansion of wealth and the weather beaten cottage of poverty" (ibid.). The columnist here expresses a concern about the great inequalities that displayed themselves at the turn of the century. But the hopeful solution of transportation access appears comical in the face of disparities between "the stately mansion of wealth and the weather beaten cottage of poverty." The author chastises the middle-class "lady" for looking down on her fellow riders: "Then there is my lady who hates the common people, and believes that she reveals her social altitude in expressing her hates in the public conveyance she might have avoided" (ibid.). However, the humor of the column serves to downplay the seriousness of the divide. The columnist also fails to see how this very dislike of some to mix with common people may prove the downfall of public transportation. That is, the ideal of social integration can be easily thwarted if riders who wish to avoid it can find a form of transportation as convenient as the trolley but that allows a private space: for example, the automobile.

ESCAPE FROM INDUSTRIALISM

It is significant that simultaneous to these celebrations of the trolley, many writers in popular magazines celebrated the introduction of the automobile for some of the same reasons they praised the trolley. "The trolley has caught up the people who had settled down to stolid city life and is carrying them off with enthusiasm into the byways of the country, where the steam car had no means of conveying them. The automobile will hurry this tide countrywide with accelerating speed" (*The Independent* 1903a: 1162).

In a 1903 special issue of *Munsey's Magazine* devoted to the automobile, one article describes how this new form of mobility would extend the opportunities for city residents to live in the suburbs that were already being created by the railroad and trolley:

> The man of moderate means who finds living in the city a detriment to health and comfort will seek in the automobile a better mode of travel between home and office than he can obtain under present conditions. Why should men be compelled to live within a stone's throw of a railroad or streetcar line? Why should some of the most beautiful and healthful portions of the country be practically uninhabited, or at best occupied only by summer visitors, while the flat lands where railroad building is easy are swarming with residents? (Scarritt 1903: 179)

Like the trolley, the automobile in this narrative restores health to residents of the city by bringing people to the country.

Some stories claimed the car restored health not just through the access it provided to the country but also simply through the process of driving. In contrast to the confinement the train creates, since the early automobile was open to the air, it brought the rider in direct contact with the environment. *Munsey's Magazine* publisher, Frank Munsey, in the automobile issue describes it as "the greatest health giving invention of a thousand years. The cubic feet of fresh air that are literally forced into one while automobiling rehabilitate worn-out nerves and drive out worry, insomnia, and indigestion. It will renew the life and youth of the overworked man or woman, and will make the thin fat and the fat—but I forbear" (1903: 183).

This view adds another dimension to the escape from the industrial environment: it expresses a pleasure in the power of technology absent its accompanying exhaustion. Both the trolley and the automobile provided an environmental escape from the conditions of the industrial city—the trolley by reducing the smog of the steam railroad and the automobile by escaping the enclosure of the train—but they also provided another dimension of escape.

More than simply distancing the rider and suburban resident from the signs of mechanization and industry, the trolley and automobile were viewed as actually controlling the elements of mechanization and enabling enjoyment from them.

The trolley and automobile made the connection between technology and pleasure direct by creating the joyride. Frank Munsey's description of "the cubic feet of fresh air that are literally forced into one" evokes the fun derived from riding in an open-top vehicle; he perfectly describes the joyride when he writes, "The fact is the automobile when 'let out' on a smooth road gives one precisely the delightful sensation of coasting" (1903: 181).

The trolley could also be a site for riding pleasure. An article in *McClure* describes a cool summer evening when people rode to the end of the trolley line and nobody got off: "The passengers merely turn over the seats and ride back. They were not going anywhere—they were simply enjoying a spin in the people's automobile. That is a new luxury of modern life. Neither a horse car nor locomotive ever provided it. The need in human nature to which it responds went unsupplied until the trolley car came into existence to fill it" (Moffet 1903: 460). Its label as the "people's automobile" indicates that the trolley was seen as something that classes of people excluded from automobile ownership could enjoy. At the same time, this label signals the trolley's inferiority in the eyes of those who owned an automobile—and the trolley's eventual abandonment.

The descriptions of pleasure rides hint at what came to be characterized as the automobile's key improvement over the trolley: creating a feeling of autonomy. The discomforts of industry involved not just the physical strains of the noise and dirt but also the uncomfortable restrictions industry imposed on daily life.[6] Modern life disciplined both office and factory workers to arrive at work and leave at a particular time, and the railroad required an equally precise regulation by the clock. The trolley partially broke from this regulation by eliminating the necessity of reading a time schedule. Because the trolley could efficiently carry small numbers of passengers, it was economical to run more frequently than the steam railroad. If the trolley was missed, the rider could feel sure that another one would come along soon. "The marvel of this new method [of transportation] is that you can go any time of day without consulting timetables" (*The Independent* 1903b: 1048).

The automobile extended this freedom from regulation both temporally and geographically. In *Munsey's Magazine*, J. P. Holland (1903: 174) contrasts the problems of both rail and horse with the pleasures of the automobile:

Where the locomotive is hard bound to the narrow gage of a carefully laid and expensive road, the automobile is free to come and go by highways and byways, up hill and down dale, over stubble field or through morass, unhampered, free, and trustworthy as a faithful hound. Time tables and beaten paths are not for it. Obedient to man's will as never was horse or dog, it will bear its master through difficulties which no quadruped could surmount: and withal it never murmurs, never wearies, and scarce requires the attention given to an equine or canine companion.

Even more than with the trolley, the automobile is unregulated by a time-table. The driver can leave at any time, change destinations after departing and decide when and where to stop. "[The automobile] has the immense advantage of being able to travel any road and reach private residences. This deliverance from steel tracks, at first thought associates the automobile with the old style carriage: but it is, on the contrary, not a stride backward, but a stage of progress ahead of the steam car or the trolley" (*The Independent* 1903a: 1162). While the trolley reduced anxiety by eliminating the noise, smoke, and rough ride of the steam railroad, it could not eliminate the actual control the machine had over the body. One's body moved according to the restrictions of the track, but the automobile was not dependent on tracks and provided control over the travel mechanism.

The automobile represented the possibility of controlling at least part of this industrialism, but it was also another industrial intrusion into the city. Munsey (1903: 181) expresses this tension when comparing the attitudes of those who have not yet driven an automobile with those who have:

The man who knows [the automobile] from the outside only despises it and damns it on general principles. There is nothing too uncomplimentary to say of it and of the one driving it. It is an invention of the devil, as he sees it from the outside, and it has no place or rights in a civilized community . . . but once inside of a really first rate automobile, a marvelous change of heart comes over him. This other view point is a revelation. He finds himself lost in admiration and wonder. The motion, the feeling of strength and power, the speed, and the obedience to the driver, thrill and delight him.

In this celebration, the automobile thrills the driver who as a pedestrian found the automobile a dangerous nuisance. Moreover, in contrast to horses, which do not obey completely, the automobile preserves the driver's ability to maintain control.

Controlling one's own automobile also meant escaping the control of transportation by large railroad companies. This power was demonstrated when national time zones were established in 1883. Previously, each town determined time differently, depending on when the sun indicated noon. This made creating a time schedule among cities difficult. The completion of the transcontinental railroad in 1869 expanded the complexity of time schedules and led each company to establish its own set of standard times. In 1883 the railroad companies acted collectively, without government sanction, to create the four time zones that now exist in the continental United States (Trachtenberg 1982: 60). Although the impact of this change on most people's lives may have been minimal, it reinforced the image of these companies dictating the conditions of daily life.

In contrast to the railroads, the first streetcar companies were small businesses. Multiple companies competed in cities, some of them running as few as one or two lines. However, by the first decade of the twentieth century, one or two companies dominated most cities. This benefited riders by allowing them to transfer freely among a single company's lines, but it also meant these companies became more like the large railroads in their power and in their ability to disregard the needs of patrons.

The increasing congestion on trolley cars powerfully symbolized a disregard for riders. While trolleys were initially celebrated for helping to resolve the problem of crowding in the cities, they soon came to exemplify the worst of urban crowding. Simply put, economies of scale meant transit companies made more money if their cars were full. Charles Yerkes, who built a transit monopoly in Chicago, told his stockholders, "The short hauls and the people who hang on the straps are the ones we make our money out of" (quoted in Barrett 1983: 18).[7]

At the same time, many transit financiers were more concerned about profits from real estate speculation than about maintaining quality service on their streetcars. Investors F. M. "Broax" Smith in Oakland, Henry E. Huntington in Los Angeles, and Senator Francis G. Newlands in Washington, DC, were among those who set up trolley companies explicitly to serve subdivisions they purchased on the urban periphery (Jackson 1985: 120–124). Consequently, lines were built without the expectation that they would make a profit. This increased the need to crowd lines that did make a profit.

Speculation could also increase residential congestion within the city. Better transportation encouraged the centralization of business activities, which increased the value of land near the city center. Owners of residential property in or near the central business district could profit most by converting it to commercial use. Consequently, these owners subdivided their tenements and crowded their residents into smaller spaces. At the same time, they ignored maintenance and waited for their buildings to fall apart so new office buildings could take their place (Fairfield 1993: 66–67).

While trolley financiers profited handsomely from land speculation, trolley company employees worked long hours for little pay, leading to frequent strikes for union recognition. This had disturbing parallels to the late-nineteenth-century labor troubles associated with large railroad companies. The most widely publicized of these, the Pullman strike of 1894, led to riots throughout Chicago. At their extreme, strikes were a physical threat to middle-class commuters, but even if they did not lead to violence, they could disrupt service. Moreover, as John Fairfield shows, demonstrations by streetcar workers could expose divisions between commuters and the laboring classes:

> When the disorder reached the business districts, the conflicting interests of the poor and the commuting middle class became clear. When the Grand Street cars in New York's 1886 strike reached Broadway, white collar workers, presumably commuters, leaned out of office windows 'to applaud the police,' while shirt making women from nearby sweatshops jeered. (Ibid.: 72)

The same divisiveness surrounding striking streetcar employees came out in the struggle over municipal ownership of public transportation. Robert Fogelson (2001) categorizes arguments opposing municipal ownership into those that were political, economic, and ideological. First, opponents argued that public officials had a history of using government contracts for personal and political gain, so placing transit in their hands was asking for corruption. Second, it was believed that the need to earn a profit would force a private company to manage transit more efficiently than a city government. Finally, some claimed that operating transit with public funds ran counter to American principles of free enterprise and might lead to socialism. This last argument had the greatest potential to provoke fear among the middle class. Some proponents of public ownership countered this fear by defending the general principals of private enterprise while claiming that transit, like other utilities, is exceptional because of its central place in urban life (Fogelson 2001: 72–74).

Other leaders celebrated the radical ideals behind municipal ownership. In fact, municipal ownership played an important role in mobilizing working-class participation in urban politics. Discussion of public ownership led to calls for other forms of aid to help the poor. "The rapid transit debate, social reformers found, led naturally to larger issues, especially the connection between realty values and the housing problem, the benefits of the single tax, and the plausibility of the garden city ideal" (Fairfield 1993: 92). While much of the middle class supported better transportation to decrease the crowded conditions of tenements, they rejected reforms that gave direct economic aid to the poor. Just as middle-class commuters expressed their discomfort with railway strikes, conservative urban reformers considered the movement for municipal ownership to be stirring class conflict (ibid.: 88).

Meanwhile, the automobile faced little resistance as an alternative method of encouraging decentralization and reducing congestion. Automobile-centered transportation plans in Chicago, Seattle, and Detroit inspired dramatic street improvements throughout urban America by World War I (Foster 1981: 43).

THE AUTOMOBILE AND RESPONSIBILITY

Relying on the automobile to reduce congestion allowed the middle class to continue supporting reform while avoiding issues of economic inequality. The automobile driver could avoid confronting poor people within the crowded trolley car and could escape being delayed by striking laborers. At the same time, "reformers" could avoid addressing the impact on the urban poor of low wages and periods of extensive unemployment. Instead, they promoted the automobile as a means to achieve success through individual hard work.

In restoring personal responsibility to the city, the automobile, like the trolley, became part of a project to restore the republican ideals of farm life that were lost in the process of industrialization. The automobile's project reconstructs these ideals not just by bringing people in contact with rural life but also by restoring the control over one's labor offered by farm life. Like small farmers who worked their own land, those who maintained their own cars controlled the pace, intensity, and hours of their work.

The pleasure derived from self-directed work is evident in several articles on car maintenance. A writer for *Munsey's Magazine* claims that boys in particular would enjoy knowing how to take care of cars, even without owning cars themselves: "Just as the boys of five or ten years ago learned to take their bicycles to pieces, clean them, and put them together again, so it will soon be part of a boy's education to understand all the intricacies of an automobile, even to the fine points of its necessarily elaborate mechanism" (Scarritt 1903: 178).

The focus on youth is interesting in several ways. The article tells a story in which boys who learn to work on automobiles will develop the same type of resourcefulness found in the yeoman farmer. In noting the popularity of home projects at the turn of the century, John Stilgoe writes, "In the borderlands of large lots and roomy cellars, and soon garages, professional men might remain in touch with an essential element of American character lost to office work—the making and remaking of built form—and transmit it to sons and even daughters" (1988: 268). Moreover, since young people need not own automobiles to become interested in maintaining them, the automobile takes on the role of preparing youth for democratic citizenship.

> Nor will this knowledge be confined to the sons of men who are able to afford an automobile. Youth is democratic . . . Public school education is not confined to the lessons taught in school hours, nor is the best of it to be learned from books. Many a bright lad who is going to school to-day, the son of parents to whom the possession of an automobile seems as remote as the moon, will grow to manhood imbued with knowledge of the machine's value and determined to possess one for himself. (Scarritt 1903: 178)

The aspiration to own an automobile prepares one for the role of citizenship just as aspiring to landownership does. Furthermore, just as at the turn of the nineteenth century many believed anybody who worked hard could have a farm, at the turn of the twentieth century many believed anybody could acquire a car, or at least one's children could. In other words, the narrative being constructed around the automobile here is a narrative of upward mobility. In this story, through hard work and discipline, anyone can escape poverty and become part of the middle class, in this case signaled by car ownership.

For advocates of self-reliance, the automobile provided a measure of individual worth. In his critique of speed limits, Frank Munsey (1903: 182–183), argues that they both restrict personal freedom and shift responsibility for safety away from the driver. For Munsey, those who wish to impose speed limits on autos lack an inside understanding of the automobile. "It is not fair for men who know nothing of an automobile from the inside to undertake to say just how fast it shall go. It is not fair for the reason that they know nothing of its capabilities—how readily it responds to the will of the driver." The automobile "responds to the will of the driver," so any accident can only be blamed on the driver. "I don't believe in hard and fast speed laws. I believe instead, in the strictest kind of responsibility—responsibility for all accidents and injuries caused by the recklessness or lack of skill on the part of the driver."

Although theoretically the automobile allows all drivers to prove their reliability, the views of some writers make this ideal of equal access problematic. For example, coachmen as a group are depicted as incapable of proper car maintenance. A piece in *Overland Monthly* cautions readers that after one's first automobile purchase he or she must learn how to drive the automobile and not let the coachman drive it: "When you get your machine, don't lend it or allow your coachman to run it. The latter will either ruin your automobile or your horse, after running the auto" (Johnson 1902: 170). Similarly, an article in *Review of Reviews* emphasizes that "the driver must learn to [drive] himself: cannot possibly pay some one else to do it for him. He (or she) must know how to fire up: how to leave the engine during a stop for luncheon: how to turn the starting crank briskly in the gasoline carriage after a stop . . . He (or she) must have a practical familiarity with each working part, and know what to do if something goes wrong and what not to do: also be willing to face oil and grime with hand and clothes" (Moffet 1900: 706).

The implications of these articles are twofold. First, they reaffirm the importance that driving the automobile oneself has in restoring a feeling of individual autonomy. This is best indicated in an essay from *Cosmopolitan* stating that "the personal equation enters into motor driving, as into pretty nearly everything else in life. . . . It would be quite unsafe to warrant the life of an automobile in the hands of a careless owner or driver. One man will damage his almost inappreciably, another in the same time will wear his completely out" (Speed 1900: 151). Second, the reason one should not let the coachman drive is because he will ruin the car. The unworthy owner is marked by class and race.

While the celebration of rural individualism depended on the exclusion of native peoples, here the exclusion is directed at African Americans and immigrants. Jay Rubin (1978) notes that in the antebellum North, blacks held a niche in low-paying service jobs such as domestics and coachmen, but with the arrival of low-skilled immigrants from Ireland, the competition for these jobs increased. After the Civil War, according to a statistical analysis conducted in the 1890s (Salmon 1892), the majority of domestic workers, including coachmen, were foreign-born. Although the study did not measure the number of native-born service workers who were black, based on earlier patterns it is likely that a large number of them were. In addition, a historical study of Pittsburgh in the early twentieth century found that African Americans dominated jobs in service, presumably including coachmen, as well as in transportation, such as teamsters and draymen (Bodnar, Weber, and Simon 1988).

The race and class distinctions are made clear in several discussions about the cost of maintaining a car. A commentator in *World's Work* distinguishes between two owners' abilities to keep a car:

> One owner will keep no account, allow his driver to take the machine to a repair shop as often as he likes, make no attempt to understand it himself and bring his own more educated intelligence to bear upon its problems. . . . The other will study his engine till he knows what it is doing and what should not be done to it, keep every want of his machine regularly supplied, find a keen pleasure in doing all trifling repairs at home. (Norman 1903: 3502)

Maintaining the automobile oneself is thus a way of both asserting autonomy and differentiating oneself from the worker who lacks the same capacities.

The servant's incompetence is also depicted in a cost comparison between horse carriage and automobile in *Scientific American* (1903: 354). After summarizing the costs of purchasing an automobile, the editors write,

> The coachman, moreover, has no horses to clean or feed, no harness to wash, no necessity for going constantly to the farrier and wasting precious time of his mistress while the horses are being shod, and no good excuse to offer why he should not always be on hand at the request of the employer. He cannot keep for himself, as his little perquisites, his monthly commissions on feed, stabling or shoeing, nor can he get his percentage on all new horses bought to replace lame or sick ones.

Here, the primary benefit of maintaining the car by the owner is to avoid the skimming that coachmen engage in. The distinction between those who are capable of driving and maintaining the automobile and those who are not legitimates a class and racial hierarchy that views some groups as more suited for work subservient to a machine and others as more suited to controlling machines. In the discourse of republicanism, it deems the former group ultimately incapable of becoming the responsible thinker required of a democracy.

At the turn of the century, there was considerable debate over who exactly was appropriate for inclusion as a U.S. citizen. The last decade of the nineteenth century saw a dramatic increase in immigrants from southern and eastern Europe, who were frequently stereotyped as criminals and instigators of labor unrest. This led Massachusetts Congressman Henry Cabot Lodge and New Hampshire Senator William Chandler to call for a requirement that new immigrants be literate. This idea was made popular nationally by a group

of Harvard graduates who formed the Immigration Restriction League (IRL).
As John Higham writes,

> [The League's] first publication referred elliptically to the great danger
> of a change in America's race lines, but its arguments centered chiefly
> around data designed to prove that southern and eastern Europe—in
> sharp contrast to northwestern Europe—was dumping on the United
> States an alarming number of illiterates, paupers, criminals, and mad-
> men who endangered the "American character" and "American Citi-
> zenship." (1963: 103)

Matthew Jacobson (1999) builds on Higham's analysis to show that a central component of the immigration debate concerned the question of whether
particular races were capable of self-government. In this context race meant
not just black or white; it was assumed that within Europe there existed many
different races, from Slavs and Hebrews to Italians and Celts. According to
politicians like Lodge, new immigrants were not of the same racial stock as
the Anglo-Saxons who founded the nation. This view was supported by members of the IRL, who were part of the educated elite, and it was legitimized by
scholars of eugenics such as Henry Orfield, who stated in 1924: "[The idea
that] all men are born with equal rights and duties has been confused with
the political sophistry that all men are born with equal character and ability
to govern themselves and others" (quoted in Jacobson 1999: 84). The latter
belief, according to Orfield and the IRL, was clearly false.

Despite the skepticism expressed toward new immigrants' capacity for
self-governance, under the terms of the 1790 and 1875 Naturalization Acts,
these immigrants were considered white and therefore allowed to become
citizens. Significantly, court decisions following the 1875 act included some
non-Europeans such as Armenians, but the courts barred immigrants from
southern and eastern Asia from naturalization. Indeed, while the 1875 act
made a point to include Africans, congressmen from western states would
not allow "white person" to be struck from the Naturalization Act because
they wished to exclude Chinese, who were immigrating in large numbers to
the West (Jacobson 1999: 73).

The right of white immigrants to become citizens is significant because
unlike Asians—excluded from naturalization—and African Americans—
the majority of whom continued to live in the Jim Crow South—these immigrants could translate their citizenship into political power. However, as
new immigrants gained influence in urban politics, some reformers began to
blame political corruption on their supposed lack of patriotism. In particular, Catholic immigrants were thought to be loyal to the pontiff and unable

to think independently (Higham 1963: 41). Calls for restrictions on enfranchisement failed, but conservative reformers found other ways to weaken the influence of these groups.[8] Steven Diner (1998: 231) notes that "stricter voter registration laws, designed to prevent corruption, made it more difficult for Americans, especially from working-class and immigrant backgrounds, to vote."

In the case of urban transportation, this weakening could be done by isolating transit regulation from city politics. For example, in 1894 the New York state legislature established the Board of Rapid Transit Railroad Commissioners with five members of the Chamber of Commerce sitting on the eight-member board and gave the board sole power to name their replacements. Despite widespread opposition by labor unions, the makeup of the board was ratified in a citywide referendum (Hood 1993: 61–66). As will be discussed in Chapter 5, immigrants eventually did acquire a voice in the management of New York's subways, leading to a municipally operated line. However, the politics behind New York's subways were in some ways exceptional since, unlike trolleys, subways did not compete with automobiles for the space of the street.

A more representative example of mass transit's development in the United States can be found in Chicago. In the years before a decisive 1907 referendum on transit policy, voters several times indicated their support for municipal ownership. Despite this, the so-called Ordinances of 1907 strongly favored a privately run system. Paul Barrett (1983: 40, 93) shows that public ownership failed in part because its strongest advocate, Chicago Mayor Edward Dunne, was linked to socialists and striking unions. However, a primary reason voters chose the 1907 deal was its promise to overcome political controversy by placing decisions in the hands of engineers.

Fairfield argues that municipal ownership of public transit failed to gain support throughout the United States partly because it involved leaving power with politicians who were viewed as corrupt and inefficient. In its place, "municipal innovators" saw urban planning as encouraging efficiency and overcoming political controversy (1993: 107–108). Planning might involve streets for automobiles *and* mass transit, but streets proved easier to get built. Daniel Burnham's 1909 plan for Chicago helped popularize the view that a network of streets is essential to the health of a city. As Barrett puts it, "Streets were to do more than edify, inspire, and promote easy movement. They were to take over transit's role as a weapon against slums" (1983: 73). Significantly, Burnham's plan called for a transit system, but this was regarded as secondary to the improvement of streets. Thus, while Chicago resisted direct financing of streetcars, incurring debt for street construction went unchallenged (ibid.: 76). Moreover, while Burnham intended that automobiles, trolleys, and pedestrians share the street, regulating motorists proved difficult, and over time automobiles were clearly given preference.[9]

The favoritism Chicago showed toward the automobile typified public policy in cities throughout the United States. Building roads for the automobile appeared to help address the same problems of the city that the trolley did, and professional engineers rather than corrupt politicians would control their design. Moreover, while transit was considered a business and therefore could be taxed, roads were considered a service to be provided by the government. Consequently, transit companies actually helped pay for street improvements that benefited automobile drivers. These companies also paid burdensome franchise fees and were required to clean and repair the streets their trolleys used (St. Clair 1986: 106). In short, although transit systems were treated as if they had a monopoly, they actually competed with the automobile. Not surprisingly, as the automobile's popularity grew, fare revenues dropped, causing a cyclical decline in the level of transit service throughout U.S. cities (Flink 1988: 367).

THE DEMOCRACY OF TRANSIT'S DECLINE

The topic of mass transit's decline in the United States has sparked significant debate among those who research the city. One popular theory, which can be traced to a 1974 Senate investigation led by Bradford Snell, holds that automobile interests—including General Motors, Firestone, and Standard Oil—replaced trolleys with buses in cities across the country. This led people to abandon mass transit for automobiles (Flink 1988: 364–367). Scott Bottles (1987) dismantles this theory by showing that trolleys had been in decline for years by the time they were replaced by buses. Furthermore, most riders regarded gasoline-powered buses as more convenient and comfortable than trolleys. According to Bottles, the primary reason for transit's decline was simply people's preference for an automobile's convenience.

Those who hold Bottles' view do not deny that public policy favored autos over mass transit, but they claim that this favoritism was a democratic choice. For example, historian Erik Monkkonen (1988: 168) writes, "While the need for and convenience of fixed rail transit should not be minimized, it is important to keep in mind that deliberate urban policy, in the form of street surfacing, encouraged automobile and truck traffic. . . . Cities and the people in them to a large extent chose their forms of transportation."

Bottles and Monkkonen are certainly correct in claiming that the support for autos over transit was political, but to suggest that this support was a "democratic choice" glosses over the ways urban politics can favor elites.[10] Monkkonen dismisses writers who maintain that the decline of transit harmed the poor. He points out that in many cases workers could not afford to commute via streetcars and claims that in Milwaukee, for example, "control of fixed rail transit did not concern working class politicians very much" (1988: 161). However, his example of Milwaukee is misleading because it conflicts with the history of struggle to maintain low fares in other cities.[11]

Furthermore, while it is true that streetcars were initially of primary benefit to the middle class, by the 1930s this had changed. Especially in large cities like Chicago and New York, mass transit became essential to the working class, not only for commuting to and from work but also for shopping and recreation (Barrett 1983: 106–107, Hood 1993: 179–180). Not until the 1950s did a majority of the urban working class own automobiles, so up to this time most still walked or took mass transit to their jobs (Flink 1988: 359).

When race and gender are considered, the claim that transit choices were democratic becomes even more problematic. During the early part of the twentieth century, when crucial decisions were being made that shaped the future of urban transportation, a large segment of the U.S. population was excluded from political participation. Despite the growing presence of Asian Americans in cities such as San Francisco and New York, because Asian immigrants were barred from naturalization until 1952, they had little say in local or national politics (Takaki 1998). By 1908, most of the South found ways to circumvent the Fourteenth Amendment and prevent blacks from voting (McDonagh 1999: 157). Since almost 90 percent of African Americans still lived in southern states in 1910, this meant the vast majority were disenfranchised (New York Public Library 1999: 100–101).

For African Americans who moved to northern cities, political power did translate into representation on the local level. However, this representation was often merely a token element of the urban machine. As David Moberg (1990) shows, in Chicago blacks garnered a few patronage jobs but had little say over citywide policy. Mexican Americans experienced discrimination similar to that of blacks. In the early twentieth century, "whites only" primaries were held in some Texas counties and were extended statewide in 1923. Texas also charged a poll tax that few Mexican workers could afford. When Mexican Americans did acquire representation at the municipal level, as with blacks, this representation failed to translate into a significant voice in urban policy (Gutiérrez 1995: 27).

Of course, in most states women were excluded from voting entirely until the Nineteenth Amendment was ratified in 1920. When women did receive the vote, it was achieved largely by arguing that women brought a distinctively maternal contribution to democracy. Consequently, as Eileen McDonagh (1999) argues, women continued to be marginalized in the public sphere.

Significantly, the desire for women to be shielded from urban crowds led many community leaders to condemn streetcars. Of particular concern was the mixing of middle-class women with working-class men. Placing homes in the suburbs partially solved this problem, but women would still need to shop in the city. The automobile's advantage was its ability to provide access to the city while sheltering women from the laboring classes and foreign elements of the urban population (Scharff 1991: 24). Virginia Scharff writes, "Beneath the welter of political conflicts, there lurked the idea that the very character of mass transit set it on a collision course with bourgeois ladyhood. The trolley was simply too public a vehicle for the female personification of privacy" (ibid.: 7). When trolleys became the center of social conflict, for example during transit-worker strikes, women's endangerment became even more explicit. A 1919 strike in Los Angeles led a local working-class paper to condemn the replacement workers for putting the safety of women at risk (ibid.: 154).

Ironically, while the automobile might isolate women from these types of disturbances, the independence automobile ownership provided also led to criticisms of women driving. Clay McShane (1994: 161) writes, "If the automobile symbolized liberation and men were driving to escape traditional social constraints, they must have feared that their wives or daughters, whom prevailing values confined much more sharply, would also adopt the technology as an escape." Thus, while the number of households with automobiles grew rapidly in the 1920s, many women in these households were not permitted to drive. The point here is that while women were excluded from a voice in urban transportation policy that favored the automobile, they continued to rely on public transit.

This was even more true for working-class women and women of color who were frequently required to work outside the home. In San Francisco, Chinese American women often took the streetcar outside of Chinatown to work in garment factories, sometimes carrying small children on their backs (Takaki 1998: 255). Black women were often relegated to the lowest-paying jobs, and, whether living in the North or South, they either walked or relied on public transit. Most famously, Rosa Parks worked as a seamstress, and the impact of the boycott she led in the 1950s revealed the importance of public transportation for African American women and men (Jones 1986: 278). In sum, women and people of color had little say over supposedly "democratic choices" leading to transit's decline and were generally the ones harmed most by this decline.

However, the point of this chapter is not to defend mass transit as counterhegemonic and condemn the automobile as a product of white middle- and upper-class power. Policy decisions and the arguments promoting them emerge out of complex conditions that vary from city to city. The concern here is less with the specific political struggles than with the common ideals underlying these struggles. Moreover, it must be emphasized, policies toward *both* trolleys and automobiles were designed primarily in the interest of the white middle class.[12] At the same time, as Clay McShane argues, supporting these policies proved easier when it was thought that workers would benefit: "Support for policies favoring technological changes, like . . . automobility, allowed middle-class residents to flee the center city, and, simultaneously, believe that there was no self-interest in their policies" (1994: 227).

While proponents of both trolleys and automobiles claimed these technologies would uplift the urban working class, the automobile fit more easily with a middle-class American view of how this uplift could best take place. In contrast to the trolley, the automobile required individuals to prove their right to the benefits of transportation by learning how to maintain and operate a mobile machine, even if they could not yet afford to own one. In other words, the automobile is linked to the American ideal that individuals have the capacity to make their own destiny. This ideal is actually expressed quite well by Monkkonen, who claims automobiles are a symbol of progress because of their "accessibility": "The poor and rich alike can own and shape their automobiles" (1988: 166). This myth of equal access hides profound inequalities.

The need to isolate the consequences of these inequalities explains another appeal of the automobile. While both the trolley and automobile were celebrated as relieving the stressful conditions of the city, only the latter allowed middle-class residents to avoid directly confronting these conditions—physically, through contact with working-class residents and employees on the trains, and politically, through municipal policies to improve the lives of the working poor.

The ultimate preference given to the automobile establishes the link between transportation and public participation in the city. That is, individual participation and individual control over the automobile were valued, but collective control over the built environment in the form of publicly owned transit was not. Resistance to collective control is revealed in a slightly different manner in the next chapter, where the plans of Lewis Mumford and his colleagues at the Regional Planning Association of America are discussed. In this case, governments resist taking on the call for greater public control of land speculation. At the same time, the automobile-centered plans themselves have the potential to hinder certain elements of public participation.

CHAPTER 2

TOWNLESS HIGHWAYS AND
HIGHWAYLESS TOWNS

The October revolution of the automobile, which will effectually transform the physical means of life and make possible a higher type of civilization, has hardly begun.   MACKAYE AND MUMFORD 1931: 347

In short, the American has sacrificed his life as a whole to the motorcar, like someone who, demented with passion, wrecks his home in order to lavish his income on a capricious mistress who promises delights he can only occasionally enjoy.   MUMFORD 1953: 235

In less than thirty years, what had been an oddity on city streets became common: the value of owning an automobile was no longer questioned; rather the question had become how to accommodate the rapid growth in car ownership. The premise of this question was even accepted by Lewis Mumford, who, as the longtime *New Yorker* architecture critic, is likely best known for frequently attacking the automobile's dominance of the city. In particular, he was an outspoken critic of the highways being built in and around New York City by Robert Moses (Caro 1975). But the first quote above reveals that Mumford took part in the enthusiasm of the 1920s that accompanied the dramatic increase in car ownership, and he envisioned the automobile having a positive impact on modern life. Like earlier proponents of the automobile, Mumford saw its primary benefit in allowing the decentralization of urban populations. In addition, Mumford and his colleague Benton MacKaye believed the automobile's flexibility might be ideal for traveling through uneven topography; thus the car suited their call for regional development in accord with the natural contours of the landscape.

Ironically, accommodation of the automobile eventually led to sprawling development and the drastic razing of the natural landscape, which Mumford and MacKaye had specifically warned against.

The limited ability of Mumford, MacKaye, and the Regional Planning Association of America (RPAA)—which they helped found—to influence urban development reflects deep resistance in America to the redistributive efforts of planners. It was not through lack of effort that the RPAA was unable to achieve many of its goals. Members were active in the early planning associations and lobbied governments to implement their plans. Most notably, Clarence Stein, as chairman of the New York State Commission on Housing and Regional Planning, called for state-sponsored low-income housing projects and restrictions on development. But this required substantial government intervention in the real estate market, and this intervention was vociferously opposed by powerful interests who benefited from land speculation (Luccarelli 1995: 147).

However, while the redistributive goals of the RPAA largely failed to take shape, cities did appropriate elements of their design goals. In particular, the plans developed for Radburn, New Jersey, in the late 1920s introduced important techniques for eliminating the conflict between automobiles and pedestrians, and these techniques were frequently incorporated into later suburban developments (see Figure 1). While some elements of Radburn, such as homes that faced away from the street and inward toward a shared park, never caught on, the use of cul-de-sacs became quite common (Relph 1987: 65–67).

The transportation principles incorporated into Radburn were expanded upon by Benton MacKaye in a 1930 article for *The New Republic* titled "The Townless Highway" and further developed a year later with the aid of Mumford in *Harper's*. Despite the radical ideals of these planners, their proposal for townless highways was an attempt to solve problems of the modern city in a way that was largely consistent with the perspective of conservative reformers. Furthermore, their plan failed to account for how political and social realities might make the automobile a tool of social exclusion and as a consequence help sustain housing inequalities that Mumford and his colleagues wanted to address.

SUPERHIGHWAYS AND SUPERBLOCKS

MacKaye and Mumford's design for townless highways came at a time of both growing alarm about problems created by the automobile and an increasing number of proposed solutions. While proponents of the automobile

Figure 1. The 1929 plan for Radburn, with its network of cul de sacs, looks very similar to the typical tract housing of today. Courtesy of the Radburn Association.

had hoped it would resolve tensions centered around the industrial city, by 1930 it had created a new one—what the title of a 1931 article for *The Outlook and Independent* calls "This Motor Ache." (The two religious magazines were now merged.) The author summarizes the predicament: "Today there are more automobiles by three million than there were horses, mules, asses and burros in 1900, from which it is concluded that there are many times the number of vehicles in the streets today. Result, more traffic congestion" (Duffy 1931: 491).

For this and other writers of the late 1920s and early 1930s, the solution was emerging in the construction of superhighways, controlled-access roads containing no stops and no grade crossings. In these proposals for superhighways, the benefits of the automobile are no longer promoted as they were in articles from the turn of the century; instead they are assumed. "It is not a case of deciding whether or not the automobile is a vital part of modern civilization. . . . The automobile has demonstrated that it is a highly desirable adjunct to the steam engine, Pullman and box car" (ibid.). As in the early discourses surrounding the automobile, a primary goal of these superhighways was to provide access to the countryside. "A large city's motor transportation problem is of a dual nature: the problem of providing ample motoring space from its borders to the open country, and the problem of supplying adequate intra-city facilities" (ibid.: 492).

MacKaye and Mumford foresee a similar goal for their townless highways. The desire to escape from the city's industrial environment is embodied in the name "townless highway." In this name MacKaye and Mumford also acknowledge that the automobile, while permitting an escape from certain industrial elements of the city, is itself industrial. That is, although automobile driving may be empowering and pleasing for the driver, for suburban residents who live near the road, especially a busy one, it brings the signs and sounds of industry they had hoped to escape. "Living on a trunk motor road is like living on the railroad. More and more the sensible property owner is shying off the wide and handsome highway. He wants to travel on it, not settle there" (MacKaye and Mumford 1931: 351).

While the automobile was celebrated for its safety in comparison to the horse and carriage, it also brought new dangers to the city. Because it could attain much higher speeds than horses and, unlike a trolley, could change lanes freely, the automobile made crossing streets very dangerous.

> There is scarcely a street leading to a school where, unless the motorist does crawl [sic], he may not kill a thoughtless child: there is hardly a major crossing or a bottle-neck on our modern highways where, in the daily confusion, a car may not be wrecked or a body maimed in someone's impatience to move swiftly where movement is almost impossible. (MacKaye and Mumford 1931: 347)

MacKaye and Mumford argue that the solution to this danger is to separate the heavy automobile traffic from the neighborhoods and eliminate the mixing of automobile and pedestrian traffic completely.

Already people are demanding to be rid of the endless stream of gasoline locomotives that pass under domestic windows—the private locomotive, pleasure car, or truck with its hum, its dust, its exhaust,
its constant threat to the lives of little children who have for the moment escaped the eye of their mothers and nurses, to say nothing
of grown adults, confronted by much greater hazards on the peaceful
highway than the bold highwaymen who terrorized the Pony Express.
(Ibid.: 350)

Thus, the townless highway provides shelter from the industrial and
safety from the mechanical. In order to accomplish this, roads would be separated from footpaths—something that Frederick Law Olmsted had introduced into the design of Central Park. Mumford comments, "Three consid-
erations must have been in [Olmsted's] mind: the safety of the pedestrian,
the convenience of the driver, and the desirability of avoiding the bustle and
noise in parts of the city designed for relaxation and repose" (1931: 42).

Olmsted's dual emphasis on technical design and aesthetics influenced
many of the early controlled-access highways. Sidney Waldon, chairman of
the commission that developed Detroit's superhighway plan, said the plan
would help create "a new kind of city, with magnificent buildings acquiring
a special dignity by reason of such settings as only a tree-ornamented superhighway can give" (quoted in Foster 1981: 109). Likewise, two primary concerns—efficiency and aesthetics—are found in the title of a 1931 article in
American City: "Facilitating Traffic and Preventing Blight by Spacious Planning in Express Highways" (Whitten 1931). It is also significant that the first
controlled-access highway open to the public in the United States was the
Bronx River Parkway, completed in 1925. This parkway embeds into its form
a primary function of the superhighway's efficiency—enabling residents' escape from the demoralizing aspects of the city to the healthful environment
of the suburbs. In short, making the expressway a parkway would shield it
from symbols of the city along its side and augment its function of carrying
drivers away from the city.

Concerned about the destructive potential of industrial growth, MacKaye
and Mumford hoped to show how technology could be used toward human
rather than mechanical ends: "Whether he is traveling for sheer pleasure or
to get somewhere, his major purposes are served by the Townless Highway:
the motor car has become an honor to our mechanical civilization and not a
reproach to it" (MacKaye and Mumford 1931: 356). Moreover, MacKaye and
Mumford hoped the highway would not only permit an urban escape but
also create a new kind of city. This city would be built from "superblocks"
where residences are turned inward toward a communal park from which

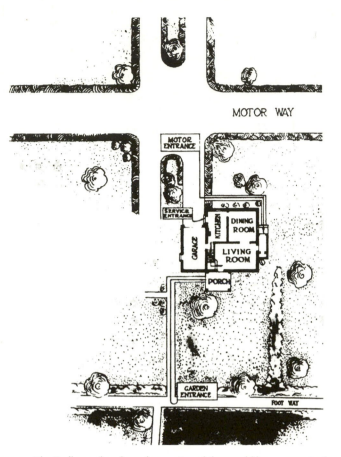

Figure 2. The Radburn plan shows how automobiles would have access to the back of the home and the front facing a footpath. The garage entrance pre- figured contemporary suburban housing. Courtesy of the Radburn Association.

automobiles are excluded, while automobiles and roads are given access to the rear of the homes (see Figure 2).

MacKaye and Mumford's notion of a superblock is embodied in a plan for the city of Radburn. "In Radburn, through traffic is confined to the through avenues; from these main avenues, which define the Radburn superblocks, there stems a system of motor lanes each of which comes to a dead end. The greater number of residences can be reached only by motor lanes, and no car is tempted to enter a motor lane unless the driver had definite business there" (ibid.: 353). All schools, stores, and community services were planned within the superblock, so it would no longer be necessary to cross a street when attending school, shopping, or visiting a neighbor.

Members of the RPAA were not the only ones to conceive of separating pedestrian and vehicular traffic. Most notably, Le Corbusier developed a similar concept in his "Radiant City" plan originally published in 1933. Much like the superblock, his residential sectors would contain housing surrounded by parks and linked to stores and other facilities by internal walkways (Le Corbusier 1933/1967: 163). Besides sharing a practical concern about the conflict between pedestrians and cars, Le Corbusier shared with Mumford and the RPAA similar ideas about responding to the industrial city's problems. Like Mumford, Le Corbusier believed in the need to bring the health-giving aspects of the country back to the city, so his plans called for high residential towers on pilotis, or piers, that would allow the greatest amount of green space for recreation. Both Mumford and Le Corbusier were also concerned about the destructive impact of speculative development; much like Mumford, Le Corbusier called for state regulation of land to assure affordable housing (Holston 1989: 44–46).

However, the large-scale towers designed by Le Corbusier were antithetical to Mumford's conception of small villages. Mumford was inspired most by the English planner Ebenezer Howard, who developed a plan for "garden cities." Howard's goal was to combine the economic and cultural benefits of the city with the health and beauty of the country. Garden cities were intended to be self-sufficient with separate zones for shopping, residence, and industry. Population would be restricted to thirty thousand inhabitants, and a surrounding greenbelt would both prevent sprawling development and contain farms to supply food (Howard 1898/1960: 50–57). For Mumford, the plans of Howard could be furthered by new technologies, including the automobile: "[Howard's] plan for decentralizing industry and setting up both city and industry within a rural matrix, the whole planned to a human scale, is technologically far more feasible to-day than it was forty or fifty years ago. For in the meanwhile, our new means of instantaneous communication have multiplied; likewise our means for swift transport" (Mumford 1960: 38).

Mumford believed technology would allow the creation of a "new regionalism," permitting greater distribution of a city's benefits while eliminating the problems associated with large, crowded populations. "The radio, the moving picture, the airplane, the telephone, electric power, the automobile— all these modern utilities have only increased the potential advantages of the region as a whole over the metropolis: for with these instruments, the unique superiority of the more congested areas is removed and their benefits are equalized and distributed" (Mumford 1986a: 215).

Significantly, while suburbs may appear to fit this regional design, Mumford was highly critical of the form suburban development took in the

United States. As Catherine Jurca (2001: 50) shows, Mumford was one of several critics from the 1920s who saw suburbs degrading civic life by encouraging smugness and consumerism. "Mumford had made explicit that the problem of the suburb was also the problem of the suburbanite, who put up with an inhumane environment that had more respect for machinery as such than for the people it was meant to serve."

Ironically, while technology might make suburbanites complacent, Mumford initially saw it helping to create places that fostered public participation and revitalized civic sensibilities. He disliked the form suburbs took in the United States, first because they simply extended the size of the city rather than creating a smaller alternative, and second because as mere satellites they were deprived of the city's cultural benefits. Mumford imagined multiple small cities in a region, each locally controlled but sharing their material and cultural resources.

> The new regional pattern will be a constellation of related cities separated by parks and permanent agricultural areas, and united for common projects by a regional authority. Each city would have all the local institutions necessary to its own effective life, local shops, schools, auditoriums, theaters, churches, clubs: and in addition each center would perhaps tend to specialize in some one institution of culture or social life, a museum of natural history in one center, a radio broadcasting station in another, a university in a third. Modern transportation and communication remove the necessity for the continuous urban agglomeration: they make this new pattern of cities possible. (Mumford 1986a: 214)

A similar idea was hinted at in earlier narratives surrounding the trolley:

> The trouble of the past half-century has been social differentiation. Cities grew, not only because of their industries, but grew at the cost of the country . . . . Wealth and enterprise went to the crowded districts; farm depression followed, and rural life was held in contempt. But the new age begins to look both ways—distributing advantages more evenly. There will be an ease of interchange between the denser and less dense districts: breaking up the local sentiments, and local morals, which now concentrate and develop in districts. (*The Independent* 1901: 1995)

Here, as with Mumford, the city is celebrated for its cosmopolitanism, and better transportation is seen as providing access to it for those who live outside major cities.

Still, Mumford's celebration of urban culture is limited. He rejects the urban mass culture found in the twentieth-century city. This rejection is found when he discusses "Broadway as Symbol." He complains that the cultural degradation embodied in New York's famous street is recreated on a smaller scale in cities throughout the country: "Up and down these second hand Broadways, from one in the afternoon until past ten at night, drifts a more or less aimless mass of human beings, bent upon extracting such joy as is possible from the sights in the windows, the contacts with other human beings, the occasional or systematic flirtations, and the risks and adventures of purchase" (Mumford 1945: 12).

It is clear that Mumford is uncomfortable with commodity culture. Part of this discomfort comes from its association with the materialism of capitalism. For Mumford the immorality of the market comes from its indiscriminate exploitation of the land. This is seen in his characterization of New York after the Civil War: "the water and the soil, as the prime environment of life, were becoming 'immaterial,' that is to say, they were of no use to the canny minds that were promoting the metropolis, unless they could be described in a legal document, appraised quantitatively, and converted ultimately into cash" (Mumford 1945: 32).

MacKaye and Mumford directly address this distaste for signs of the commercial. Describing the country highway they write: "There is the scorching ugliness of badly planned and laid out concrete roads peppered with impudent billboards: there is this vast, spreading metropolitan slum of multiple gas stations and hot-dog stands" (1931: 347). What they call "the motor slum" develops when companies purchase land by the side of the road on which to construct billboards and shops that attract drivers. Instead MacKaye and Mumford recommend that all land adjoining the highway be government-owned, which would eliminate what they call a "blight" on the country. According to their proposal, service stations would only be built at ten-mile intervals, along with a "well equipped restaurant which has supplanted the half a dozen greasy hot dog incubators," and these businesses would be placed on a frontage road separate from the highway, keeping entrances and exits from slowing traffic (see Figure 3).

While the desire to eliminate advertising may have sprung largely from a distaste for commercial society, it also served to further the escape from urban troubles. The uncertainties of business and the market could cause stress much like the noises and smells associated with industry could. MacKaye and Mumford viewed their design as reducing both types of strain: "With no danger of anyone suddenly cutting across, with no officious advertiser begging him to halt and change his tires or his underwear, or to patronize a

Figure 3. Illustration of "Townless Highway" shows how development is separated from the main road. "Townless Highways," *American City*, May 1930.

hotel in the town he has just left, with unobstructed right of way and unobstructed vision, our motorist has less anxiety and more safety at sixty miles an hour than he used to have in the old roadtown confusion at twenty-five" (1931: 355). In short, the townless highway was intended as a shield both from the physical disturbances of the industrial city and the psychological pressures of the commercial city.

HIGHWAY TO DOMESTICITY

The "ideology of domesticity," which gained prominence in the mid-nineteenth century through the writings of Catharine Beecher, called for the home to be a refuge from the pressures of the rapidly expanding economy. Margaret Marsh (1990: 74–82) shows that the manner to best achieve this refuge varied among its advocates and over time. Initially many women believed that an ideal home could be created in the city, but in part due to the increasing amount of labor unrest and its association with new immigrants, by the turn of the twentieth century the goals of domesticity were viewed as best achieved at a distance from the city. More specifically, creating a positive environment for children took on increasing importance in the twentieth century. Men were encouraged to take a greater role in raising children and to participate in home-centered activities. MacKaye and Mumford echo these sentiments when they assert the need to think about the automobile as a "family locomotive" that links the space of transportation to the space of the home. At the same time, they emphasize that young people, when not in the automobile, must be shielded from its dangers. They describe how the design of Radburn helps create this shield and facilitates the construction of a space to best nurture children. "The point to remember is this: it is only by a deliberate separation of local and through roads, of traffic and residential functions, that the motor road itself can attain its maximum efficiency in the number of vehicles served at the highest safe speed, and that the community can attain its maximum efficiency as a place for living, recreation, sleep, and the care of the young" (1931: 354).

While this ideal of domesticity had men playing a role within the home, women were still expected to be the primary caretakers. Radburn's design helps construct a nurturing home "where pedestrian traffic must cross motor traffic within the great superblocks that make up the residential sections, the deadly grade crossing is eliminated. . . . Since playgrounds, a school, and other community facilities are provided in each superblock, no child need ever cross a traffic artery on its way to school or to the playground: indeed, the housewife who goes to market on foot is equally safe" (ibid.: 353).

MacKaye and Mumford wrote this at a time, the end of the 1920s, when the social status of women was undergoing rapid change. A decline in birthrate and household size, combined with an increase in mass-produced goods and mechanized housework, required much less work in the home (Kessler-Harris 1982: 110). At the same time, home designs began to entail simpler upkeep (Wright 1981: 172). But feminist leaders such as Charlotte Perkins Gilman demanded more than small, efficiently designed kitchens; they suggested that houses and neighborhoods be planned for women who worked outside the home and had an active role in public life. In order to be free from domestic requirements and the secluded space of the home, Gilman called for child-care facilities and collective kitchens (ibid.: 172–173). Likewise, Ebenezer Howard's original concept of a garden city included cooperative child care and meal preparation, but these aspects were not incorporated into the RPAA's plans for Sunnyside, New York (the first and smaller of their developments), or for Radburn (Hayden 2002: 172–174).

The failure of the RPAA to take up these aspects of the garden city acceded to popular demands that the increasing number of working women return home. World War I had allowed women to enter jobs previously held only by men, and although many women were forced to give their jobs back to men after the war, new opportunities emerged in the increasingly mechanized office to become receptionists, typists, and stenographers. In addition, professional careers in education and health care had been opening up to women since the turn of the century (Kessler-Harris 1982: 224). At the same time, many women had gained self-confidence from the successful movement for their suffrage. The combination of these changes inspired a common fear that women would leave the home for a career. Responding to this fear, home economics courses in the 1920s taught college women that their happiness depended on choosing a family over a career (Marsh 1990: 136). Elizabeth Wilson (1991: 111) shows that a similar popular desire to see women return home after World War II is reflected in Mumford's comments on the Abercrombie Plan in Britain:

> Fortunately (from his point of view) he was able to report that among his most brilliant and promising female students in the United States he had observed "a radical change in attitude from their mothers' generation: babies and family life have become central again, and the attractions of a professional career . . . have become secondary."

Mumford bemoaned the declining value given to the traditional work of the homemaker and the tendency of women to pursue less noble jobs for a wage: "From the standpoint of current fashion, it is more important to write a dishonest piece of publicity or a bad poem, to spend eight hours at a typewriter or sewing in a dressmaking factory, or even to stand all day at a counter in a dry-goods store than to make a bed properly, diaper a baby neatly, or grow a beautiful stalk of snapdragons" (1955: 266–267). According to Mumford, the primary way the value of these humble pursuits can be restored is by relocating to a house near the country where women have access to a garden and children have a safe place to play. "Life succeeds only in an environment of life. The sterile felicity of the urban apartment house . . . is not, can never be, a substitute for living space" (268).

Besides being sexist, Mumford's essay reveals an ignorance of the millions of women who, even in times of economic prosperity such as the 1920s, had no choice but to work outside the home. Young working-class women who lived at home were expected to use their wages for household expenses, and not every married woman could rely on her husband's income to support the family. This was especially true for women of color. As Sarah Jane Deutsch (2000: 431–435) points out, when writers and politicians of the 1920s called for women to stay at home, they typically meant white women. Mexican American women worked in the fields picking fruits and vegetables or in factories where produce was canned. Discrimination against African American women who had left the rural South limited them primarily to domestic service work, whether that meant cooking, washing clothes, or cleaning homes. And Chinese American and Japanese American women often worked beside their husbands in family businesses (Takaki 1998: 254).

Besides his discomfort with women working outside the home, Mumford shared with conservatives a dislike of the urban entertainments that attracted women out of the home (Marsh 1990: 136). Young working-class women and women of color in particular found great pleasure and freedom in the early-twentieth-century city. In their free time, white women went to amusement parks, theaters, and dance halls (Peiss 1986). While they faced discrimination at many venues, African American women enjoyed the freedoms of northern city life that they lacked in the rural South (Jones 1986: 192). And as Vicki Ruiz (1992) shows in her interviews with Mexican American women, urban popular culture of the 1920s and 1930s often gave them the confidence to assert their independence from the restrictive roles imposed on them by traditional families. Thus, critics of commercial culture like Mumford, who believed women's proper place was in the home, had good reason to be concerned.

The commercial culture of the city also provided moments of freedom for middle- and upper-class women. The new industrial economy required that shopping become a central part of domestic labor; thus the department store became a place of social interaction among these women. As directors of family consumption, women could exercise a small amount of power and escape the tedium of the home in these elegant stores (Barth 1980: 129). According to Roswitha Mueller (2002: 35), city planners found women's presence in the city troubling not just because the women might be tempted to take jobs outside the home but also because their presence undermined attempts to impose order on the city: "Many of the shortcomings of city planning in the twentieth century have their roots in a mechanistic mindset, bent on orderliness, controllability and power over what was perceived as chaotic and irrational."

This conflict between order and disorder is found in Mumford's criticisms of Jane Jacobs' influential *The Death and Life of Great American Cities* (1961). While Mumford shared with Jacobs an antagonism toward urban redevelopment in the form of highways and high-rise housing projects, he strongly disagreed with her attachment to the unplanned chaos of city streets (Mumford 1968: 197). Mumford wished to segregate pedestrians on interior walkways and leave roads to the cars, but Jacobs (1961: 51) saw streets as the center of urban culture, and she appreciated the easy access women had to this urban culture. Although, as Wilson (1991) notes, Jacobs failed to understand how the political economy of 1950s deindustrialization created her ideal neighborhood of Greenwich Village, the point here is that Mumford's criticism of Jacobs once again reveals his desire to segregate women from urban life.

Mumford was not so naïve as to think that women would not have to leave the home for shopping, so to keep women from entering the city in that case, he suggested bringing the stores to the suburbs. In their townless highway article, MacKaye and Mumford reveal a preference for women not having to travel beyond the safety of their "superblock," but they acknowledge this may not be feasible initially. Consequently, they suggest as an alternative that stores be located within a short driving distance of home. To maintain the principle of separating pedestrians from roads designed for automobiles, parking lots would have to be built for these stores: "Local traffic needs ample parking space, as the Sears Roebuck stores have been intelligent enough to discover and to provide for in the layout of their new buildings" (MacKaye and Mumford 1931: 350). Older department stores required that shoppers park downtown and then walk on the street to the store's entrance; the design of Sears shielded women from this experience. Sears created an isolated link from the home to the department store, and the influence of this design soon meant most shopping was done by car (see Figure 4).

The spread of this design throughout the United States meant that the car went from a convenience to a necessity for a majority of Americans. Ruth Schwartz Cowan (1983: 85) writes, "The automobile had become, to the American housewife of the middle classes, what the cast-iron stove in the kitchen would have been to her counterpart of 1850—the vehicle through which she did much of her most significant work, and the work locale where she could most often be found." Thus, in addition to being more restricted from the space of the city, women took on the new burden of chauffeur and courier—a burden that they continue to carry today, even when most work full-time.

AUTOMOBILE AS SUBURBAN POLITICAL MACHINE

Equally important to the construction of a domestic sphere was the need to restore a feeling of autonomy lost in the mechanization of large industry and the unpredictability of the market. In Chapter 1 I discussed how the assertion of one's ability to drive and maintain a car helped create this sense of autonomy. The handiness and independence encouraged by the automobile

Figure 4. Parking lots made driving to Sears more convenient than walking. Photo by M. L. Fotsch.

echoes themes found in the works of Ralph Waldo Emerson and Henry David Thoreau, both of whom Mumford revered. The desire to maintain one's own automobile matches these authors' high regard for practicality and independent thinking, traits Mumford (1926: 93) considered typically American: "[Emerson and Thoreau] fathomed the possibility, these Americans, of a modern basis for culture, and fathoming it, were nearer to the sources of culture, nearer to the formative thinkers and poets of the past, than those who sought to restore the past." Both Emerson and Thoreau celebrated self-reliance and associated the country with an empty slate upon which to discover and create oneself and a new society.

Mumford saw the fostering of individualism as beneficial to society. He rejected selfishness but supported a type of individual creativity that showed concern for the entire community: "The individualism of an Emerson or a Thoreau was the necessary complement of the thoroughly socialized existence of the New England town; it was what prevented these towns from becoming collections of yes-men, with never an opinion or an emotion that differed from their neighbors" (ibid.: 117–118). In other words, according to these writers, individualism is necessary for social democracy, and individualism is developed through a creative interaction with nature.[1] At the same time, Thoreau saw the contributions of social institutions as vital to the enrichment of the individual: "As the nobleman of cultivated taste surrounds himself with whatever conduces to his culture—genius—learning—wit—books—paintings—statuary—music—philosophical instruments, and the like: so let the village do . . . . To act collectively is according to the spirit of our institutions" (Thoreau quoted in Mumford 1926: 118). The townless highway reasserted this necessary contact with nature but also permitted the fostering of civic institutions. It maintained rather than eliminated the cultural benefits of the city and, equally important, the political benefits of the city: the ability to come together and directly interact with neighbors.

The significance of this link between individual creativity and small-scale democracy further sheds light on Mumford's discomfort with commodity culture. Forms of mass-produced culture—movies, amusement parks, and five-and-dime stores—lack the "originality and creativity" linked to the works of Thoreau. As Walter Benjamin explains in his famous essay, mechanical reproduction destroys the "aura" attached to works of art (Benjamin 1955/1969). This authenticity is precisely what makes forms of "high culture" valuable to Mumford, and he describes the problem with mechanically produced objects in terms not that different from Benjamin's: "The craftsman literally possesses his work, in the sense that the Bible says a body is possessed by a familiar spirit" (Mumford 1924: 217). Again sounding like Benjamin, Mumford indicates the distancing effect this authenticity can have: "There is something in man that compels him to respect the human imprint of art: he lives more nobly surrounded by his reflections as a god might live" (ibid.: 221). However, while Benjamin saw the elimination of the aura allowing a critique of traditional authority, Mumford simply saw it as culturally degrading.

According to Mumford, mechanical reproduction by itself does not destroy the work's aura; thus he celebrates the photographs of Stieglitz. Mumford believes that for Stieglitz, "from the beginning the machine was as subordinate to his human direction, through his understanding of its potentialities and capacities, as is the breathing of a Hindu guru" (1945: 46). In contrast, the machine or mechanized processes dominate the entertainments of the working class:

The urban worker escapes the mechanical routine of his daily job only to find an equally mechanical substitute for life and growth and experience in his amusements. The Gay White Way with its stupendous blaze of lights, and Coney Island, with its fear-stimulating roller coasters and chute-the-chutes, are characteristic by-products of an age that has renounced the task of actively humanizing the machine, and of creating an environment in which all the fruitful impulses of the community may be expressed. (Ibid.: 17)

This degraded culture of the city prevents the intellectual development that Mumford sees as crucial to democracy.

Mumford sees the failure of the big city to produce positive democratic institutions embodied in the "machine" politics of the turn of the century. In particular, he describes late-nineteenth-century New York as dominated by this type of politics: "Beer saloons, four to as many corners in most parts of the city, brought together in their more squalid forms the ancient forces of hunger and love and politics: 'free lunch,' 'ladies' entrance,' and the political boss and his underlings. The main duty of the latter was to protect vice and crime and to levy a constant tax upon virtue in whatever offensive form it might take—as justice, as public spirit, as intelligence" (29). This image reveals a clear middle-class bias. Daniel Czitrom (1991) has pointed out that although based on patronage and questionable electoral practices, machine politics in large cities like New York could provide a unified political base and help create cross-ethnic coalitions. Machine politicians were often more progressive in their concern for the betterment of those who lived in the slums than "progressive" reformers who tended to be more discriminating about who deserved assistance.

Elizabeth Wilson (1991: 100) argues that most "progressive" planners ignored the economic conditions that created the poverty and unhealthy conditions of the city slum and hoped to erase these conditions purely through design: "Like the Victorian philanthropists they so despised, the twentieth-century planners displaced the general problem of poverty—ultimately of social and economic inequality—on to housing and urban chaos, but would also purge the disorderly aspects of working class life, such as gambling, street entertainments, prostitution and unlicensed street trading." Mumford did not think that design was the solution to poverty—as already noted, he believed in a more equitable distribution of resources—but at the same time, much like the planners Wilson describes, he had little regard for the culture of the urban working class.

Perhaps the most troubling aspect of Mumford's disregard for the activities of this group is how it paralleled nativist attitudes of the period. For example, although his celebration of a past American aesthetic was meant to be inclusive, similar appeals to American heritage had been used to call for restrictions on immigration. Nativism of the 1920s culminated in the explicitly racist Immigration Act of 1924. This act excluded all immigrants ineligible for citizenship—which meant Asians—and by basing immigration on national origin linked to the 1890 Census favored northern and western Europeans over southern and eastern Europeans. White middle-class Americans supported this act because, as noted earlier, they feared immigrant radicalism and the rise of immigrant political power in the cities (Daniels 1990: 279). Perhaps the worst manifestation of nativism from this period was the rise of the Ku Klux Klan in northern cities. While the KKK is usually associated with the rural South and violence toward blacks, it became a powerful political force in northern cities of the 1920s, arising partially in response to the dramatic increase in Catholic immigrants. By 1924, 40 percent of the KKK's membership resided in Ohio, Indiana, and Illinois, and half its members lived in cities of more than fifty thousand (Judd 1988: 124).

Mumford was not a nativist; his attitude toward immigrants and their culture was complex. He both recognized their exploitation and saw immigrant neighborhoods on the lower East Side of Manhattan as closer to what a community should look like.

> [New York] threw open its doors to the Irish of the [eighteen-]forties, to the Germans of the fifties and sixties, later to the Italians, and to the Russians and Jews of Eastern Europe: the outside world, contemptuous but hopeful, sneering but credulous, sent many of its finest children to New York. . . . But the congested East Side, for all its poverty and dirt, was not the poorest part of the city: it still had its open markets with their color, its narrow streets with their sociability and their vivid common life and neighborly help, its synagogues with at least the dried remnants of a common vision. (1945: 35)

But Mumford expresses a subtle discomfort with immigration in his desire for a "permanent community." He uses ecological terms to argue for cultural stability:[2]

> Regional planning is the New Conservation—the conservation of human values hand in hand with natural resources . . . . Permanent agriculture instead of land skinning, permanent forestry instead of timber mining, permanent human communities, dedicated to life,

liberty and human happiness, instead of camps of squatter settlements, and to stable building, instead of the scantling and false work of our "go-ahead" communities. (Mumford 1986a: 209)

The emphasis on permanence, in one sense, anticipates today's movement for sustainable development, but it also projects a future utopia without accounting for the dramatic shifts in population and culture linked to the modern economy.

While Mumford's condemnation of urban popular culture ignored the significance it had for new immigrants, his promotion of residential decentralization missed how suburbs might hinder the political unification corresponding to this culture. Just as automobile-centered developments could effectively confine women, they might also serve to neutralize the working class. For example, Glenn Yago (1984: 36–37) argues that this was the case in Nazi Germany where Autobahn-centered residential development was designed to help eradicate the radical tendencies of urban labor:

By dispersing the working class to various settlements on the outskirts of major cities under the Nazi formula, suburbanization would ensure a measure of social peace and redefinition of classes in a nationalist framework. Through motorization, the building of highways, the construction of the "people's automobile," and the general improvements associated with these policies, fascism would provide physical and geographic mobility for a disciplined work force instead of social mobility.

In the United States both labor and corporate leaders held similar goals in the 1920s. In response to the continuing labor unrest that had taken place in major cities throughout the United States going back to the 1880s, suburbanization was promoted as a way of appeasing white male workers. Dolores Hayden (2002: 49) quotes a corporate official saying, "Get them to invest their savings in homes and own them. Then they won't leave and they won't strike. It ties them down so they have a stake in our prosperity."

Once again it becomes clear how the underlying ideals of Mumford and the RPAA are lost while surface elements of their designs are implemented in ways that undermine some of these ideals. While Mumford condemned typical suburbanization for ignoring the need to cultivate community, decentralization easily fell into a suburban form and possibly served to legitimize and sustain a profit-oriented economy.

The potential for suburbs to neutralize the working class came not just from the new economic dependency they created but also from the divisions they facilitated. The appeasement of white male workers was based on the exclusion of women from the workforce and of nonwhites from most suburban housing. This second exclusion was enforced in part through racially restrictive covenants officially endorsed by the National Association of Real Estate Brokers in its code of ethics from 1924 (Massey and Denton 1993: 19). Although most urban laborers were not able to purchase a suburban home in the 1920s, after World War II suburbanization much like that envisioned by corporate leaders became the norm. This was facilitated by the 1934 National Housing Act, which subsidized low-interest loans but systematically excluded people of color from these loans.

Another tool of division that Mumford failed to recognize was municipal separation. He viewed the sprawling metropolis as democratically unmanageable and advocated the separate incorporation of suburbs as a solution. For Mumford, small towns independent of the city would be more hospitable to democratic participation. However, new suburban towns could also deny access to socially, economically, or racially different groups.

Sam Bass Warner (1962) describes how the creation of Boston's early suburbs permitted a class segregation that enabled residents to benefit from the wealth of the city without sharing in its burdens. Because only the wealthy could afford to live in the outermost suburbs, they in effect excluded poorer members of society; and because of the municipal independence of these upper-middle-class suburbs from central Boston, the suburban tax base did not have to fund any of the technical and social services of the central city. As a result, Warner argues, the city services increasingly decayed: "The growing parochialism and fragmentation resulted in a steady relative weakening of social agencies. Weakness, in turn, convinced more and more individuals that local community action was hopeless or irrelevant. From this conviction came the further weakening of the public agencies" (160). In other words, precisely the type of community segregation—in this case enabled by streetcars but eventually by express highways—that Mumford advocated brought about further social divisions. Perhaps in Mumford's ideal society, where wealth was redistributed, socially diverse suburbs would exist; but as implemented in the United States, municipal separation could easily serve to worsen material inequalities.

By the time of *The City in History*, published in 1961, Mumford had recognized the gap between the intentions of his plans and how they had been implemented. In particular, like Warner, he criticizes how suburbs have become enclaves of the wealthy where the problems of the poor can be ignored: "In the suburb one might live and die without marring the image of an innocent world, except when some shadow of its evil fell over a column in the newspaper. Thus the suburb served as an asylum for the preservation of an illusion. Here domesticity could flourish, forgetful of the exploitation on which so much of it was based" (494). The tension with his earlier celebration of domesticity is clear, and yet a later passage reveals a strange ambivalence about suburban exclusivity: "When the suburb served only a favored minority it neither spoiled the countryside nor threatened the city. But now that the drift to the outer ring has become a mass movement, it tends to destroy the value of both environments without producing anything but a dreary substitute, devoid of form and even more devoid of the original suburban values" (506). Here it seems the problem is not so much suburban isolation from the city but rather that the suburb has become too much like the city—crowded and chaotic.

Mumford attributed the failures of both suburb and city to misguided government policies. In the 1930s he criticized New Deal housing policies, arguing that they would primarily benefit real estate speculators. However, he said nothing about how federal rules systematically discriminated against people of color. In 1967 Mumford made clear his pessimism about government ventures in a statement to the Senate Committee on Governmental Expenditures arguing against large investments in housing projects. He cautioned, "Go slow! Experiment with small measures and small units, until you have time to prepare better plans and to organize new public agencies to carry out those plans. Whatever you do in extending the policies followed in the past will almost surely meet with the same embarrassments and the same failures" (Mumford 1968: 226). One example of those failures was "what happened to MacKaye's conception of the townless highway":

> When he put forward this proposal, he sought to apply to the motorway efficient transportation principles, like that of an independent right of way, with access only at wide intervals, that had long been incorporated in the railroad line . . . . Unfortunately, the highway engineers took over every feature of MacKaye's plan except the most important one: that it should be "townless," that is, that it should bypass every urban center, small or big. (216)

However, Mumford did not provide an alternative to massive government bureaucracy; in particular, he did not suggest a political alternative, for example, where those in need of housing might direct the building agency themselves.

Most troublingly, Mumford revealed a complete ignorance of the systemic racism underlying the failed state of both cities and suburbs. Like many public intellectuals of the late 1960s, he tried to make sense of the civil disturbances that seemed to emerge every summer in ghettos throughout the United States, and his answer drew upon his earlier critique of the declining traditional family. While not denying that urban unemployment was a problem, in the end, he argued, "no adequate renewal program will be possible until the restoration of the basic family constellation is taken as one of the essential goals of adequate housing" (252). Mumford's attitude echoed the arguments of leading white liberals such as Daniel Patrick Moynihan. In his influential 1965 report *The Negro Family: The Case for National Action*, Moynihan saw poverty as key to understanding urban turmoil, but he also blamed pathologies of the black family, such as female-headed households (Hodgson 1978: 263–267). While Moynihan and his colleague Nathan Glazer attributed the problems faced by African Americans to the legacy of slavery (Steinberg 1989: 119), Mumford not surprisingly attributed their problems to the degraded environment of the city: "The mere increase in urbanization has in fact automatically increased the incidence of pathological social phenomenon" (Mumford 1968: 232).

Mumford also followed Moynihan in arguing that the difficulties faced by African Americans and Puerto Ricans were equivalent to those faced by immigrants in the early twentieth century: "Faced with this influx of two depressed minorities . . . American municipalities experienced, in even more acute form, the same difficulties that mass migration from Europe had caused between 1870 and 1920" (231). This confusion matches what Michael Omi and Howard Winant (1994) describe as the "ethnicity paradigm" introduced by Robert Park in the 1920s. According to Park, immigrant groups that started on the economic margins and settled in ethnic enclaves would eventually move to middle-class residences in the suburbs. Moynihan claimed that this model would apply to blacks once civil rights laws were passed to give them the same opportunities as whites, as Omi and Winant (1994: 19) describe: "Once equal opportunity legislation along with its judicial and administrative enforcement were accomplished facts, it fell to blacks to follow in their predecessors' footsteps." For Mumford, the progress of "minorities" would come once they escaped their depressed neighborhoods to more wholesome surroundings.

The primary question, according to Mumford (1968: 248), "that must be answered, by the minorities themselves, is whether they are willing to move out of their present neighborhoods." In his view, African Americans and Puerto Ricans chose to live in the ghetto because they preferred to live among people similar to themselves. For someone who spent his life studying the city, it would seem that Mumford was surprisingly blind to housing discrimination. On the other hand, some awareness is revealed when he states, "No open housing or school busing can overcome the isolation and resultant self-segregation that sheer numbers have produced" (ibid.). What is to be made of this blatantly contradictory statement? Mumford must have recognized at some level that discrimination kept blacks from moving into white neighborhoods, since this is precisely what open housing and school busing was meant to challenge. Yet, he reaffirmed the myth that ghettos were a result of "self-segregation." Clearly Mumford, like many white liberals then and now (see Meyer 2000), would have been happy to see people of color in better living conditions, as long as he could still exclude them from his own neighborhood.

In this light, perhaps it is not surprising that the most glaring oversight in MacKaye and Mumford's advocacy for townless highways was their failure to recognize how the social inequalities of the 1920s were embodied in automobile ownership. At the time MacKaye conceived of the townless highway, most urban laborers, white and nonwhite, did not own cars. In 1929 the ratio of persons to cars was still only five to one, and most cars were owned by farmers, professionals, or wealthy residents of the city (Flink 1988: 140–141). Moreover, urban car owners frequently drove automobiles of ostentation until the Great Depression made it disrespectable and dangerous because the poor stoned them in the streets (ibid.: 218). In cities especially, the automobile was a mark of social success and exclusivity before 1930. In contrast, as it became available to a large majority of whites after World War II, lacking one became a sign of failure. This postwar shift signaled the development of new types of poverty in neighborhoods with low rates of car ownership.

The consensus of city planners through the first half of the twentieth century coincided with the ideal of townless highways: planners viewed decentralization as crucial to the elimination of urban instability. Mark Foster (1981) writes, "In the early years of the planning movement, few doubted that decentralization was anything but a blessing, and they welcomed any technological advances that assisted such a pattern of growth" (44). Yet, he writes, while building roads to encourage decentralization was popular among planners, "for a variety of reasons, many of them beyond their direct control, planners exerted only a limited impact in shaping the twentieth-century city" (5). Thus, while writers like Mumford had plans to incorporate multiple modes of transportation, when elements of these plans were implemented, the original goals were undermined. This in part explains the tension between Mumford's early and later attitude toward cars.

Ultimately, only part of the Radburn development was completed because financing fell through with the stock market crash of 1929. At the same time, the Great Depression inspired an important new element in the discourse surrounding highway construction. Not only would the automobile and road bring access to a better life in the country, construction would provide jobs by sparking automobile-centered consumption and economic recovery. The Futurama exhibit at the 1939 World's Fair, which embodied this vision, was inspired in part by the ideas of Mumford. But the commercialism on which this vision was based ran counter to Mumford's distrust of the private market. This consumerist dream evoked similar concerns among a group of German social theorists who had come to the United States to escape Nazi persecution. However, unlike Mumford, they were not interested in designing a technical solution to modern crises. Rather, for them the unquestioned acceptance of technical design revealed flaws within modern society as much as consumerism did. Amid a time of world crisis, while Norman Bel Geddes built Futurama to inspire a future prosperity centered on the automobile, German refugees Max Horkheimer and Theodor Adorno saw technical utopias based on capitalism leading to the reification of daily life.

PART 2

GERMAN CRITICAL THEORY
MEETS AMERICAN CARTOPIA

■ ■

CHAPTER 3

THE BUILDING OF A SUPERHIGHWAY
FUTURE AT THE NEW YORK WORLD'S FAIR

A free-flowing movement of people and goods across our nation is a requirement of modern living and prosperity.   GEDDES 1941: 10

Futurama, a diorama designed by Norman Bel Geddes and sponsored by
General Motors was the most popular exhibit at the 1939 New York World's
Fair. During the 1930s a few urban highways had been built, but this exhibit
was spectacular by comparison. It depicted the United States in the year
1960 with multilane superhighways crossing the country. Viewers stood
in line for hours to enter it. Upon entering, they were seated on moving
benches with built-in speakers that transmitted explanations for each element of the diorama. *Business Week* (1939: 27) described the scene: "More
than 30,000 persons daily, the show's capacity, inch along the sizzling pave-
ment in long queues until they reach the chairs which transport them to a
tourist's paradise. It unfolds a prophecy of cities, towns, and countrysides
served by a comprehensive road system. Somewhere in the rolling davenport
a disembodied angel explains the elysium" (see Figures 5 and 6).

The exhibit, like the fair as a whole, emphasized hope for the future at a
time when daily life for many held fear and uncertainty. The United States
had endured a decade of depression; war had erupted in Europe, where fascism
and communism were expanding; and the instability of the economy seemed
to fuel the growth of radical movements in the United States. In his opening
address to the fair, President Franklin Roosevelt expressed hope that global
instability would be overcome: "The eyes of the United States are fixed on the
future. Our wagon is hitched to a star. But it is a star of good will, a star of
progress for mankind, a star of greater happiness and less hardship, a star of

Figure 5. Moving benches at the Futurama exhibit.

Figure 6. Diorama of a 1960 Midwestern metropolis at the Futurama exhibit.

international good will, and above all, a star of peace. May the months to come carry us forward in the rays of that hope" (quoted in Zim, Lerner, and Rolfes 1988: 9). Many saw new technology helping to bring on this better future, and technological progress was embodied in the rapid progression of cars in the Futurama. The exhibit sped time past contemporary crises just as it increased the traveling speed of the automobile to one hundred miles per hour. The problems of the "modern world" were linked to the problem of traffic congestion, so superhighways, by creating "a free flowing movement of people and goods" could resolve the nation's problems and bring "prosperity."

Although the crises of the 1930s were felt not only in the city, urban problems were the key concern of Geddes's project. Many elements he depicted in Futurama were later implemented in the Interstate Highway Act of 1956; while some specific design elements were not implemented, the exhibit undoubtedly helped popularize the concept of the superhighway and build the foundation for the eventual construction of the largest public works project in history. Even if Futurama did not directly influence the construction of the interstates, analyzing its popularity can help explain why these highways were allowed to restructure U.S. cities. Built into the design of Futurama was the assumption that expanded consumption sparked by massive federal investment in highway construction would best bring the economy out of its slump, and in many ways this was an accurate prediction: although it was federal investment in defense that provided the first boost, the postwar economy was aided greatly by the growth of automobile production and highways.

A few critics saw an underside to this expansionist economy. Futurama embodied in many ways what philosophers-in-exile Max Horkheimer and Theodor Adorno found most disturbing about American consumer culture. On the one hand, Futurama perfectly blended information and promotion, and on the other, it uncritically celebrated the use of technology for corporate interests. New highways might bring postwar suburban consumerism and economic stability, but they might also serve to sustain exploitative and oppressive social relations.

MAGIC MOTORWAYS

The origins of Futurama can be traced to 1936, when J. Walter Thompson solicited Geddes's help in forming an advertising campaign for Shell Oil that would present innovative solutions to problems of city traffic. Jeffrey Meikle (1984: 7) writes, "With characteristic enthusiasm, he went far beyond his original mandate. Eventually he and the members of his firm designed both an interstate highway system and an entire metropolis." Not only was this version of the diorama used in a 1937 Shell advertising campaign, it went on display for a while in New York and was exhibited in several other large cities. In addition, a film presenting the ideas it espoused was loaned to organizations in smaller communities. "Throughout the fall [of 1937] while Shell's magazine advertisements were running, showings of the film triggered articles and editorials about the highway problem in dozens of small daily newspapers" (ibid.: 30–31). The publicity encouraged General Motors to hire Geddes to construct an exhibit several times larger and much more elaborate. This exhibit became Futurama.

In the book he wrote to detail the vision of Futurama, *Magic Motorways,* Geddes (1941) explained the popularity of his exhibit this way:

> All of these thousands of people who stood in line ride in motor cars and therefore are harassed by the daily task of getting from one place to another, by the nuisance of intersectional jams, narrow, congested bottle necks, dangerous night driving, annoying policemen's whistles, honking horns, blinking traffic lights, confusing highway signs, and irritating traffic regulations; they are appalled by the daily toll of highway accidents and deaths, and they are eager to find a sensible way out of this planless, suicidal mess. The Futurama gave them a dramatic and graphic solution to a problem which they all faced. (4)

Here, the city is represented as a place of chaos, noise, and arbitrary rules. The superhighway provides an escape from this in its design and through its role in allowing people to live in small-scale residential neighborhoods away from signs of the industrial city. Describing this role, Geddes writes, "By opening up the sections surrounding the center, by reclaiming them from misuse and blight, people were drawn out, distributing more evenly both population and traffic" (213).

The theme of the Futurama exhibit fit closely with the fair's overall theme, The World of Tomorrow, not just in its emphasis on the future but also in its redesign of the American landscape. Lewis Mumford, who was on the fair's theme committee, explained to the New York City Club in 1939: "The story we have to tell . . . and which will bring people from all over the world to New York, not merely from the United States, is the story of this planned environment, this planned industry, this planned civilization" (quoted in Cusker 1980: 4). The theme exhibit, the second most popular at the fair, was a diorama designed by Henry Dreyfus centered around a city of the future, much like in Geddes's exhibit. Similar to the Futurama, Drey-

Figure 7. The theme exhibit designed by Henry Dreyfus. Photograph by Richard Wurts. "Democracity," New York 1939 World's Fair. Museum of the City of New York. The Wurts Collection.

fus's Democracity featured high-speed parkways to enable residents to live in small towns outside the center city (see Figure 7).

Both Geddes's and Dreyfus's exhibits have many features that parallel the work of Mumford. Like Mumford, these designers support the movement away from what they consider the congested and unhealthy environment of the city, and they contend that typical suburban development lacks planning and simply replicates the chaos of the city. Geddes (1941: 206) quotes directly from Mumford's 1938 *The Culture of Cities:*

> The original residential areas are eaten into from within, as if by termites, as the original inhabitants move out and are replaced by lower economic strata; then these overcrowded quarters, serving as an area of transition between the commercial center and the better dormitory areas, become in their disorder and their misery special breeding points for disease and crime.

The text of the Democracity brochure similarly condemns past development by invoking the future as "no longer a planless jumble of slums and grime and smoke, but town and country joined for work and play in sunlight and good air" (Seldes 1939: 20). For Geddes and Dreyfus, cities and their surroundings needed to be planned in coordination, in Mumford's terms by "regional planning."

For Geddes, this planning would segregate the superhighway from the town in ways similar to the townless highway of MacKaye and Mumford. First, the roads linking the superhighway and city would be bordered by parks "to prevent the tendency of industry and small business alike to spread out along the right of way and exploit it" (Geddes 1941: 213). Second, the superhighway would avoid going directly through the city. "A great motorway has no business cutting a wide swath right through a town or city and destroying values there: its place is in the country where there is ample room for it and where its landscaping is designed to harmonize with the land around it. Its presence will not, like that of a railroad, destroy the beauty of the land. It will help maintain it" (211).

Herein lies a slight difference between Futurama and Democracity, as Dreyfus is more willing to allow his parkways to go directly through the city. However, this difference is less significant than the goals they share—to erase the signs of the city and replace them with signs of the country or village. Both Geddes and Dreyfus make a point of hiding the images of urban disorder from the traveler. Like Futurama, Dreyfus's Democracity emphasizes the need to hide signs of the city from the commuter. It contrasts railroad trains, which ran "through desolate slums and unsightly dump heaps," with parkways and "an underground high speed artery to the business center," thus avoiding urban or industrial environments (Seldes 1939: 15).

Geddes further links himself to Mumford by celebrating Radburn, New Jersey, and the garden cities of Ebenezer Howard. Geddes (1941) writes of Radburn, "Here homes turn their back doors to the streets, fronting instead on green parks and safe playgrounds inside the large residential blocks. These neighborhood units are united by a single community center, where all shopping and business can be attended to without the necessity of having to repark the car several times in front of scattered shops" (196). At the same time, Geddes believes that all business could not be contained within residential units; instead work and home should be separated. Following the inspiration of Robert Owen, Geddes regards "the city as a *working* entity and the country as a *living* entity [his emphasis]" (209). Applying this concept to a mill town where "thousands of families live alongside the grimy mills," he writes, "with an adequate highway system to transport them back and forth, these families could be moved 30 to 50 miles away from their place of work. A day will come when factory labor lives not in shanties on the other side of the tracks, but in healthy uplands between forest and stream" (292).

Again, similar ideas are put forth in the Democracity exhibit. First, there is the parallel concern of segregating foot traffic from car traffic: "The streets are built for motor traffic; when you want to walk, you walk through connecting parks around which are offices and stores and museums" (Seldes 1939: 8). Democracity presents a more detailed vision of the relationship between work and home. Dreyfus constructs a city with six interconnected elements, but interestingly, while residents of "Pleasantville" are segregated from the business center and industrial regions, industrial workers live near factories in "Millville." Still, if residents of Millville do not avoid industry, the country is brought to them in the form of greenery and gardens surrounding their homes. "Certain things you've been accustomed to, you'll miss in Democracity. . . . You'll miss the slums. . . . and all the nervous discomfort of overgrown cities and the smoky air and the dark rooms and sunless streets. . . . and the noise" (ibid.). Similarly, Geddes (1941: 292) approvingly cites the sociologist Charles H. Cooley, who argues, "'The extreme concentration of population at centers has deplorable effects upon health, intelligence and morals of people.'" Geddes continues, "When the time comes and transportation finally realizes its purpose—namely, to free men from bondage to their immediate surroundings—it is not only their bodies that will be restored by sun and air and contact with nature. It is their minds as well."

By 1939 the goal of providing urban residents with better road access to the country was already being fulfilled in New York City. The popularity of the Futurama exhibit in New York was fitting, since the city's parks commissioner, Robert Moses, was one of the most effective road builders of the era. Moses's most impressive project of the 1930s was the Henry Hudson Parkway, which brought him national recognition (Caro 1975: 569). Between 1924 and 1936, Moses oversaw the successful construction of one hundred miles of parkways (515), providing access to the grand beaches and parks of Long Island, the construction of which he also oversaw.[1] Like the proponents of highways at the fair, Moses wished to facilitate access to the country and permit an escape from crowded city conditions.

Moses also used the popular desire for grand highway and park projects to subvert public debate. He relied on the publicity gained from successful projects to build support for future plans. Although Moses owed his rise to Governor Al Smith, a machine politician, his power derived from being portrayed as a reformer able to cut through politics and get things done. As John Mollenkopf (1983) puts it, "Moses created effective links with local Democratic bosses, but he also responded to middle class reformers by building organizations with large, highly qualified staffs which produced results" (72). The press labeled critics of his highway plans "obstructionists" and "politicians" who were motivated by narrow self-interest (Caro 1975: 500–575).

Geddes (1941) uses similar rhetoric to explain the problems often faced by road projects. He argues that highways had often been overly expensive and poorly planned because of graft and local political control: "Possibly even more ruinous than the outright theft of highway funds is the 'political road'—the road routed not where it can be of most service, but where it will most profitably serve the interests of those in political authority" (169).

Geddes's and Moses's attitudes toward politics were a legacy of progressivism. While machine politics were based on patronage, progressive politics claimed to be based on objectivity and merit. Fiorello La Guardia, the mayor of New York, expressed his belief in the ideals of progressivism in a state of the city report released for the World's Fair: "In the first issue of *New York Advancing* it was frankly conceded that my theory of non-political municipal administration for New York was an experiment and made no claim to originality. . . . I now dare to venture the statement that the experiment has succeeded" (La Guardia 1939: xv). A "non-political" administration was a label used to contrast his New York City administration with past ones controlled by Tammany Hall's vote-buying techniques. Geddes (1941: 177) expressed his alliance with progressive administrations by enumerating multiple examples of "graft" in highway production, including by former New York Mayor William Tweed. Moses invoked this same discourse when denouncing opponents of his West Side Highway project by claiming they owned land near a proposed alternative route (Caro 1975: 547).

An autocratic style did not alone make Moses effective: the federal government boosted the power of regional administrators by allocating money to them directly rather than to local governments (Wallock 1991). Geddes supported this superseding of local control because he believed it would prevent politicians from deciding a highway's route based on local interests. Geddes presupposed that engineers knew better than local residents what would benefit them most.

At the same time, Geddes disagreed with Moses's plan to bring highways directly through cities, and Moses's criticisms of Geddes's exhibit led to a dispute recorded in the *New York Times* (Gelernter 1995: 364). Despite this, in the end Geddes and Moses agreed that urban chaos could best be overcome through the effective designs of engineers, without the intervention of politicians.

STABILIZATION THROUGH PROGRESS

Futurama proposed overcoming urban problems through engineering and technology; at the same time, it addressed the chaotic ways technology had been used and called for improved planning to achieve technology's full potential. This paralleled the fair's overall theme. Members of the fair's theme committee hoped to educate people about the possibilities that technology provided and to encourage them to support its advancement. Grover Whalen, the fair's president, declared the aim of the fair "to place en route the world's resources in a gigantic crusade against man's chief foes: inertia, lassitude and chance" (quoted in Heller 1989: 2). In this view, technology could help solve the economic and social problems of the country if people believed in it and were motivated to appropriate its benefits.

The automobile was key in motivating people to recognize the need to accommodate technology's advance. The subtitles of "The World of Tomorrow," Pearl E. Levinson's Official Poem of the New York World's Fair, 1939, were "Hub," "Spokes," and "Wheel." The section "Wheel" made the connection between progress and road construction:

> *Knowing far traveling is not traveling*
> *Far if eyes be turned to where we were.*
> *We cannot stand at intersection of a road*
> *Remembering only the detoured hour*
> *That was good and the easy solitude.*
> *It is time and later is too late.* (Levinson 1939: 10)

The poem describes a challenge to face the future and its possibilities; this requires accepting technological changes and learning how they can benefit people. The automobile had become a familiar symbol of the potential to go beyond the "intersection" toward places where technology is clearly benefiting people. It also is used to bring together these themes in John Black's "At the Fair II," a Song of the World's Fair:

> *These loves of mine, these people, materials,—wheels!—*
> *(Circling eternities of man's advance).*
> *Would I might capture in a song*
> *The Magic of these ways and worlds . . . .*
> *O engineering, open door*
> *To worlds unknown before.* (Black 1939: 15)

The automobile focus of the fair was also found in the many buildings with streamlined designs, including the central buildings of the transportation section by General Motors and Ford. By the late 1930s, the designers of automobile bodies used streamlining—fashioned on airplanes—to give cars the image of speed. Streamlining and the automobile gave technology a familiar, popular, and exciting image, which could help overcome people's discomfort about its advancement.

Education could also help fulfill this goal. Donald Slesinger, the designer of the fair's education exhibit, describes education as an "intellectual safeguard for the individual against the confusions, maladjustments, and misconceptions of a changing civilization" (quoted in Cusker 1980: 12). One method of education, best demonstrated by Futurama, was to better acquaint people with the use of technology in daily life. Geddes notes at the beginning of *Magic Motorways* (1941: 4): "One of the best ways to make a solution understandable to everybody is to make it visual, to dramatize it. Futurama did just this: it was a visual dramatization of a solution to the complex tangle of American roadways." Building familiarity with technology and enthusiasm for its possibilities, Geddes and others hoped, would overcome inertia that prevented the country from benefiting from new technologies.

For Geddes, the inertia was Americans' hesitation to embark on large projects such as his that would aid technology. "What holds America back from doing vital deeds today is not, as in some countries, exhaustion or even, primarily, fear of war. There is no lack of individual courage. But there exists a certain public suspicion of united effort" (292). Instead of people making a united effort, Geddes views them as acting chaotically and awkwardly. Describing the migration from city to suburb he writes, "Like swarms of locusts they proceeded to devour that land, digesting it in the forms of suburbs, 'developments,' unplanned areas overbuilt with cheap speculative housing, until these areas in turn left disorder, blight and new slums, and people had to march out still further" (206).

But the inertia of people also comes out in their unwillingness to take initiative. In particular, Geddes blames the failure to develop the potential of the automobile on laziness: "People who have achieved a partial success are often inclined to sit back self-satisfied and blind themselves to the fact that the success is only partial. Because we today move more freely than our ancestors, we have a tendency to overlook the fact that we should be able to move ten times more freely" (10). Geddes represents this inertia in a montage of three photos containing large aggregations of people, sheep, and cars. The caption reads "MEN MACHINES OR SHEEP?" The image implies that once people are shown the importance of building a superhighway system, they will take control of the machine and become "men." Central here is the theme of controlling technology in order to assert individual autonomy lost in mechanized culture, reasserting a theme found in the earlier discourse surrounding automobiles.

Geddes's language also parallels criticisms of the New Deal that claimed financial relief to the poor would produce laziness. Even at the worst moments of the Depression, many argued that giving direct aid would make people content not to work, just as in Geddes's image of people satisfied with "partial success." By 1934 the federal government eliminated direct relief to the poor out of concern that those who remained unemployed were simply unwilling to work or did not try hard enough to find a job (Piven and Cloward 1979: 82).

A similar perspective can be found in the promoters of modern industrial design. Walter Teague, who designed the Ford Exhibit and several others at the fair, saw "slovenly workmanship" as being endemic to industrial society and believed industrial design was central to the restoration of democracy (Cusker 1980: 12). In this image, modern industry makes people passive, and this passivity in turn leads to poorly designed goods: goods made with little creativity but that can be produced cheaply and easily. To counter this regressive cycle, designers like Teague and Geddes believed industry must begin to create a better-designed machine.

Geddes contrasts men to sheep and machines, but his project demonstrated a need to adapt men to machines before they could benefit from and gain control of machines. In fact, his motorway would automatically control the speed and steering of the car.[2] Geddes (1941) believes this control was necessary due to human fallibility: "Human nature itself, unaided, does not make for efficient driving. Human beings, even when at the wheel, are prone to talk, wave to their friends, make love, day dream, listen to the radio, stare at striking billboards, light cigarettes, take chances" (48).

For Geddes, cars should be controlled more like trains. "The locomotive engineer is not likely to make a mistake as a result of wrong judgment. . . . An efficient system of automatic signals keeps him thoroughly acquainted with the situation ahead of him, informs him of emergencies which are not visible to the human eye" (54). What had been viewed as a central benefit of the automobile—an individual's ability to control a machine—was now viewed as the automobile's dangerous flaw.

The desire to eliminate driver control may be explained in part by the faster automobile and heavier traffic, which caused problems in the 1930s not found during the car's introduction at the turn of the century. Moreover, Geddes emphasizes the danger posed by other drivers; this danger impinged on the freedom the automobile provided. On the "magic motorways," one could be free to leisurely enjoy the trip as in a train, but with the privacy and independence of an automobile. Business Week (1939: 28) provided an apt description: "Most revolutionary is the proposal for control of cars, not by the driver but by operators in towers, at regular intervals across the highways. It would be impossible for a drunk or sleeping motorist to leave the road. Drivers could bowl along with their hands off the wheel free to enjoy the scenery or hug their girls." The Futurama vision still provides drivers the privacy to "hug their girls" and the freedom to travel when and where they wish.

At the same time, the fear of accidents can be seen as mirroring the fear of instability in the economy. In this context, motorways could provide the stability and safety that is lacking at a time when the economy fluctuates and jobs are threatened. In other words, the motorway provides a different sort of freedom, similar to the freedom of job security. Safety in this case also implies safety from demonstrations by the unemployed. The image of crowds demanding financial relief or striking workers demanding better salaries and working conditions is reflected in Geddes's description of "swarms of locusts."

In contrast to a unified protest by workers and the poor demanding economic security, Geddes calls for unity through "freedom and understanding." However, this unity would not come until the motorway system was first constructed because poorly built roads harm human freedom. Put differently, the individuals who are not uniting toward a better future need to be directed by industrial designers, educators, or intellectuals toward this future. To achieve freedom, it must first be sacrificed.

The irony is epitomized in his chapter "Eliminate the Human Factor in Driving." Geddes (1941: 56) calls for eliminating human control not only over the automobile but also over the construction of the system—except of course by professional engineers:

> But with the changes in the car, will the driver too be changed? Will he have lost one bad trait which made him years ago a menace to his own safety and a nuisance to others? Don't count on it. But these cars of 1960 and the highways on which they drive will have devices which will correct the faults of human beings as drivers. . . . Everything will be designed by engineering, not by legislation, not in piecemeal fashion, but as a complete job.

The fair's theme exhibit lays even greater emphasis on the importance of unity and overcoming chaos. Although Democracity lacks the same kind of distrust in human activity shown by Geddes, the reiteration of the theme of "interdependence" reads as a fear of social division parallel to Geddes's fear of social chaos. Describing the fair's theme, Grover Whalen (1939: 1) writes, "It is a theme of building the World of Tomorrow—a world which can only be built by the interdependent co-operation of men and of nations." This interdependence is contrasted with chaos in the description of a mural above the Democracity diorama: "On one side is the World of Tomorrow built by millions of free men and women independent and interdependent. . . . On the other side is chaos" (Seldes 1939: 11). While the Democracity exhibit depicted "giant figures. . . . with arms linked" working to build the World of Tomorrow, the social divisions of the contemporary world marked themselves on the fair, where maintenance workers went on strike and other workers threatened to go with them (New York Times 1939b). Warren Susman (1980: 18) notes that the idea of unity at the fair was a way to overcome divisions that seemed salient throughout the United States in the 1930s. According to popular culture of the time, "divisions within society seemed superficial. Somehow, if they could only be allowed to talk or be instructed in what to say, the people could easily speak out in one voice."

The Futurama and Democracity exhibits revealed both a fear of social divisions and a very concrete way of overcoming these divisions, that is, through the creation of massive public works projects. The construction of an extensive highway system could create a common goal and pacify a large group through the security of employment. In the 1930s, highway projects were viewed in large part as a way of providing jobs to the unemployed. Primarily through the Works Progress Administration (WPA), money was given to local governments to improve infrastructure and create jobs. It was also intended to replace direct relief, which had been cut off. However, in reality, as Frances Fox Piven and Richard Cloward (1979: 84–85) point out, the WPA reduced unemployment very little. Instead, the program served primarily as a rhetorical device to defend the view that the unemployed were simply unwilling to work. Road construction could be used to promote the idea that the federal government was doing all that it could to help the jobless. Mark Rose (1990: 10) writes that although President Roosevelt did not believe highway projects were more effective than other methods of taking care of the unemployed, "on April 14, 1938, as joblessness and the prospect of Democratic losses mounted, Roosevelt urged appropriation of an additional $100 million 'only for [highway] projects which can be definitely started this calendar year.'"

Even if highway construction alone could not solve the crisis of unemployment, it represented a strategy to achieve better economic times by providing an immediate boost in employment and facilitating market expansion over the long term, as Geddes (1941) notes: "A national motorway system maintaining a high grade of efficiency will maintain the flow of goods to the consumer without interruption. Demand can be more easily predicted: supply will be more uniform, and to that extent business will grow more stable" (289). At a time when many were worried about keeping their jobs, Geddes presented a future in which jobs were abundant again. The spread of the motorway would push the spread of new industry: "The lifeblood of industry is constant expansion. Economic recovery and prosperity are achieved, not by suppressing industry but by creating new industry. More industry puts more people to work" (291).

Futurama demonstrates what David Harvey describes as spatial and temporal displacement resolving a crisis of overaccumulation. Harvey (1989: 184–185) argues that before World War II, the tendency of capitalism to produce more than the economy could absorb caused cycles of depression. Highways could slow this tendency by aiding the expansion of industry and housing into the suburbs, providing new space for economic development. At the same time, federal investment in defense industries, which were frequently located on the urban periphery along new highways, could absorb productive capacity by increasing debt over time. Mark Rose (1990: 71) writes, "Economists and those interested in economic planning evaluated road-building formulas in light of long-range business trends. Traffic relief, they thought, was necessary to encourage growth. . . . At the same time, massive road construction, if timed properly, offered a useful device in a program for controlling economic swings."

Alfred P. Sloan, General Motors chairman of the board, argued that automobile consumption would play an important role in economic recovery. In a statement to the Temporary Economic Committee in 1939, Sloan reported that "with a rise in the national income there can be a considerable expansion in production because automobile sales increase considerably faster than the national income rises" (quoted in Crider 1939). In fact, automobile ownership doubled in the ten years following World War II (Rae 1965: 192). General Motors facilitated this growth by financing the purchase of its cars with consumer loans, another example of temporal displacement. The postwar economy boomed in part due to the increase in automobile consumption and a new ethic of consumption. By 1968 one out of six Americans had occupations linked to motor vehicles (Goddard 1994: 214).

Some critics of the fair contended that the goal of promoting consumption superseded the fair's ideal of promoting a better future. Peter J. Kuznick (1994: 341) notes that members of the scientific community struggled to place an educationally oriented science exhibit at the fair, but they were disappointed to find the fair dominated by corporations that "narrowly defined science in terms of gadgets, commodities, and magic." The Futurama exhibit in particular has been criticized as a blatant promotion for the sale of automobiles. In his biography of La Guardia, Thomas Kessner (1989: 438) writes, "At the fair for the common people, the World of Tomorrow was interpreted by General Motors, the Edison Co., Eastman Kodak, and AT&T, by the polished hawkers of a consumer society. . . . General Motors' futuristic paean to the automobile in modern life, not Democracity, was the fair's most popular exhibit—rank commercialism dressed up in the shiny idiom of 'American Progress.'"

On the other hand, David Gelernter, author of *1939: The Lost World of the Fair* (1995), contends that historians like Kessner are mistaken; contemporary commentators on the fair recognized that the most popular exhibits were those that did not have a commercial bent. Even "commercial exhibits" were noncommercial. For example, according to an article in the *New Yorker* written during the fair, "automobile manufacturers seem to take the same attitude towards their exhibitions that they do toward their radio programs. In both cases they remind the public from time to time that they are in the business of making motorcars, but the emphasis is on entertainment and not, as it is so frankly at the annual Automobile Show, on the product" (quoted in Gelernter 1995: 361). Thus, Gelernter argues, critics miss the point—that cars and other products were popular in themselves without advertising. "Could it possibly be that Americans 'yearned for television sets, superhighways, foreign foods, and a streamlined life' because they *wanted* television sets, superhighways, foreign foods and a streamlined life?" (363).

CRITICS OF CONSENSUS

The consensus Gelernter imagines at the World's Fair was challenged, ironically, by one of the founders of the theme committee, Lewis Mumford. Although Mumford supported the redirection of people to planned small-scale towns, his vision of the economy was antithetical to that of General Motors' expansionism. According to biographer Donald Miller (1989: 296),

> Mumford was not unaware of the role technology could play in reducing poverty; poverty was more dehumanizing, in his view, than any machine. Nonetheless, he continued to describe the good life in nonmaterial terms, and to advocate constraints on economic growth, even at a time when one out of five American workers was unemployed. . . . Mumford's proposed stationary state challenged the standard American approach to social justice—an approach emphasizing expansion rather than fair division.

Mumford was not the only one to oppose the underlying premise of economic expansion: émigrés from Germany who brought their Frankfurt Institute to the United States in the 1930s to escape Nazi persecution were trenchant critics of the trends toward consumerism they saw in American culture.
Despite their appreciation for the refuge offered by the United States and their
willingness to work on state-sponsored research projects, central figures of
the Frankfurt School such as Theodor Adorno and Max Horkheimer criticized
precisely the images of stability based on consumerism projected in the Futurama exhibit—a stability not unlike what appeared to develop in the 1950s
as construction of the interstate system began.

The similarities in thought of Mumford and members of the Frankfurt
School are striking, beginning with their common rejection of a revolution
based on economic contradictions and a proletarian uprising. This common
rejection led them to focus more on "superstructural" elements of society—
in particular, artifacts of culture. For Mumford (1986b: 305) this method
of analysis ran counter to Marxist theory: "Karl Marx was in error in giving
Material instruments of production the central place and directive function in human development." In contrast to Mumford, whose view of Marxism was strongly influenced by experiences with the American Communist
Party, members of the Frankfurt School interpreted Marx as understanding
capitalism in more than economistic terms. In particular, Horkheimer and
Adorno saw Marx's theory of commodity fetishism as fundamental to the
understanding of social relations under capitalist society. Marx argued that
under capitalism, relations between objects determined relations between
people. For example, people's ability to labor and receive a wage is determined by the price of commodities on the market. At the same time, the
structuring of human relations by the market is seen as natural. "Through
the countless agencies of mass production and its culture the conventional-
ized modes of behavior are impressed on the individual as the only natural,
respectable, and rational ones" (Horkheimer and Adorno 1944/1989: 28).
The critique of this rationality's power to control dissent and its control of
culture is central to Horkheimer and Adorno's project in *Dialectic of Enlightenment* (1944), much of which was written during their exile in the
United States.

Despite their differing views on Marx, Mumford and members of the
Frankfurt Institute shared a critical attitude toward the profit motive's power.
Adorno (1945: 210) writes, "We live in a society of commodities—that is,
a society in which production of goods is taking place, not primarily to satisfy human wants and needs, but for profit." Mumford (1938: 289) describes
"the city under the influence of a capitalistic mythos" in a similar fashion:

"The owners of the instruments of production and distribution subordinate every other fact in life to the achievement of riches and the display of wealth." For Mumford this results in "standardization, largely in pecuniary terms, of the cultural products themselves in art, literature, architecture and language" (ibid.). Likewise, Horkheimer and Adorno are concerned about the impact of mass production on cultural items, but for them this impact comes not simply from the greed of the capitalists but more importantly from the penetration of the logic of commodity fetishism into "mass culture." Mumford and the émigrés also picture similar consequences from commodity culture. Adorno (1938/1988: 280) states, "The sacrifice of individuality, which accommodates itself to the regularity of the successful, the doing of what everybody does, follows from the basic fact that in broad areas the same thing is offered to everybody by the standardized production of consumption goods."

At the same time, for Horkheimer and Adorno, not only had mass culture been standardized in the pursuit of efficiency, it also provided continuity between the experience of routine mechanized labor in the contemporary workplace and leisure time. For them, leisure is occupied by the continual distraction of the culture industry, thus preventing critical reflection. "[Amusement] is sought after as an escape from the mechanized work process. . . . But at the same time mechanization has such power over man's leisure and happiness, and so profoundly determines the manufacture of amusement goods, that his experiences are inevitably afterimages of the work process itself" (1944/1989: 137). It is in this sense that the Futurama exhibit is marked by the ideas of mass production in a more direct manner than other forms of mass culture. The experience of the exhibit parallels the experience of a factory. Viewers become parts in a factory to be processed: first, they wait in line for up to three hours to enter the exhibit, at which point they are carried through the diorama in seats that roll on tracks like a conveyor belt taking riders from one region of the country to another.

An article in *Popular Science* magazine that illustrates visually the inner workings of the exhibit, describes it with the same fascination that might be directed at an efficient factory:

> Each sound track, a separate recording of the talk describing the diorama, is synchronized to the movement of a group of four chairs and is transmitted to the built-in loudspeakers by an ingenious system of 'third rails' and pick-up shoes beneath the cars. Thus, each spectator hears a running description of the exhibit perfectly timed to the progress of the chair in which he is sitting. (Van Duyne 1939: 104)

This article echoes the goal of the exhibit and the fair as a whole to make people more comfortable and familiar with new technologies. But the uncritical acceptance of mechanization in everyday life and the simple pleasures that it can create are precisely what concerned Horkheimer and Adorno. From this perspective the exhibit that Geddes hoped would encourage people to become active and "demand a comprehensive, basic solution to a comprehensive, basic problem" (1941: 11) might actually make visitors more passive.

Horkheimer and Adorno draw a connection between sound movies and passivity that could be applied to the construction of the sound system in the Futurama exhibit: "The sound film, far surpassing the theater of illusion, leaves no room for imagination or reflection on the part of the audience, who is unable to respond within the structure of the film, yet deviate from its precise detail without losing the thread of the story: hence the film forces its victims to equate it directly with reality" (1944/1989: 126). Similarly, in Futurama, passengers have their own speakers, discouraging interaction among viewers and encouraging a silent reception. Although Futurama narration does not play the same role as dialogue does in sound film, many other elements of the diorama function to blend the interior world of the diorama and the contemporary exterior world. The three-dimensionality, the simulation of real time, and the prosaic display of a diorama provide an element of reality that films lack. The most striking aspect of the Futurama creators' attempt to blend the exhibit with the exterior world was the exit. E. L. Doctorow describes it in his novel *World's Fair* (1985):

> And then the amazing thing was that at the end you saw a particular model street intersection and the show was over, and with your I HAVE SEEN THE FUTURE button in your hand you came out into the sun and you were standing on precisely the corner you had just seen, the future was right where you were standing and what was small had become big, the scale had enlarged and you were no longer looking down at it, but standing in it, on this corner of the future, right here in the World's Fair. (325)

Horkheimer and Adorno have been rightly criticized for failing to see the contradictory elements of popular culture, its potential for opposition, and the diverse responses to it (Kellner 1989: 140–145). In fact, Lizabeth Cohen (1990) credits mass culture, including movies and network radio, with helping to create a common understanding across diverse ethnic groups, enabling a successful working-class movement to develop in the 1930s. However, some examples of mass culture work more like Horkheimer and Adorno's description of the culture industry than others. In particular, Futurama exemplifies perfectly how entertainment could subtly promote particular corporate interests.

The exhibit displays what Horkheimer and Adorno describe as the overlapping of amusement and advertising. Because Futurama does not appear to be an advertisement, it functions more effectively as one. By not directly promoting General Motors cars, the vision it creates of an automobile-dominated world is made to seem scientific and not something sponsored by a car company. While the text that is heard through the speakers during the tour appears to be purely informational, it is actually an advertisement for GM cars and for cars in general. As Horkheimer and Adorno write of popular magazines, "In the most influential American magazines, *Life* and *Fortune*, a quick glance can now scarcely distinguish advertising from editorial picture and text" (1944/1989: 163).

Moreover, the exhibit was not easily separated from the theme exhibit of the fair, which was intended to be educational and had no corporate connection. The similarity between Futurama and Democracity is revealed in a collection of reflections by fair attendees. Several misidentify the Futurama as The World Of Tomorrow. One woman states,

> A highlight was seeing the World of Tomorrow—superhighways with overpasses and underpasses, loops seemed to go everywhere as model cars sped along. Harvey and I marveled at these 'speedways' . . . Mother told us this would never happen in our lifetime, much less in 1960. How wrong she was! She is still alive and, up until a few years ago, she drove on the Los Angeles freeways. (Quoted in Cohen, Heller, and Chwast 1989: 16)

The visitor does not just fail to distinguish between exhibits that promote a particular company and exhibits intended to be impartial, she confuses the GM exhibit with the central exhibit of the fair—the *theme* exhibit.

Futurama managed to appropriate the status of "theme exhibit" and become the most celebrated part of the fair through its ability to blend amusement, information, and promotion. The primacy of promotion could be seen in the building design, which more effectively created publicity than informed large numbers of people. Its limited capacity of six hundred led to long lines at the entrance and made getting in more exceptional, thereby adding to its popular image (see Figure 8). As described in *Business Week* (1939: 22), "The speed with which the chairs traveled around the Futurama

Figure 8. Entrance ramp to General Motors Futurama exhibit. GM Corporation 1978. Courtesy of GM Media Archives.

made it impossible to accommodate more than 28,000 a day—many of whom had to wait two or three hours—while other less expensive exhibits attracted and accommodated much greater crowds." That the crowds in themselves could add to the exhibit's popularity is indicated in another visitor's reflection: "The most popular attraction was called the World of the Future, sponsored by General Motors. It was one of the few we were willing to stand in line for, as if one hadn't really seen the fair without attending this attraction" (quoted in Cohen, Heller, and Chwast 1989: 15). Here it seems that standing in line is precisely what makes the exhibit so much worth seeing. Doctorow presents a similar picture: "The General Motors exhibit was the most popular in the whole fair, and so I didn't mind the long wait we had, practically an hour" (Doctorow 1985: 323).

The consensus on the popularity of Geddes's exhibit foreshadowed the consensus that formed around the construction of an interstate highway system in the 1950s.[3] Moreover, as predicted by Geddes, the project would require a significant contribution by the federal government for its construction. Equally fundamental for the automobile industry to the promotion of car buying was the need to dramatically increase the government's investment in highway building. Thus, while General Motors did not promote its product directly, by promoting the construction of a transportation infrastructure it promoted the sale of its product. Walter Lippmann (1939: 51) famously commented on the use of public investment for private industry: "GM has spent a small fortune to convince the American Public that if it wishes to enjoy the full benefit of private enterprise in motor manufacturing, it will have to rebuild its cities and highways by public enterprise."

Lippmann's assessment, according to Gelernter (1995: 363), is the "modern fair historian's all time favorite citation." Gelernter disagrees with critics who argue that Futurama was an elaborate scheme to encourage automobile sales, but those critics misread Lippmann. Rather than criticizing General Motors, Lippmann is celebrating the ability of private companies like GM to build such extraordinary exhibits. Lippmann (1939: 50) contrasts this ability with the limits of communist and fascist countries: "This is what private enterprise can do, and the best that the Italians or Russians have to show is no more than a feeble approximation." His apparent criticism of General Motors' demand is actually a clarification and assertion that public investment is necessary to support private enterprise. "So one comes away feeling that men are right when they affirm the value of private enterprises and when they affirm the necessity of public enterprise; where they go wrong is in denying that both are necessary and that their collaboration is indispensable" (51).

This coordination of private and public is a key theme not only of Futurama but also of the Democracity exhibit. Both imply an important role for the state in assisting and regulating the private economy. It is put most explicitly in the program for the Democracity exhibit: "If Democracity were Utopia, government would be superfluous. But Democracity is an entirely practical city. . . . And there can be a dozen or a hundred such groups of towns and villages and centers in the United States, each with commercial and agricultural and industrial interests. The government exists to see that these interests harmonize" (Seldes 1939: 12). Central to this coordination is the transportation system, and the Futurama exhibit presents the transportation system as a key area in which the federal government must participate, as Geddes (1941: 181) writes: "There is a Federal obligation to develop the country's resources of land, water power, and natural wealth. And there is no single undertaking more important to these obligations than the development of facilities for national transportation."

The increasing intervention in the economy by government was central to the cultural theory of Horkheimer and Adorno. Due to this intervention, the inevitable economic crisis, which traditional Marxist theory saw as bringing capitalism to an end, could be delayed and possibly averted completely. The state's ability to control economic crises gave importance to the analysis of the cultural realm of society. Horkheimer and Adorno dedicated *Dialectic of*

Enlightenment to Friedrich Pollock, who wrote a pivotal essay on "state capitalism." Pollock (1941/1988: 75) argues that to replace the inconsistencies of the market system, the first rule of state capitalism calls for a general plan:

A general plan gives the direction for production, consumption, saving and investment. The introduction of the principle of planning into the economic process means that a plan is to be constructed for achieving on a national scale certain chosen ends with all available resources. It does not necessarily imply that all details are planned in advance or that no freedom of choice at all is given to the consumer.

Geddes (1941: 272) implies very similar ideas in his plan for the future:

Today, just as the participation and encouragement of government in the work of science has grown steadily more important, so grows the need of its participation in long-term planning. Thousands of private enterprises, utilities and industries have set up agencies to study and coordinate their work, but none has gone as far as setting down a series of over-all principles. It has remained for government to do this.

The cooperation of state and private industry is accompanied by the dramatic growth of corporations like General Motors whose size gave them tremendous influence on the market. Thus, it is appropriate for General Motors to sponsor the design of a state project and that this design closely resembles the publicly sponsored Democracity exhibit. This conforms to Pollock's view that large corporations were operating more like states, and states were operating more like large corporations: "In all spheres of state activity (and under state capitalism that means in all spheres of social life as a whole) guesswork and improvisation give place to the principles of scientific management. This rule is in conformity with state capitalism's basic conception of society as an integrated unit comparable to one of the modern giants in steel, chemical or motorcar production" (1941/1988: 77).

MOTORWAY DISCIPLINE

Although the Great Depression brought much greater intervention by the U.S. government in the economy—through work programs, assistance to homeowners, regulation of farm prices, and protections for organized labor—the dramatic intervention that best matched state capitalism took place in Nazi Germany (ibid.). It is thus significant that one totalitarian country Lippmann did not mention when contrasting the capabilities of private industry was Germany. On the one hand, he could not compare a German exhibit to that provided by General Motors since Germany did not provide a pavilion for the fair. On the other hand, the failure to mention Germany is significant since Germany had in some sense done better than simply construct a model of a future highway system. Germany, since 1933 under the direction of Adolf Hitler, had already embarked on a project similar to what Geddes had planned for the United States.

U.S. planners and officials, including Roosevelt, Truman, and Eisenhower, were aware of and impressed by Germany's construction of the Autobahn (Foster 1981: 162; Goddard 1994: 158, 181). Thus, the liability of Futurama's similarity to the Autobahn is perhaps not unnoticed by Geddes, who in several places makes a point to distinguish the construction of his project from a totalitarian one. The "suspicion of public effort" he sees in the United States might arise in part from fear of a powerful fascist government. He attempts to reduce this suspicion by distinguishing America's fundamental mores from those of European countries. Geddes celebrates America as a country of diversity that the motorway system would help unite:

> And diversity—whether racial or geographic—is a basic heritage of America. And out of that very interchange of diversity will come another thing—something that in this era of misunderstanding and conflict and war may be the most essential thing of all. Our country was founded on it. We call it *unity*. It is not a unity imposed from above, such as exists under dictatorships, but a unity based on freedom and understanding. (1941: 295)

Yet some of Geddes's proposals might also be viewed suspiciously. His call for overriding local politics with federal authority and professional engineers sounds similar to totalitarianism. Even more troubling are his depictions of irrational and passive crowds throughout his book, betraying a desire to control the social divisions that were salient in America during the 1930s. The same desire to control social divisions—to control social dissent—epitomized the goals of fascism.

We have seen that decentralization with the Autobahn was a strategy to neutralize working-class organizations. The implication of Geddes's project is the same. Moreover, his system would help disperse the chaotic crowds he depicts throughout his book and perpetuate their isolation while traveling. Dispersal and isolation make organizing for social protest more difficult.

Perhaps more than any element of Geddes's design, the control of cars by operators in towers looks totalitarian,[4] and it points to the central contradiction in the fair's glorification of the automobile: the automobile had freed people from the disciplines of mechanization only to require new disciplines. During its turn-of-the-century introduction, the automobile was acclaimed for providing an opportunity to control a machine in a world where machines increasingly shaped daily life. However, the automobile required self-discipline, conforming to the rules of the road, and controlling the direction and speed of the car to avoid accidents. The control tower eliminated this need for self-discipline, but it also eliminated a central reason people enjoyed the automobile. Thus, one critic of Futurama attacked "the remote control idea as destroying the chief reason for car owning—the pleasure of handling a powerful, free-moving vehicle" (*Business Week* 1939: 28). The automobile fulfilled the desire to control mechanization in daily life, but the Futurama plan leaves this desire unsatisfied.

This contradiction can be traced to the logic of progress on which the Futurama exhibit is premised. This progress is based on a faith in technical rationality. For Horkheimer and Adorno, this faith has become irrational, just like the religious myths that scientific thought had originally tried to undermine: "The principle of immanence, the explanation of every event as repetition, that the Enlightenment upholds against mythic imagination, is the principle of myth itself" (1944/1989: 12). The Enlightenment, like myth, was embraced as an escape from the domination of nature, but, through science, it began to dominate nature. In the process of dominating nature, human beings became subservient to scientific rules. "The absurdity of a state of affairs in which the enforced power of the system over men grows with every step that takes it out of the power of nature, denounces the rationality of the rational society as obsolete" (39). There is no better illustration of this than an automobile driver who must ultimately submit to the demands of driving.

The similarity of driving to the domination of the factory extends beyond the routinization of behavior it creates. The automobile also exploits labor. Workers are not paid for the labor necessary to drive to and from the job. As Ruth Schwartz Cowan (1983) points out, the automobile added labor to the shopping habits of middle-class housewives; household staples were less often delivered or purchased at the corner store and instead required multiple car trips.[5] Of course, sometimes driving is done for pleasure, and waiting for the bus to arrive or struggling to find a seat on a crowded subway is uncompensated work as well. However, the automobile is promoted precisely as an escape from this labor. Because driving may sometimes be fun, the labor time it requires is not recognized.

The automobile allowed the restoration of control over production, but to the extent this production was an uncompensated requirement, it also allowed one's self-exploitation. "The more the process of self preservation is effected by the bourgeois division of labor, the more it requires the self alienation of the individuals who must model their body and soul according to the technical apparatus" (Horkheimer and Adorno 1944/1989: 29–30). The key point here is that this "adaptation to the technical apparatus" has become naturalized, and Geddes's project epitomizes this naturalization; for, despite the superhighway's new constraints on the freedom of the driver, Geddes continues to portray automobile driving as liberation: "Motoring is one of the most popular recreations there is. It promotes the sense of freedom that comes from greater mobility" (1941: 293).

UNITY AND EXCLUSION

Freedom to travel in Geddes's eyes would lead to more social exchange. As in Mumford's vision of regional developments, such freedom would break down parochialism by allowing better understanding among different groups, Geddes writes:

> This freedom of movement, this opening up of what is congested, this discarding of what is obsolete all add up to one thing: interchange— interchange of people, places, ways of life, and therefore modes of thought. The American nation is not going to be able to solve the major problems facing it until its people of various classes and regions—the workers, the intellectuals, the farmers, business men—get to know each other better and to understand each other's problems. (1941: 294)

The equalization of all people's problems, the reduction of all problems to "misunderstandings," allows the resolution of differences to take on a mechanical form.

Yet, despite Geddes's emphasis on interchange, the Futurama exhibit is loaded with implied barriers. Just as the exhibit prefigures the consensus to be formed in the 1950s around freeways, it also prefigures the exclusions on which this consensus is based. On one level, the fair itself implemented these exclusions. The cost of attending the fair was prohibitive for many people. Gardner Harding (1939: 197) of *Harper's* magazine points out that after seeing some of the key exhibits and eating "two reasonable meals for two people— there isn't much left of a ten dollar bill before you get to the Amusement Zone at all." For this reason, Harding continues, "the amusement concessionaires have already begged the fair to cut the price for general admission during the evening from 75 cents to 50 cents, and this is symptomatic of a general discontent with the whole price structure." By comparison, it still cost only five cents to take the elevated rail to Coney Island.

The exclusivity of the intended audience is also indicated by the high expense of the theme exhibit, which cost twenty-five cents to enter. "No American likes to be thought cheap, and Grover Whalen. . . . seems to have picked the higher unit price as contributing in some way to the prestige and dignity of his privileged conception of the World of Tomorrow. But he forgets that the World of To-day around him objects to paying high prices" (ibid.: 198). Harding's sarcasm subtly points to the contradiction in constructing a model solution to contemporary economic instabilities that ignores the practical impact of these instabilities.

Not only was the admission price for the fair exclusive, but the fair also limited those permitted to express themselves through an exhibit. Harding asked an "administrative official" why there was very little "community" representation compared to the amount of business representation. The official replied, "to be fully representative of community interests, the Fair should include the co-operative movement, the granges and farmers' groups, the many useful and important social organizations that make up life in every American community. But you can't sell space to those folks. They haven't any money." Harding comments, "This perfectly sound answer raises the whole question of whether a Fair bold enough to embark on so many wholly unconventional ventures, might have realized the flatness of its appeal to people who 'haven't any money'" (196). The favoring of those with business connections extended into the Futurama exhibit. According to one fair attendee,

> Favored customers, friends, press, or V.I.P.'s waited in a lovely, air-conditioned reception room tended by attractive hostesses. There were snacks, coffee, or drinks. Every few minutes, a hostess would usher a small party into a darkened tunnel. The crowds who were waiting in the hot sun for all those hours entered a darkened tunnel, too. These tunnels merged about twenty feet in, mingling those who sweated on line for four or five hours with some who just enjoyed a drink in an air-conditioned lounge several minutes earlier. No one ever wrote about this. (Quoted in Cohen, Heller, and Chwast 1989: 17)

Equally important, the exhibit showed the potential for exclusion in the same way that Radburn, New Jersey, did. While efficiency was the stated goal of neighborhood design, the possibilities for segregation were implied. "The idea of progressive town-traffic planning is this: Of all the vehicles on the road, only those shall enter the community which actually have business there; and of those which do enter the community, only those shall enter a given street which actually are being used in connection with people living in that street" (Geddes 1941: 197).

Rather than encouraging interaction, Geddes's design shows how the automobile could be used to exploit the resources of the city while avoiding its problems: "Radburn effectively shows how a community can preserve its privacy and at the same time maintain full contact with the rest of the world" (196–197). The design of Democracity belies a similar tension: while it segregates middle-class residents from the industrial and central business districts, factory workers—whose labor presumably brings significant wealth to the city—are housed near their places of work and segregated from the middle class.

The key component in creating exclusive neighborhoods was housing. Radburn barred the working class because the cost of housing was prohibitive. Affordability was also a problem with the "Town of Tomorrow" exhibit at the fair. Again it was Harding who claimed that the model homes on display were too expensive for the majority of those who attended the fair: "For that three-quarters of our people for example, which doesn't earn three thousand dollars a year, Tomorrow Town, one of the most industriously publicized features of the Fair, is in point of fact a definite breach of faith" (196).

What Harding failed to see was that despite the limited affordability of the homes on display, the exhibit displayed its creators' foresight into the role homeownership would have in the post–World War II era. Federal Housing Administrator Stewart MacDonald had a better understanding of this as he predicted that homes would become available to the "underprivileged" in a speech at the opening of the Town of Tomorrow exhibit. Quoted in the *New York Times* (1939a), MacDonald said, "The old fashioned 'heart breaking' mortgage system with its frequent foreclosures during times of economic depression, has been broken up by the Federal Government. . . . In other words, home ownership has been made accessible, as far as financing is concerned, to families which could never have contemplated the purchase of their own homes a few years ago."

MacDonald's address at the Town of Tomorrow reaffirms the corporate strategy to prevent strikes by encouraging indebtedness among workers. He lists the most important goal of greater homeownership not as "stimulation of industry" but rather as the "social values" that homeownership entails: "A nation of home owners provides insurance against unrest and social upheaval." MacDonald openly voices the implicit goals of decentralized development: as workers become invested in suburban homes, they come to identify themselves more as property owners.

MacDonald's idea that homeownership prevents social unrest became ironic in the 1940s when white homeownership was a principal motivation for violence directed at African Americans. During the first decades of the twentieth century, the threat of violence against blacks attempting to rent or purchase homes in white neighborhoods was a primary means of maintaining the borders of the ghetto. Violence became a reality when blacks migrated north by the thousands to take jobs created by World War II, leading to unbearably crowded conditions in the limited housing available to them. In February 1942 violence erupted when black families moved into a project located in a white neighborhood of Detroit, and this led the Detroit Housing Commission to set a policy keeping blacks out of public housing located in white neighborhoods (Sugrue 1996: 74). In Chicago, the years 1944 through 1946 saw attacks on forty-six blacks attempting to move outside the ghettos. African Americans risked this violence to escape outrageous rents and dilapidated buildings that sometimes housed ten families in a single apartment (Hirsch 1983: 53).

More than racism, this violence was sparked by white homeowners' desire to maintain property values, which they feared would drop rapidly if blacks moved next door. The federal housing policies praised by MacDonald supported this fear because they barred government-backed loans in neighborhoods with even a single African American resident. This redlining underpinned not just the value of property but also the ability of prospective homebuyers and current homeowners to get federally subsidized loans. The need to guarantee access to these loans led one developer in Detroit to build a half-mile-long wall to assure the Federal Housing Administration (FHA) that these homes for whites would be unconnected to an adjacent African American neighborhood (Sugrue 1996: 64). While in his speech MacDonald expresses hope that federal policies would expand the privileges of homeownership, tellingly, he does not demand these privileges for all, without regard to race.

The messages of the fair on the issue of integration were mixed. While the logic of freeway-based development promoted by the fair's transportation exhibits eased the formation of exclusionary neighborhoods, the designers of these exhibits claimed to support social integration. At the same time, the federal housing policies endorsed at the fair clearly supported segregation, and it was these policies that made postwar suburban homeownership available to whites while simultaneously denying this privilege to blacks.

A preview of this duality was made concrete in the 1939–1940 New York World's Fair exhibit on "Typical American Families." To promote the fair, contests were held across the United States to select families most representative of America. These families were selected to live on the fairgrounds in homes built by the FHA. The exhibit was sponsored in part by the Ford Motor Company, and winners were given a trip to the fair in a new Ford automobile: on arrival, they lived in homes built by the FHA on the fairgrounds. Thus, home and automobile ownership were linked as essential to American families. But systemic exclusion from this ideal was also embodied in the contest, as Robert Rydell (1993: 57) writes:

> To help local civic leaders judge contest winners, world's fair authorities circulated a questionnaire that included "racial origin" as one of the categories to be considered. World's fair authorities also made clear that they hoped each family unit selected would "consist of parents and two children." The results were predictable. "Typical" American families were native-born white Americans.

The construction of the "typical American family" also meant affirming the role of women as homemakers, a role that was also written into the designs of the highway-based developments. Geddes (1941: 290) writes of the positive transformations new motorways would have on women's domestic role:

> City housewives, buying a staple such as eggs, will not have to depend either on the products of what may be inferior nearby poultrymen or on "fresh" eggs that have taken a week to get to the city, via truck, terminal, train, and then terminal and truck again. High-speed trucks will transport the most perishable foods overnight directly from one point to another eliminating the in-between delays.

While it is unclear if Geddes expects women to shop via automobile, Futurama does assume drivers are primarily men, just as does the writer for *Business Week* who describes drivers who "hug their girls." In short, the tension within Futurama's portrayal of increased interaction alongside its potential for increased isolation leans more toward isolation for women.

The potential for isolation and exclusion implicit in the Futurama exhibit in many ways was realized in 1950s highway-based suburbanization, and the gaps in the utopia of Futurama would become salient in multiple ways by the early 1960s. But while Geddes's vision was for most a dream in 1939, at the same time on the other coast of the United States, a city designed around the automobile was much closer to being realized. In 1941 Adorno moved to Southern California, where the automobile was more prevalent than in any other region of the country. The year Adorno arrived, the Los Angeles Department of City Planning endorsed a comprehensive regional parkway plan that would further support the automobile's dominance of the city. It was in Los Angeles that Horkheimer and Adorno wrote *Dialectic of Enlightenment*, which is appropriate, given the book's critique of the commodified lifestyle—a lifestyle that would eventually center on the automobile.

Another critical voice came from their fellow exile from Nazi Germany: the director Billy Wilder, who had been living in Los Angeles since 1933. Two films in particular by Wilder throw a different light on the tensions found in the Futurama and Democracity exhibits. The ideas in these films, *Double Indemnity* and *Sunset Boulevard*, resonate with problems Adorno and Horkheimer found in U.S. culture. More importantly, both films expose gaps in the ideal of automobile-centered cities by dramatizing the experience of living in Los Angeles.

■ ■

CHAPTER 4

FILM NOIR AND THE HIDDEN VIOLENCE OF TRANSPORTATION IN LOS ANGELES

In 1937 the Automobile Club of Southern California produced a Los Angeles motorway plan that was to become the model for a system of "parkways" approved in 1941 by the Los Angeles Department of City Planning (Bottles 1987: 216–223). A broad consensus had developed that accommodating the automobile was the most rational form of urban design. Yet, at the peak of this enthusiasm for automobile-centered cities, voices of dissent emerged. In the year of the plan's approval, German philosopher and social theorist Theodor Adorno moved to Southern California. Here he met his colleague from Frankfurt Max Horkheimer, who had likewise escaped to the United States in 1935. Together while in Los Angeles, they wrote *Dialectic of Enlightenment*, which criticized the passive acceptance of capitalist technocratic rationality: the same rationality that underlay the parkway plan. They also criticized the prominent identification with and reliance on consumer culture in the United States; and as the center of film production and automobile consumption, Los Angeles embodied the target of this critique.

Another critique of the now-dominant pattern for cities in the United States can be found in two films made during Adorno's stay in Los Angeles, *Double Indemnity* (1944) and *Sunset Boulevard* (1950). These classic examples of film noir, directed by Billy Wilder, another exile from Nazi Germany, affirm the problems of twentieth-century capitalist culture described in *Dialectic of Enlightenment*. But Wilder's films also attach these problems to the specific locale of Los Angeles and by doing this link the depravity of modern culture to the automobile and its reconstruction of the city. These films expose not just the passivity and artificiality that *Dialectic of Enlightenment* describes but also a problem at the very center of the Los Angeles lifestyle: the problem of isolation.

While the dangerous consequence of the Los Angeles plan portrayed by *Double Indemnity* and *Sunset Boulevard* is isolation, the plan's ability to isolate and segregate simultaneously served a desire held by a large part of the Los Angeles population—a desire for racial purity. This desire was reflected in the frequent attacks on people of color in the 1930s and 1940s. While *film noir* might exaggerate the violence of social isolation, the Los Angeles transportation system actually worked to hide the brutal violence of racial segregation and also helped to maintain it.

RATIONAL ALIENATION: *DOUBLE INDEMNITY*

She was to drive so she didn't make any sudden stops, or get herself tangled in traffic. (Cain 1936/1978: 51)

Part of the automobile's appeal can be traced to a faith in technological advancement. Mark Foster writes, "An important factor behind the planners' approval of the automobile was their assumption that they could always guide its evolution as the servant of mankind" (1981: 43). The 1941 Los Angeles plan to accommodate the automobile embodied the technical rationality criticized by Horkheimer and Adorno in *Dialectic of Enlightenment*. This rationality relies faithfully on the ability of numerical information to solve societal problems. In the case of the Los Angeles regional transportation plan, highway construction was based explicitly on engineering statistics. David Brodsly (1981: 136) describes the power scientific data had on Los Angeles freeway planners: "Plans were often presented as being dictated by 'reality' and therefore as embodying the only rational option. Such planning, characterized more as a technique or a 'science' than as an art, emphasized the priority of the data and, sidestepping all political implications, obscured the possibility of choice."

Technical rationality plays an equally powerful role in the film *Double Indemnity*. In it, an insurance salesman, Walter Neff, and a woman he meets while making a sales call, Phyllis Dietrichson, conspire to take out accident insurance on her husband and kill him for the premium. They decide to make it appear that the death took place on a train because in this case the insurance policy pays double the premium—hence the title of the film, *Double Indemnity*. The logic of this murder is an ultimate corruption of Enlightenment thinking. The murder plan demonstrates the power of technocratic rationality to support the severest form of human exploitation. Everything about the murder plan is highly scientific, including the search for double indemnity. In fact, the apparent flawless rationality of the plan is a central element of its appeal to Neff. He is at first very antagonistic to the idea of helping kill Phyllis's husband, but as he begins to imagine the perfect murder plot he changes his mind. Neff recounts what he thought after she proposed the idea to him and he told her to forget about it:

> Maybe she had stopped thinking about it, but I hadn't. I couldn't. Because it all tied up with something I had been thinking about for years, since long before I ever ran into Phyllis Dietrichson. Because, in this business you can't sleep for trying to figure out the tricks they could pull on you. You're like the guy behind the roulette wheel, watching the customers to make sure they don't crook the house. And then one night, you get to thinking how you could crook the house yourself. And do it smart. Because you've got that wheel right under your hands. (Wilder and Chandler 1943: 31)

The aesthetic appeal of the perfect murder marks the ultimate detachment of scientific rationality from critical thinking. "In its neo-positivist version, science becomes aestheticism, a system of detached signs devoid of any intention that would transcend the system" (Horkheimer and Adorno 1944/1989: 18). As with the planners of the city, relentless affirmation of analytical method to displace the myths of pre-Enlightenment thought itself has been replaced by a new myth of mathematical procedure. If, as in *Double Indemnity*, all factors are calculated and the procedure is followed correctly, then its moral consequences are insignificant.[1] Neff's rationalization for murder illustrates Adorno and Horkheimer's concern that faith in scientific formulas makes the twentieth-century appropriation of Enlightenment thought totalitarian and barbaric. "The paradoxical nature of faith ultimately degenerates into a swindle and becomes the myth of the twentieth century; and its irrationality turns it into an instrument of rational administration by the wholly enlightened as they steer society toward barbarism" (ibid.: 20).

The goal of Neff's reasoned plan is to become wealthy. This exemplifies Horkheimer and Adorno's argument that the drive for profit had come to influence all aspects of social life—including romance. This drive is not the same as the American Dream of economic success. Certainly, in the context of the recent Depression and uncertain job prospects for returning war veterans, many Americans felt a real anxiety about their financial security. So, the pessimism of *film noir* might be read as a critique of American expectations for wealth. In this vein, Ken Hillis (2005) argues that *films noirs* often demonstrate failed efforts to achieve the Enlightenment dream of political subjectivity rooted in self-creation. Thus, *Double Indemnity* reveals the impossibility of attaining what Hillis calls the "brass ring" of economic independence.

However, for Horkheimer and Adorno, this Marxist critique of economic inequality is no longer very useful for understanding capitalist society since the state has come to play an increasingly important role in managing the economy. White men like Neff are quite wealthy by historical standards, and there is no indication he is concerned about his finances. Indeed, he seems to have achieved his piece of the American Dream. Horkheimer and Adorno claim not just that the American Dream is a myth but that it is a dream empty of critical reflection. This emptiness permits rationality to be deployed for financial gain without regard for consequences.

Part of Phyllis's motivation to kill is her desire to escape her husband, but what makes the murder perfect and appealing in Neff's eyes is the possibility of double indemnity—achieving the most return possible on the murdered body. The logic of commodity fetishism reaches its final consequence when murder is committed for money. The desire for profit is never questioned; the only question is how science and technology can best achieve this profit. For Adorno and Horkheimer this means men are turned into spiritless objects, and the ultimate spiritless object is the dead body. "Industrialism objectifies the spirits of men. Automatically, the economic apparatus, even before total planning, equips commodities with the values which decide human behavior. Since, with the end of free exchange, commodities lost all their economic qualities except for fetishism, the latter has extended its arthritic influence over all aspects of social life" (Horkheimer and Adorno 1944/1989: 28).

For example, the profitability of the insurance business is sustained by people's expected misfortunes. The automobile expanded the profit of insurance companies immensely as car accidents became common. The insurance premium for a train accident pays double precisely because it is so unlikely. In contrast, the frequency with which car accidents occurred helped to normalize the risk of injury and death associated with them.[2] However, if people came to accept the risk of driving an automobile, it was not simply because they viewed it as the most efficient form of transportation: the automobile was also popular because it helped transform city space. Understanding the popularity of this transformation will clarify *Double Indemnity*'s pessimistic depiction of it.

In addition to the appeal of the car's technology, Los Angeles residents supported the city's accommodation of the automobile because of their economic and cultural backgrounds. A large number of them were migrants from the Midwest and, unlike European immigrants to eastern cities, were able to afford single-family homes. At the same time, because they frequently came from small towns, they wished to retain a rural atmosphere. According to Carey McWilliams (1946: 159), "In the process of settlement, they reverted to former practices and built, not a city, but a series of connecting villages." Their conservative religious backgrounds also led them to associate cities with moral corruption. When a writer from the East mocked the puritan values of Los Angeles, several residents countered with indictments of urban immorality. One proclaimed,

> It is our departure from these "village ideals," the simple, comely life of our fathers, that has nurtured the blight of demoralizing metropolitanism, a curse alike to old and young and that embodies in its spirit all those indulgences and immoralities which [the writer] seems to think constitute a higher phase of existence than any possible extract of a village. (Quoted in Fogelson 1967/1993: 191)

This perspective on the city inspired the type of development found in Los Angeles. An engineer for the Automobile Club wrote, "The horizontal expansion of the urban community is not due to any new-found desire in urban people" (quoted in Bottles 1987: 181). The automobile, the engineer continued, had made it possible "to satisfy an inherent desire common to all people to find order, space, [and] to escape from the noise and confusion of congested living and working quarters."

The automobile permitted people to live in pastoral environs while still having access to the economic opportunities of the city. In the view of several local businessmen, this suburban lifestyle was what attracted people to Los Angeles. One said, "Los Angeles' future depends upon the suburban cities surrounding it. . . . The ideal life that we have here is the country or home life with your gardens and bungalows" (ibid.: 180).

Architectural historians David Gebhard and Harriete Von Breton (1989: 5) elaborate on the projection of the Los Angeles ideal to a broader public:

> The Los Angeles scene, as portrayed in films, weekly radio broadcasts, and the press, seemed to mirror just what most Americans throughout the country felt their world should be like. The Hollywood version of the "average" middle class American family lived in a quiet, suburban setting, in a spacious Colonial Revival house tastefully furnished in Early American reproductions, with two or more automobiles in the family garage.

By the 1940s, Los Angeles had become a model for planners who imagined that the automobile was the ideal solution to the problems of the city. A planner from Milwaukee argued that "the automobile has taught people that they can live as comfortably beyond the city's confines with all the coveted city conveniences and do so with less expense and greater benefits to themselves and their children" (quoted in Bottles 1987: 181).

Just as Los Angeles was becoming the model city for planners, movies of the *film noir* genre such as *Double Indemnity* were indicating that this paradise created instabilities for domestic relationships. In *Double Indemnity* Phyllis is trapped in a relationship with her husband and stepdaughter. A chance to escape comes through a business transaction with Neff. Phyllis's boredom and her desire to escape her domestic confines point to the isolation a woman may face in the automobile-centered suburb where, especially if she lacks her own car, she spends most of her time secluded from public life. As Phyllis describes it to Neff, "He won't let me go anywhere. He keeps me shut up. He's always been mean to me. Even that life insurance all goes to that daughter of his" (Wilder and Chandler 1943: 29). The isolation of Phyllis at home was in keeping with the suburban domestic ideal. Women were expected to maintain a home isolated from the chaos of the urban market (Marsh 1990: 8). The consequences could be depression and the desire to flee, sometimes through violence, as in Phyllis's case.[3]

The inability of women like Phyllis to escape the confines of suburban domestic life came in large part from economic dependence on their husbands. To work outside the home was seen as distracting from a woman's primary role of homemaker. Some saw working women taking jobs away from men whose role was to support a family. The film is set in 1938,[4] when the nation was still in the midst of the Great Depression. At this time, the belief that working women might threaten men's jobs was exacerbated by high rates of unemployment. Women were discouraged from seeking work, and those who did faced discrimination and were given the lowest-paying jobs (Kessler-Harris 1982: 251–253). In Los Angeles less than one-third of all women had jobs in 1940; among those with jobs, more than one-third worked in the low-wage service sector (Kasun 1954: 25–34).

During World War II, as young men went off to war, the number of women who had access to better-paying factory jobs dramatically increased. But the increased hiring of women for weapons production and other jobs formerly held by men did not reflect a change in attitude among the general population. The continued resistance to women working outside the home was reflected, first, in the frequent failure to pay women equal wages for the same work; second, in the delayed and ultimately inadequate provision of child care; and, third, in the termination of women from defense jobs at much higher rates than men after the war (Kessler-Harris 1982: 287–295). A 1946 *Fortune* survey found that a majority of both men and women believed married women, even without young children, should not work outside the home (296). Thus, even if *Double Indemnity* is read in the context of its 1944 release, it is clear that a woman like Phyllis would ultimately find it difficult to live independently. In this light, money from insurance is one of the few options that would allow Phyllis to escape dependence on her husband. At the same time, this freedom was threatened by her relationship with Neff, not just because he could expose her collaboration in the murder but also because she might still have to play the subservient role of a homemaker.

Such a sympathetic reading of Phyllis is not encouraged by her characterization in the film.[5] She is depicted as a cruel and calculating woman who possibly caused the death of her husband's first wife and now is manipulating Neff into helping kill her husband. Neff believes Phyllis has entrapped him into committing murder and that she plans to kill him next with the help of another man. In a confrontation near the end of the film Neff says to Phyllis, "You're rotten clear through. You got me to take care of your husband, and then you got Zachette to take care of Lola, and maybe take care of me too" (Wilder and Chandler 1943: 106). But the character of Phyllis is made more complex when read in conjunction with other *film noir* women in similar predicaments. For example, in *The Postman Always Rings Twice* (1946, directed by Tay Garnett), based on a novel by Cain, Cora Smith is even more dramatically isolated by the Southern California reliance on the automobile: she works with her husband at a roadside café outside of Los Angeles. Her loneliness and ennui are evident to Frank, a hitchhiker, who, like Neff in *Double Indemnity*, helps plan the murder of Cora's husband. Cora is portrayed in a much more sympathetic manner than Phyllis, with a greater emphasis placed on the tedium of her daily life and her dependence on Nick, her husband. Reading Phyllis and Cora together, one finds that both describe their lives as "boring," and this boredom can be linked to the automobile suburb. The same suburb that may shield the home and women from the mixed society and commerce of the city can produce loneliness and isolation.

Interestingly, Neff too is seeking to escape a certain familial bond—mainly with his colleague and mentor Barton Keyes, the insurance company's claims investigator. Several writers (Claire Johnston 1980; Frank Krutnik 1991; James Maxfield 1996) read Neff's decision to collaborate with Phyllis as a strategy to avoid a homoerotic bond between him and Keyes. This bond is consummated in the final scene when Neff surrenders to Keyes.

Wilder himself saw the film as a love story between Neff and Keyes (Lally 1996: 137), and it is clear the tie between the two men is central to the film.

The interaction between them reveals mutual respect and affection. At the same time, Neff expresses discomfort with Keyes's desire to watch over and advise him. When Neff receives a phone call from Phyllis while Keyes is in the office, Keyes refuses to leave the room, and after Neff ends the phone call, Keyes inquires about the woman in a disparaging manner. Later, after the murder, Keyes arrives at Neff's apartment unexpectedly, much like a nosy neighbor in a small town. Neff shows his desire to escape this bond first in his attempt to deceive Keyes and prevent him from uncovering the fraud. This betrayal signals the rejection of Keyes's intimacy. Moreover, just as money will allow Phyllis to escape her dependence on her husband, it will allow Neff to escape the dependence on his work and the bonds associated with it. Thus, *Double Indemnity* shows how the workplace can be burdened with the same obligations and moral ties associated with the home.

Kevin Lally, in his biography of Billy Wilder, describes Neff as restless and anxious "to escape a workaday rut" (1996: 137). In this view his alienation conforms to the alienation that Horkheimer and Adorno describe as part of bureaucratic capitalism. Yet, Neff's discomfort with his moral tie to Keyes seems at least as important as the tedium of his work. Keyes offers Neff a job as his assistant, which pays less but, Keyes tells him, "takes brains and integrity. It takes more guts than there is in fifty salesman." Neff replies, "It's still a desk job." If Neff was simply tired of his "workaday rut," he might enjoy taking a job that required more thought and instilled a deeper purpose in his work. The new job also might enable him to better control the outcome of the claims investigation on Phyllis, but it would also mean working more closely with Keyes and a deepening emotional connection to him. It is ironic that Neff finds the relationships at work burdensome, since work in the city can be a way of escaping the restrictions and surveillance of a small town. In fact, many of the migrants who came to Los Angeles in the first part of the century came from small towns in the Midwest where the norms of everyday life could be highly confining (Fogelson 1993: 64). Certainly one realm in which this freedom came was in social relationships, so Neff is more free to pursue Phyllis—someone he knows nothing about outside of a business relationship—because his relationships are not easily monitored by family or neighbors.

On the other hand, Neff's situation indicates that the other side of the freedom provided by large cities is desperation. In other words, one can read his affair with Phyllis as coming from a difficulty in finding relationships elsewhere. Lally (1996: 136) calls Neff a Los Angeles archetype, "the middle-class huckster/bachelor whose slick, cocky outward show wards off the pain of introspection." Frequently in *film noir*, male protagonists are depicted as loners who must make difficult moral decisions in an immoral social world (Schatz 1981: 128–129).

Carey McWilliams and Robert Fogelson, two influential historians of Los Angeles, describe social isolation as one of its central characteristics throughout the first half of the twentieth century. Part of this isolation comes from the preponderance of new migrants. In a chapter from *Southern California Country* (1946) titled "I'm a Stranger Here Myself," McWilliams points to several curious elements of Los Angeles that developed out of the predominantly migrant population. "Societies" formed around the states from which members migrated, providing a sense of belonging and a connection to the past. Cafeterias became a popular place for these societies and other single people because the informal atmosphere allowed strangers to sit and talk together. McWilliams argues that migrants could never completely feel at home in Los Angeles and draws a parallel to the immigrant's experience in America. He quotes literary critic Thomas K. Whipple: "'Emigrants turn into detached individuals, like so many grains of sand—but for a man to be severed from a social organism is for him to suffer abnormal deprivation'" (179).

Robert Fogelson claims community was slow to develop in Los Angeles for institutional reasons. Voluntary associations declined as government welfare and insurance companies began to fulfill the needs of the unfortunate. At the same time, commercial associations became more professional and less socially oriented. Perhaps most relevant, the new mobility of the middle class meant that churches and community organizations lacked stable membership and continually struggled to welcome new members. This mobility came in part from residents' efforts to keep their lifestyle standard matched to their income—as more property and larger lots became available with the automobile's help, residents continually sought better homes (Fogelson 1967/1993: 194–195).

The automobile also created an environment of isolation by making it difficult to become acquainted with neighbors and by permitting travel that is not centered on the central business district. "An amazing crisscross pattern of automobile transit has developed, with literally no relation existing between place of employment and place of residence" (McWilliams 1946: 236). Neighbors are not likely to encounter one another downtown or walking on neighborhood streets. "The widespread use of private automobiles inhibited casual contacts that formerly stimulated personal relationships" (Fogelson 1967/1993: 194).

Paul Schrader (1972), in his classic article on *film noir*, argues that the cynicism of *noir* expressed a disappointment with the American Dream of economic opportunity that had built up in the 1930s; this disappointment was exacerbated in Los Angeles, where people migrated with hopes of living a life of independence and leisure.[6] Indeed, during the Depression, the promotional literature that the Chamber of Commerce used to attract the middle class from the Midwest became a problem for the city as it began to attract dispossessed farmers and other poor migrants from Arkansas and Oklahoma (Klein 1997: 35).

At the same time, during the Depression a tension developed between the wholesome image that promoters of Los Angeles tried to portray and the city's growing reputation for the immorality of Hollywood actors or the gambling and prostitution found downtown. While city leaders were concerned that this negative image would discourage middle- and upper-income families from settling in the area, they also recognized that the city profited from the less reputable businesses (ibid.: 76). The 1941 freeway plan provided a partial solution to this tension by isolating downtown from the shopping districts of the west side. The freeway created a barrier to the blight of downtown and allowed those coming from Pasadena or other eastern suburbs to bypass it.

This segregation was legitimized by *film noir* since, as Norman Klein argues, *noir* often caricaturizes poor and nonwhite areas of the city as hopelessly corrupt slums while erasing the community life of these neighborhoods (ibid.: 79–80). A major exception can be found in Chester Himes's *If He Hollers Let Him Go* (1986), originally published in 1945. The novel describes African American life within and outside the ghetto through the eyes of shipyard mechanic Bob Jones. For Jones, Los Angeles's corruption is intimately linked to the violence and systemic discrimination blacks face. In contrast to the *noir* novels Klein describes, the Himes novel characterizes African American neighborhoods as a refuge from corruption rather than a source of it.[7]

While *film noir* mostly avoids depicting nonwhite neighborhoods, in some films urban entertainments and venues frequented by people of color provoke crime or shield dangerous activities. In *The Blue Dahlia* (1946, George Marshall) and *Criss Cross* (1949, Robert Siodmak), the male protagonists return to Los Angeles to find the women they left associating with shady characters and dancing to Latin and swing music. In *Criss Cross* the music takes on sexual implications as we see the protagonist watch his ex-wife dancing with a mobster to Latin music. In *Blue Dahlia*, Johnny returns from the war to find people dancing to swing records in his home and his wife having an affair with a nightclub owner. Both films express fear of the corrupting influence of black and Latin music. *Blue Dahlia* goes further in its condemnation of the music by depicting Johnny's friend Buzz having a war wound that is aggravated by "that monkey music." Every time he hears jazz—on the jukebox, on the radio, or in the nightclub—his head begins to pound, driving him to violence. In the final scene of the film, it appears as if it has driven him to murder Johnny's wife, but instead it only prevents him from remembering his alibi.[8]

In *D.O.A.* (1950, Rudolph Maté), it is the man who is less than faithful to his beloved. Frank Bigelow travels to San Francisco to momentarily escape his fiancée in Banning, a small town west of Palm Springs. The dance music emanating from a neighboring hotel room draws him into an evening of thrills and danger. Bigelow accompanies his hotel neighbors to a jazz club, where extreme close-ups of the black musicians laughing and sweating are mixed with shots of white listeners bouncing wildly to the music. Bigelow seems annoyed by the loud beat, and in the chaos of the club someone poisons his drink. Although the club is in San Francisco, the scene could just as easily have taken place in Los Angeles, where during the 1940s and 1950s there was a lively music scene along Central Avenue. Although it was a largely black neighborhood, clubgoers included white youth from surrounding suburbs. This racial mixing concerned many suburban whites, so they attempted to shut down clubs that permitted integration.[9]

Double Indemnity affirmed the sanctions on integration found in Los Angeles mainly by its exclusion of any nonwhite character other than janitor, porter, and parking attendant.[10] However, the scene in which Neff first takes out Lola, Phyllis's stepdaughter, makes the segregation explicit. They are eating in a restaurant as Neff narrates in the background, "I took her to dinner that evening at a Mexican joint down on Olvera Street where nobody would see us" (Wilder and Chandller 1943: 87). In 1930, Olvera Street was constructed as a Mexican marketplace for tourists in conjunction with the restoration of the area surrounding Los Angeles Plaza.[11] Neff likely chose this location because few whites travel to this part of town except as sightseers. Yet, unlike in the *films noirs* mentioned above, this neighborhood is not a source of danger. Instead, danger is found in the middle-class suburban landscape that supposedly represented an escape from the corruption of downtown.

On the one hand, *Double Indemnity* links middle-class ennui and loneliness, which Fogelson calls "endemic to Los Angeles," to murder; on the other, it exposes how the spatial configuration of the city facilitates crime. The frequent transitions in neighborhoods and the commuter lifestyle allow unfamiliarity with neighbors and make anonymous crime more feasible than in an intimate village where neighbors are aware of each other's activities. This anonymity makes meeting an acquaintance at the train station unlikely and therefore allows Phyllis to take Neff, disguised as her husband, to the train.

Large cities of the East also allow a certain anonymity, but their density and regular pedestrian traffic limit the privacy needed to commit an anonymous crime. The dispersed nature of Los Angeles neighborhoods provides a more secluded space.

Even more important for the murder plot, the automobile permits a certain amount of privacy within a public space. Phyllis drives her husband to the train station, allowing the two to be seen publicly in the car together. What cannot be seen is Neff hiding in the back of the car (see Figure 9). When they turn down a dark street, she honks the horn to cover any sounds of struggle, and Neff knocks Mr. Dietrichson from behind. It is crucial that the car is both public—appearing in a public space, which establishes the presence of the husband and wife en route to the station—and private—providing a hidden space, which allows the murder to be unobserved.

The automobile certainly plays an important role in earlier crime films. In gangster films of the early 1930s, for example, it serves as a tool for violence and plunder. But the types of crime and criminals are very different. In the gangster film, the origins of crime are clearly the degraded and corrupt city. Criminals are often depicted as products of an impoverished and violent childhood, as in *The Public Enemy* (1931, William Wellman) (Schatz 1981: 82–91). The questionable mores of working-class immigrants and the search for power and wealth pursued by illegitimate means are linked to the urban environment.

It is precisely this atmosphere that the residents and planners of Los Angeles were trying to avoid. Thus, it makes sense that the criminals are much more part of a group in gangster films than in Los Angeles–based films such as *Double Indemnity*. While the classic gangster films focus on the rise and fall of individual gangsters, they are clearly part of a gang community, and loyalty to the community is valued. Furthermore, the automobile had an impact on crime but not yet on the design of the city. In gangster films bystanders frequently witness crimes, and it is the power of the gang that protects them from prosecution. In contrast, for *films noirs* located in Southern California the automobile is frequently used to hide the crime, as in *Double Indemnity* or in *The Postman Always Rings Twice* when Cora and Frank kill Nick by rolling his car off a cliff.

The ability to hide crime in an automobile better than on public transportation is made clear in the train scene from *Double Indemnity*. After Neff boards the train he quickly proceeds to the back to have a smoke. The plan is to jump off the back at a particular point where he and Phyllis will place the husband's body on the railroad track, so it will look as if he fell and was killed by accident. There is a temporary setback when Neff finds another passenger sitting in the back of the train (see Figure 10). Neff finally

Figure 9. Neff (Fred McMurray) poised to commit murder in an automobile. *Double Indemnity* (1944, Billy Wilder).

Figure 10. In the back of the train, Neff tries to avoid identification by a fellow passenger. *Double Indemnity* (1944, Billy Wilder).

convinces the man to leave, jumps off the back of the train, and helps Phyllis bring the body onto the track. Later in the film, the passenger who had seen Neff—albeit from the back—confirms suspicions that the dead man found on the track was not the man on the train. This convinces Neff that he will eventually be caught. In other words, it is precisely the public aspect of public transportation that undermines the murder plan's success.

SUNSET BOULEVARD: PLANNED OBSOLESCENCE

If I lose my car it's like having my legs cut off. (Joe Gillis in *Sunset Boulevard*)

Double Indemnity begins with a car speeding down the middle of a street barely avoiding several accidents before stopping at an office building. A man stumbles out of his car and gets the attention of the doorman, who takes him up the elevator to the offices of an insurance company. He finds his way into one of the offices, where he proceeds to recount the events of the film into a dictating machine as a confession to his colleague, the claims manager Keyes. Thus, when the film begins, the events of the story have already taken place and the narrative moves forward toward an inevitable end. This is a frequent characteristic of *film noir*.

A similar logic of inevitability is behind technical rationality: once the data are collected for a problem with a scientific solution, there is no room for hesitation or reflection. The automobile embodies the thrill and the danger of this inevitable drive forward; it offers the possibility of greater power through mobility, but it also threatens to overpower the driver. "Technology is making gestures precise and brutal, and with them men. It expels from movements all hesitation, deliberation, civility . . . Which driver is not tempted, merely by the power of his engine, to wipe out the vermin of the street, pedestrians, children and cyclists" (Adorno 1951/1984: 40).

This link between the automobile's drive and the fatality of *film noir* is even stronger in Wilder's film *Sunset Boulevard*. In this film the plot is triggered by the inability of Joe Gillis, the protagonist, to make his car payments. He escapes repossession agents by driving his car to an apparently deserted mansion on Sunset Boulevard (see Figure 11). The owner of the mansion, a fallen silent movie star named Norma Desmond, snares him into intimacy because he cannot use his car unless he makes the payments. Gillis thinks he will earn money by editing a script Norma has written for her dream return to the screen. The automobile thus carries him to his des-

Figure 11. Gillis pulls into the driveway of Norma Desmond to avoid having his car re-possessed. *Sunset Boulevard* (1950, Billy Wilder).

tiny directly, when he drives into the mansion driveway, and indirectly, by creating the economic demand that led to the car chase, and it keeps him held up in the mansion working on the script. When the agents eventually repossess his car and Gillis tells Norma, she replies, "Oh . . . and I thought it was a matter of life and death." Gillis responds, "It is to me. That's why I came to this house. That's why I took this job" (Brackett, Wilder, and Marshman 1949: 41).

Sunset Boulevard makes an explicit link between dependence on the automobile in Los Angeles and the social isolation and alienation created by this dependence. The movie star's home becomes a prison; the only time Gillis and Norma leave is when the chauffeur drives them in her car. The first time Gillis leaves the home by himself is on New Year's Eve, and it is the exceptionality of this evening that allows him to flag down a car that takes him to a party. Eventually, he begins a clandestine friendship with a producer's assistant, with whom he begins working on a script, but in order to maintain this relationship he must drive Norma's car (see Figure 12). This signals his dependence on a car to maintain social and economic connections and reaffirms his dependence on the movie star.

The automobile marks itself on the Los Angeles landscape in other ways. The film shows how production techniques of the automobile have worked themselves into the movie industry. These techniques existed indepen-

Figure 12. Gillis relies on Norma's car for his clandestine relationship. *Sunset Boulevard* (1950, Billy Wilder).

dently before the mass production of the automobile, but it was Henry Ford who first refined and combined the assembly line, mechanization, and continuous-flow production with the scientific management of Frederick Taylor. In fact, before 1926 "mass production" was simply known as "Fordism" (Flink 1988: 47). The film is especially scathing when it depicts the fast-paced production techniques of Hollywood. In his early encounter with the Paramount producer, Gillis rattles off a cliché plot line: "It's about a ball player, a rookie shortstop that's batting .347. The poor kid was once mixed up in a hold-up. But he's trying to go straight—except there's a bunch of gamblers who won't let him." But Betty Shaefer, a script reviewer, calls it "just a rehash of something that wasn't very good to begin with" (Brackett, Wilder, and Marshman 1949: 9–10). Gillis's presentation of this plot along with his later discussions of a script with Betty demonstrate how film scripts are often trite and contrived to fit an easily marketed mold. Wilder depicts perfectly what Adorno and Horkheimer (1944/1989: 125) see as the penetration of mass production into the "culture industry": "The details are interchangeable. The short interval sequence which was effective in a hit song, the hero's momentary fall from grace (which he accepts as good sport), the rough treatment which the beloved gets from the male star, the latter's rugged defiance of the spoilt heiress, are, like all the other details, ready-made clichés to be slotted in anywhere."

Henry Ford first refined the interchangeability of parts in his production of the Model T. Standardization allowed Ford to reduce costs in the manufacturing process because tools did not have to be redesigned or workers retrained for yearly model changes. *Sunset Boulevard* shows how methods of efficiency used for cars are carried over to the film industry. Like automobiles, films are assembled and produced with multiple technicians, each having a very specific role—writer, script reviewer, producer, director, and hundreds of others who work on making a film. According to Adorno and Horkheimer, this mass production process led to the elimination of critical and creative thought. Although perhaps not to the degree of Ford's assembly line, where workers were not allowed to smile or talk while working, workers in the film industry have been made passive to achieve technical efficiency. "A technological rationale is the rationale of domination itself. It is the coercive nature of society alienated from itself. Automobiles, bombs, and movies keep the whole thing together until their leveling element shows its strength in the very wrong which it furthered. It has made the technology of the culture industry no more than the achievement of standardization and mass production" (ibid.: 121).[12]

However, the goal of profiting from mass production does not just require efficiency; no matter how cheap the product, the consumer still must want to purchase it. In the 1920s, Ford dealers could no longer compete with General Motors, and seven out of ten began to lose money (Flink 1988: 230). Ford's ideal of mass production failed because it lacked the sophisticated marketing techniques developed in the 1920s by GM. Part of GM's promotional strategy was to manufacture and advertise a different car for every income group, primarily based on superficial distinctions. *Sunset Boulevard* indicates that films, like cars, must be both familiar and novel. In the prelude to his tale, Gillis explains, "I sat there grinding out original stories, two a week. Maybe they weren't original enough, maybe they were too original. All I know is they didn't sell" (Brackett, Wilder, and Marshman 1949: 2).

Moreover, Alfred P. Sloan, who became GM president in 1923, recognized that in order to continue selling cars after the market had become saturated, older cars had to be made obsolete, even if they continued to function. Consequently, in contrast to Ford, who refused to change his Model T and did not believe in useless style and frills, GM came up with minor design changes every year to encourage purchase of its current models. This idea of planned obsolescence was implemented in the production of films when scripts remained fundamentally the same but continually incorporated minor changes. "The movie-makers distrust any manuscript which is not reassuringly backed by a bestseller. Yet for this very reason there is neverending talk of ideas, novelty, and surprise, of what is taken for granted but has never existed" (Horkheimer and Adorno 1944/1989: 134).

Planned obsolescence also extended to film stars. Norma Desmond had disappeared from the screen not just because she was old but also because she was from the silent era. She was made obsolete by new technology. Her automobile brings this obsolescence to the forefront in a scene in which she receives a call by Paramount studios and thinks it is for her script. In reality, they are only interested in using her car. When she arrives at the studio, workers on the lot laugh at her old car as "comic," yet the car has more value as a prop than Norma does as an actress.

While Norma is made obsolete by the film industry, she is able to sustain her high level of consumption largely because of the automobile and its central role in the Los Angeles economy. When Gillis asks her to stop buying him things, she retorts, "I own three blocks downtown. I have oil in Bakersfield—pumping, pumping, pumping" (Brackett, Wilder, and Marshman 1949: 52). Both the real estate and oil industries profited greatly from the dramatic growth of car ownership in Los Angeles. The skyrocketing demand for gasoline helped make oil into black gold, and while originating in streetcar lines, real estate speculation was given even further reach as the automobile made more land accessible to transportation.

The influence of General Motors' innovation in the area of consumer credit also plays an important role in the film. In 1919 GM introduced the notion of company financing through General Motors Acceptance Corporation (GMAC), which encouraged the purchase of automobiles above one's means (Flink 1988: 87). This is the instigating event of the film: Gillis trying to escape repossession by the automobile finance company. GM's strategy spurred a new level of consumption based on the ability to use credit for large-ticket items. Adorno and Horkheimer believed this consumption was based on identification with, as much as a need for, the product: "The public is catered for with a hierarchical range of mass produced products of varying quality, thus advancing the rule of complete quantification . . . Consumers appear as statistics on research organization charts, and are divided by income groups into red, green, and blue areas" (1944/1989: 123). Most important, this identification depended on superficial differences:

> That the difference between the Chrysler range and General Motors
> products is basically illusory strikes every child with keen interest in

varieties . . . But even the differences between the more expensive and cheaper models put out by the same firm steadily diminish: for automobiles, there are such differences as the number of cylinders, cubic capacity, details of patented gadgets: and for films there are the number of stars, the extravagant use of technology, labor and equipment, and the introduction of the latest psychological formulas. (123–124)

Gillis's entanglement in Los Angeles depicts a tawdry web coming to span the city. His reliance on creating trivial mass-produced work for the film industry is from the beginning linked to his need for an automobile. Our introduction to the Fordist manner of script production occurs immediately after he avoids having his car repossessed and is desperately seeking a job at Paramount. When he fails to find work, he decides to move back to Ohio and leave his car for the collection agency. Norma enables him to continue living in Los Angeles. Although he initially resists her purchasing him various luxury items, over time he comes to accept them, including the use of her automobile, and Norma's automobile in turn allows him to work surreptitiously with Betty on another trivial script.

The falseness of this lifestyle is revealed when Norma forces Gillis to expose his living circumstances to Betty. He explains to Betty that he has become used to his indulgences and could not live with financial insecurity even with someone he loved. When Betty arrives at the mansion and asks Gillis to gather his things and leave with her, Gillis responds, "All my things? All the eighteen suits, all the custom-made shoes and the eighteen dozen shirts, and the cuff-links and the platinum key-chains, and the cigarette cases?" Betty again asks Gillis to come with her, but Gillis replies, "Come on where? Back to a one-room apartment that I can't pay for? Back to a story that may sell and very possibly will not?"

In the end, Gillis rejects his dependence on Norma and plans to return to his "newspaper job back in Ohio." He could not live in Los Angeles because in Los Angeles one needs to maintain a minimum level of consumption. Moreover, Gillis recognizes that his inability to maintain this standard would doom his relationship to Betty. In the end, the minimal standard of consumption is automobile ownership.

Much like Horkheimer and Adorno, the film portrays mass culture creating a false world based on consumption, which hides the alienation of everyday life. Wilder's concluding sequence in which a confused Norma believes the filming of her arrest is actually the filming of the climactic scene from her new movie, shows how this false world can overwhelm the real world. Descending from the staircase, Norma says, "You see, this is my life.

It always will be. There's nothing else—just us and the cameras and those wonderful people out there in the dark" (Brackett, Wilder, and Marshman 1949: 117). The "real lives" of movie stars become important because of their fictional lives on the screen, and for Norma her fictional life becomes her real life. For Horkheimer and Adorno, "Real life is becoming indistinguishable from the movies" (1944/1989: 126).

At the same time, as a Hollywood movie, *Sunset Boulevard* challenged Horkheimer and Adorno's theory of the culture industry. In contrast to their characterization of mass culture, the movie lacked either an easy or sentimental solution to the dilemmas it depicted. Nor did it provide a straightforward moral message, which for Horkheimer and Adorno typified Hollywood tragedies (152). In fact, the film's attack on the movie industry evoked an angry response at its Hollywood premier. Louis B. Mayer of MGM shouted at Wilder that he had disgraced the film industry, to which Wilder simply replied, "Fuck you."[13] In short, the culture industry did not have the totalizing ability to erase all negatives as Horkheimer and Adorno imagined. Equally important, the power of mass production and the culture industry over working people was never so complete that it could "so confine them, body and soul, that they fall helpless victims to what is offered them" (133).

George Lipsitz (1994) has shown that the decade of the 1940s was a time of great resistance among working-class Americans, both through culture and direct action. Throughout World War II, despite the official no-strike agreement made by union leaders, workers staged walkouts and other forms of protest not just to win contract concessions but also to assert and test their power over management. Moreover, "mass culture" could take on a critical edge not only in *films noirs* like those by Wilder, but also by encouraging resistance to the exact type of consumer conformity attacked by Horkheimer and Adorno.

VIOLENCE VIA AUTOMOBILE

One example of this resistance was young whites in Los Angeles helping to popularize the music and style of African American and Mexican American youth. The most defiant aspect of youth culture was the "zoot suit"— pancake hats, wide jackets, and tapered pants—worn by young blacks and Chicanos, which was seen as flaunting the conservative values of the middle class. Precisely because white youth wanted to rebel against the values of their parents, they began to wear the zoot suit and listen to the music of black and Latino communities. Ironically, by identifying with groups excluded from mainstream society, these youths tried to overcome the isolation that *film noir* characterizes as part of Los Angeles (Lipsitz 1990: 120–121; Mazón 1984: 7–8).

Suburban white hostility toward this oppositional culture erupted into outright violence in June 1943 when blacks and Chicanos were dragged from streetcars and beaten for wearing zoot suits (McWilliams 1948/1972: 224). Between June 3 and June 13, hundreds of white sailors roamed the streets of Los Angeles attacking youth of color and stripping them of their clothes. While sailors were the instigators, Mexican Americans were most often arrested. The City Council banned the wearing of zoot suits, thus implying that Mexicans were to blame. Moreover, the white press tended to condone the attacks (McWilliams 1946: 319–320; Mazón 1984: 67–77; Lipsitz 1994: 83).

The violence was not confined to those who traveled outside of segregated neighborhoods; rather, the attacks began when two hundred sailors hired taxicabs to drive into predominantly Mexican American neighborhoods and attack Chicano youth. The automobile allowed them to attack from a position of anonymity, reaffirming the logic of automotive violence from *Double Indemnity*. When the police did run into the caravan, only nine sailors were detained, and none of them were charged (McWilliams 1948/1972: 245–246).

While in *Double Indemnity* the public aspect of the train prevented Neff from hiding his crime, the public transit system in Los Angeles failed to hide a different sort of crime—the harassment faced by people of color who rode the trains. Mexican, Asian, and African Americans all faced hostility from transit employees and other riders. This hostility reflected a desire to keep people of color restricted to small, segregated parts of the city. During the war, this desire was exaggerated by the increased opportunities for interracial socializing in Los Angeles as more young women left home to work in defense industries, and servicemen from across the country came to the city. Rail service, which had declined after years of disinvestment, brought contact between these groups under crowded, uncomfortable conditions (Bottles 1987: 169).

The "zoot suit riots" demonstrate another contrast between streetcars and automobiles. Riding public transit requires contact with people in the neighborhoods along the route. Eric Avila (2004) argues that the city's abandonment of trolleys reflected a rejection of the heterosocial environment it fostered. He notes the importance of the streetcars in bringing people from across Los Angeles to the lively music scene centered around downtown in the 1930s. He even reports that a young Charles Mingus would occasionally take out his bass to jam while riding the trolley (191). In a car, however, one can keep a distance by rolling up the windows and locking the doors, or one can simply bypass certain neighborhoods altogether. The sailors who attacked from taxis chose to drive into primarily Mexican American neighborhoods, and the automobile, unlike the train, allowed them to ambush individuals and avoid confronting the residents.

It must be emphasized that the attacks on zoot suiters, the police crackdown on interracial venues, and the demonization of nonwhites in the press was not simply the paranoid reaction of West Coast residents made uneasy by the war in the Pacific. White people's desire for segregation was supported by policies at the federal and local levels during the 1930s and 1940s. As already noted, FHA policies made acquiring loans in neighborhoods that were not exclusively white more difficult—and nearly impossible if there was a single African American resident. In the context of Los Angeles, it is also important to remember that in 1942, a large Japanese American community was not just segregated but forcibly removed from the city to internment camps.

Federal and local policies that reinforced segregation had widespread support among the white public. A central argument here is that infrastructure developments were not a product of elite conspiracies that fooled the masses. Transportation developments and popular attitudes among whites bolstered each other. Perhaps more surprising is the way social research further legitimized the need for segregation. Greg Hise (2004) notes that scholars throughout the early part of the twentieth century conducted research that pathologized communities of color. One study by a sociologist from the University of Southern California (USC) characterized a section of Boyle Heights as "blighted," using the same language as the Home Owner's Loan Corporation—a description used to explain why the neighborhood should be redlined (554).

This support among social scientists for segregating Los Angeles with the aid of the automobile is especially clear in a collection of essays from 1940 aptly titled *Preface to a Master Plan*. The authors espouse the decentralized development of Los Angeles as better for its residents than the high density of eastern cities, and they foresee the unplanned sprawl emerging in Los Angeles as creating a city that would be too large to allow a community to develop (Dykstra 1940: 6; East 1940: 97; Panunzio 1940: 39–40; Zierer 1940: 58). Their solution is to regulate development and improve transportation with the use of freeways. University of California, Los Angeles (UCLA) geographer Clifford Zierer (1940: 59) advocated small-scale "satellite" developments:

> There is a need for controlling the "run-away" suburb and for encouraging the "satellite" center in the Los Angeles area. . . . Each unit should be recognized as able to care for the needs of only a definitely limited number of persons and most of their activities. . . . Circulation among the many satellite groupings may be provided by a thoroughly inte-

grated network of major highways, which are capable of extension to the full limits of the geographic area.

While the automobile may be partly responsible for the isolation in Los Angeles, here it is also the solution. At the same time, small, self-contained communities likely meant excluding people of color, and in this way the plan could facilitate segregation.

Constantine Panunzio, a sociologist at UCLA, appreciated the city's cultural diversity while also cautioning that "too much" ethnic difference would lead to disunity: "If the proportion of foreigners is too great, or if foreigners are so strong that they form blocs and have disproportionate influence on the politics or other aspects of community life, then heterogeneity develops. Too many conflicting patterns, too many sects, and conflicting groups do not make for the unity and cohesion of the community" (1940: 36). Therefore, he argues, it is important to make sure whites remain the dominant group: "The native Whites, together with the British and Canadians, belonging essentially to the Anglo-Saxon culture, guarantee the unity of the community" (37). In other words, here the reconstruction of "community," which is threatened in Los Angeles, contains an explicit racial hierarchy.

Panunzio continues by claiming that Los Angeles lacks the segregation found in other cities: "One of the striking facts regarding these minority peoples in Los Angeles is that they are not sharply segregated as they are in other metropolitan areas" (38). In fact, housing discrimination prevented people of color from living in most of Los Angeles. Restrictive covenants in Los Angeles expanded greatly in the late 1920s with the increased migration of African Americans to the area. By 1940 blacks were restricted to living in a mere 5 percent of Los Angeles residential areas (De Graf 1962: 199). Some Mexican Americans were tolerated in white middle-class suburbs, but most remained restricted to Boyle Heights, East Los Angeles, and Chavez Ravine (Avila 2004: 52). Asian Americans were confined to Chinatown and Little Tokyo on the edge of downtown (Laslett 1996: 43).

Civil rights activists challenged the restrictive covenants, but until the 1948 U.S. Supreme Court decision declaring them unenforceable, courts frequently defended the right to exclude nonwhites from owning or renting in parts of the city (Bass 1960: 95–113). Where restrictive covenants were not enforced, white homeowners and the Ku Klux Klan used threats and violence. In the 1930s the Klan held protest marches and sent threatening notes to blacks who attempted to move into white neighborhoods (De Graf 1962: 88). In 1945, a week after receiving threats, a black family was killed when their Fontana home was burned to the ground—the parents and their two children perished in the fire (Bass 1960: 135).

The desire to exclude nonwhites from suburban developments was not only manifest in housing discrimination; people of color were also discouraged from entering white public spaces. Despite laws against discrimination, people of color were routinely denied service at hotels, restaurants, and theaters (Bass 1960: 70; Collins 1980: 77; De Graf 1962: 87). In the 1930s Pasadena allowed nonwhites to use only one public swimming pool and on only one day a week. A suit to overturn this restriction led surrounding cities to increase restrictive covenants and place similar restrictions on their public pools (De Graf 1962: 87). If people of color were found in white areas of town, they often faced abuse and were arrested by the police for fabricated or minor charges such as vagrancy (De Graf 1962: 204). In 1943, after being attacked by police in Venice Beach, Alfred Barela complained in a letter to a Los Angeles judge, "We're tired of being told we can't go to this show or that dance hall because we're Mexican or that we better not be seen on the beach front, or that we can't wear draped pants or have our hair cut the way we want to" (quoted in Sánchez 1993: 253).

Whites also wished to exclude people of color from attending the same schools as their children. In 1941 black students were burned in effigy at Fremont High School to protest their integration with whites. A leaflet passed out at the protest read, "IT'S TOO LATE NOW; THE NIGGERS KNOW THEY HAVE WON GROUND AND THEY'LL BE FLOCKING TO THIS SECTION. . . . THEN JUST LET A WHITE GIRL WALK SO MUCH AS DOWN THE STREET AT NIGHT OR EVEN AT DUSK" (Bass 1960: 119).

The everyday violence of segregation made steady employment difficult. Most new jobs were located between ten and fifteen miles from central Los Angeles in Long Beach or Santa Monica. In order to apply for a job, blacks and Latinos needed to take the Pacific Electric Red Car, which many could not afford. African Americans fared somewhat better when they successfully moved into the Watts neighborhood in South Los Angeles, and protests by civil rights leaders forced defense industries to hire more blacks. Still, when blacks did find jobs, in addition to the hostility they faced from transit workers and other passengers, the Red Car frequently broke down or was delayed, making it an unreliable means of getting to work on time. Those who worked night shifts had additional difficulties getting to work, since the Red Car did not run after midnight and cabs refused to serve the ghetto (Collins 1980: 56–59).

Linked to Panunzio's failure to recognize the high level of segregation is his failure to recognize the conditions under which this segregated population lived: "Here is a city which has no slums to speak of, at least not the slum areas which mar all the larger cities, while such slum conditions as do exist can be corrected more easily because of the absence of large tenements and highly congested areas" (1940: 39). He failed to see how discrimination forced blacks into crowded and poor-quality housing. Property owners often divided homes into several units to make the most of their property, and owners often avoided maintaining their buildings since they knew that if blacks did not like their conditions, they had little else to choose from.[14]

Not all writers in the collection were so dismissive of the poor housing in some areas of the city. In his introduction, Clarence Dykstra (1940: 9) writes, "It is important that the citizens of Los Angeles—of any city—understand their city, its functions, its organic structure, and the means by which it may be improved. . . . Let us reconstruct our slums and rehabilitate our blighted areas." But the solutions suggested to the problem of "slums" still conceal the discrimination that created them. Richard Neutra calls for the construction of subsidized housing to replace blighted "Mexican" and "Negro" neighborhoods. But Neutra (1940: 193) also implies that these groups chose to live in their crowded conditions:

> Immigrated largely from middle western and eastern cities, rather than from the plantation south, this population does not depend by any special reason of childhood conditioning on a type of rehousing in thinly spread, one-story structures. . . . To abandon the present slums and transplant these colored families much farther outward offers distinct disadvantages. Less motorized than any other group and in most instances dependent upon the combined earnings of both husband and wife, they must rely upon public carrier systems to take them to the railroad yards, hotels, and office buildings which typically employ the men, and to homes in the western section of the city where the women can find domestic service.

Here Neutra naturalizes racial segregation and economic inequality. This naturalization accepts discrimination since "these colored families" are better off where they are. And as long as there is a way to keep their conditions from spreading, other residents can ignore them.

Together, these articles reveal how the plan for freeway-connected neighborhoods facilitated the concealment of racial discrimination. They show how the creation of "community" can be used to exclude. Moreover, these authors provided a social scientific rationale corresponding to the engineering rationale for the 1941 freeway plan. As with the engineers, the solutions for social scientists had an inevitability based on empirical observation—returning us to the logic of technocratic rationality criticized by Horkheimer and Adorno. Finally, just as these observations ignore the living conditions for populations of color, the freeways facilitate continued ignorance of these conditions by allowing whites to drive around segregated neighborhoods.

The dominant culture of consumerism braced by the technology of the automobile contained multiple gaps and incongruities. *Double Indemnity* and *Sunset Boulevard* exposed an underside to the planners' idealized vision of Los Angeles. The underside for people of color was exposed most dramatically in the attack on zoot suiters in 1943 and later in the civil unrest of 1965 and 1992. Yet, despite these dark moments—these manifestations of *noir*—Horkheimer and Adorno were correct in foreseeing the power of the Los Angeles ideal. Not only did this culture successfully restructure the landscape of Los Angeles, it ultimately came to restructure the landscape of urban America.

However, in turning to the contemporary landscape, the last part of this study focuses not just on the destructive legacy of earlier transportation goals but also on the resistance that developed out of this legacy. While the first two parts focused primarily on expressions of the dominant and most influential transportation ideals, Part III focuses on the expressions that emerge in the fissures of built systems. The theoretical seeds of resistance found in the work of German refugees have grown—like the weeds that expand in asphalt cracks—to create multiple uneven voices of opposition to both the systems and the ideals that they embody.

Part III also marks a shift in the discussion of transportation's impact on the public. Parts I and II considered how plans could discourage political activism by placing transportation decisions in the hands of engineers or encourage political divisions by excluding some from the suburban consumerism that came to define success in the United States. Part III considers how the public makes use of transportation infrastructure for expressions and, through this, struggles over both the meaning of this infrastructure and the contemporary city in the United States.

PART 3

THE PUBLIC'S FEARS
OF URBAN GRIDLOCK

■ ■

CHAPTER 5

STORIES OF THE MTA: CONTESTING MEANINGS OF SUBWAY SPACE

In the early 1980s the introduction to *Saturday Night Live* began with "Live from New York, the most dangerous city in America." In an episode of the "Rocket Report" on one of these programs, guest host Charlene Tilton takes a ride through the subways with Charles Rocket. Rocket stands by with microphone in hand to report Tilton's impressions as she excitedly steps onto a graffiti-covered subway car. After a brief ride, the two step off the train and Rocket asks what Tilton thinks. A smiling Tilton is in disbelief. "My wallet is still there!" she exclaims, almost disappointed.

A decade later, the PaineWebber Art Gallery in Midtown Manhattan presented an exhibit entitled Art en Route: MTA Arts for Transit. The exhibit offered examples of artwork that had been built into the subway system after the capital rebuilding program was established in 1982. The 1994 exhibit provided a dramatically different characterization of the New York subway from the *SNL* sketch. Rather than a place of urban danger, the exhibit depicted the subway as a place that aids in "making the arts more accessible to a larger audience" (MTA Arts for Transit 1994: 5). The organizers of the exhibition viewed the Arts for Transit project as one step toward reviving the ideals behind the construction of the original subway lines. Peter Stangl, then chairman and chief executive officer of the Metropolitan Transit Authority (MTA), declared that "Arts for Transit signals a renewed commitment to the ideals of the original subway builders—that public spaces and public services are at their best when they are both functional and attractive" (ibid.: 4).

In many ways the goals behind the reconstruction of the subway parallel those that inspired its original construction: both projects set out to rescue a city that was collapsing in multiple ways. At the end of the nineteenth century the problems faced by many large cities—poor sanitation, inadequate housing, lack of open space—were perhaps nowhere more evident than in lower Manhattan. Crowding made it increasingly difficult to conduct business and was blamed for the poor living conditions of new immigrants. The first subway lines were seen as a solution to the economic and social consequences of overcrowding: according to its promoters, the subway would establish and maintain the city's position as the center of business in the United States.

In a similar way, when the capital rebuilding program began in 1982, the city was recovering from a major fiscal crisis and had gained a reputation for being dirty and dangerous. According to the MTA, the rebuilding program would help ensure the economic competitiveness of the city and region. In a 1990 assessment of capital needs, the MTA calculated the enormous economic damage that poor transportation and traffic congestion has on the regional economy, and rebuilding regional rapid transit was linked to the economic competitiveness of the region:

> The measure of New York's success in resolving its mobility challenges will be economic growth. This region could enter the 21st century with the most efficient and balanced transportation network in this country. That would mean a more mobile society, a healthier environment, a more efficient work force, and an economy that is much more competitive in the world marketplace. (MTA 1990: 10)

Although the ideals shaping the subway's reconstruction in many ways echo those behind the original subway lines, the historical context from which these ideals emerge is very different. In the late nineteenth century, industry and population were expanding in cities across the United States. Rapid growth caused problems, but for most commentators, the city's future appeared to be bright (Beauregard 2003: 31). In contrast, by 1982 U.S. cities had passed through several decades of decline, with jobs and residents moving to the suburbs. Many analysts viewed cities like New York as highly inefficient and believed that for these cities to compete, services would have to be drastically cut (ibid.: 192). The condition of the subways in 1982 revealed the legacy of urban decline.

The subway displays another side to the preference for the automobile over public transit in the United States: it signals the type of environment that driving an automobile rejects. New York is an especially appropriate location to study this rejection since it is the only U.S. city where a majority of commuters use public transportation (American Public Transportation

Association 2003). At the same time, the subway's renovation provides a useful place to explore attempts to reverse the movement away from central cities and public transit. The ability of New York to regenerate what had become such a symbol of urban decline may indicate the potential for a revival of other cities and their mass transit systems.

As a sign, the subway represents the city in a way a car and highway cannot. While the condition of automobiles largely reflects the wealth of their individual owners, because the subway serves all residents of the city it reflects the well-being of the entire city. Roads may vary greatly among neighborhoods, often depending on the income of their residents, but in the subway poorly maintained track in one area can cause delays at a location miles down the track. As Jim Dwyer (1991: 4) puts it, "Every rank of New Yorker is indentured to the subway. Nobody rides first class."

The subway is also a public forum in which diverse groups and individuals express themselves and experience the expression of others; the use of this forum has an important impact on the subway's image. It is for this reason that the MTA encourages particular voices, such as Arts for Transit, while trying to restrict others, most notably of graffiti writers. The strategies used by the MTA to reconstruct the image of the subway in many ways reflect an attempt to displace signs of the historical depravation of central cities with the highly controlled atmosphere of a shopping mall. The pressure to reshape the subway in this fashion comes from the current political and economic climate affecting cities throughout the United States. But the strategies used to attract residents and consumers back to the city—and riders back to the subway—have limits. These limits are rooted in the nature of the subway: a confined space where diverse expressions cannot easily be avoided.

THE RISE AND DECLINE OF THE NEW YORK SUBWAY'S IMAGE

I wanted to show that what we're doing today in many ways is being done in the very same spirit in which the original subway was built . . . The first subway line was built under the philosophy of the City Beautiful movement, which was that if you created beautiful spaces, they would bring out people's better impulses, their higher nature. (Sandra Bloodworth,[1] quoted in Scheier 1994)

Although many ideals invoked by contemporary promoters of the MTA were common to those behind the original subway construction, the first subway also emerged out of conflict: conflict over who would build and operate it, where the lines would be built, and how it would be regulated. This conflict manifested in the development of three competing lines that were not unified until 1940. Recalling the differing attitudes behind the support for these lines makes the appeals by contemporary officials to a single vision behind the subway's original construction problematic. Furthermore, tracing the conditions that led to the subway's decline shows how the subway marks broader inequalities in the United States that renovation cannot address.

According to historian Clifton Hood (1993), the entrepreneurs behind the first line, the IRT (Interborough Rapid Transit Company), were concerned most of all with increasing the tax base through expanded settlement in upper Manhattan and reducing the congestion that hindered commerce on the lower part of the island. Most of these entrepreneurs were members of the elite who had little regard for working-class residents of the city. After construction of the first line was completed in 1904, subway cars quickly became overcrowded, but the IRT opposed the construction of additional lines because it would reduce profits. Turn-of-the-century reformers saw this blatant disregard for the interests of riders as a consequence of government collaboration with private businesses. Thus, in 1907 the Board of Rapid Transit Commissioners was replaced by the Public Service Commission, which took a stronger regulatory position toward large transit corporations (Hood 1993: 126–131).

Under pressure from reformers, a second line was finally approved for construction in 1913. Progressives like George McAney, who negotiated the new contracts, supported subway expansion for the same reason middle-class reformers supported trolley construction. Transit permitted the working class to escape the crowded tenements of downtown for recreation or better housing, first uptown and then in the outer boroughs. At the same time, the attitudes of progressives toward the poor were often more paternalistic than democratic. They wished to disperse immigrants from crowded neighborhoods of Lower Manhattan not only to improve public health but also to reduce the social volatility of these neighborhoods. Hood (1993: 127) observes, "As hotbeds of crime, pauperism, and radicalism, these colonies threatened to eradicate traditional American social harmony and replace it with the kind of rigid, violence-ridden class structure that had already spread across Europe."

Because a lack of trust in urban immigrant voters discouraged progressives from advocating a municipally run subway,[2] the first subway lines were privately constructed; however, they were also meant to be a public monument that would represent the city's status. This reflected their emergence at the height of the City Beautiful movement, the goal of which was to improve the image of cities by building inspirational public structures.[3] For this reason aesthetics was an important element in the construction of both initial subway lines. The Rapid Transit Commission contract with the IRT in 1900 stated:

> The railway and its equipment as contemplated by the contract constitute a great public work. All parts of the structure where exposed shall therefore be designed, constructed, and maintained with a view to the beauty of their appearance, as well as to their efficiency. (Quoted in Stookey 1992: 14)

Subway stations included moldings in the ceilings, faience or terra cotta cornices, mosaics in distinctive patterns for each station, and ceramic plaques with images or designs meant to signify a station's location.[4] The beauty of the stations also helped ease the fear of traveling underground. A *House and Garden* article declared of the City Hall station: "The broad structural vaults satisfy the esthetic and scientific imagination that a necessary strength has been created underground in the proximity of the Post office and the skyscrapers of Park Row" (quoted in Stookey 1992: 15).

The aesthetic grandeur of the subways did not prevent the companies that controlled them from developing a poor image. In addition to complaints about overcrowding, people questioned the right of private companies to profit from a system built with public funds. In part because his support came from working-class immigrants, Mayor John Hylan supported the construction of a subway run by the city.[5] But while Hylan's vision for the subways was democratic, as a model it could not solve the problems that were already causing the subways to deteriorate. At the root of these problems was the assumption that public transit would be able to sustain itself on fare revenues. This became more difficult after World War I when expenses increased but contracts required the subway lines to maintain their fare at five cents. Hylan fought hard to keep the five-cent fare, claiming that the publicly run Independent Subway System (IND) would prove that difficulties faced by the private companies were due to inefficiencies. He believed the competition of a publicly run subway would force the owners of private lines to sell to the city (Hood 1993: 203).

The IND opened its first line in 1932, but during the Depression falling ridership caused declining revenues and the further delay of subway maintenance. At the same time, Mayor Fiorello LaGuardia continued to believe that the subways could support themselves without financial subsidies. Just

as Hylan claimed the IND would solve the problems the subways faced, La-
Guardia argued that unification, achieved in 1940, would allow the subways
to be self-sustaining and maintain the five-cent fare. "Unification of the
three lines would be the salvation of the subways, LaGuardia and others had
declared. It would reduce costs, eliminate competition that wasted money
by having several lines stop within a block or so of each other, and generally
improve the life of the beleaguered straphanger" (Dwyer 1991: 66). Although
gas rationing during World War II sparked a brief growth in ridership, after
the war deterioration accelerated. The fare became ten cents in 1947, but
this change was not enough to revive the system, given the requirement that
it balance its budget without subsidies. By the time this requirement was
changed in 1967—with the formation of the MTA and the use of Triborough
Bridge and Tunnel Authority funds to support the system—decades of un-
derfunding had taken their toll.

While LaGuardia failed to see the need to subsidize transit, he eagerly
supported Robert Moses in his efforts to rebuild the city around the automobile. Over the course of three decades, Moses directed the construction
of multiple expressways and bridges around New York. Because these projects neither included mass transit construction nor permitted space for
them in the future, not only did they encourage the use of the automobile,
but in some cases they made it imperative.[6] Through his administrative influence, Moses slowed the implementation of Transit Authority subsidies.
In short, the policies Moses helped institute accelerated a vicious cycle: lack
of funds led to worsening service, which led to declining ridership, which
led to a further decline in funds (Caro 1975; Fischler 1979).

However, Moses was not the only leader who supported better automobile access to the city. As shown earlier, most politicians and planners saw
accommodating the automobile as essential to urban progress. "With the
numbers of motor vehicles growing geometrically between 1900 and 1920,
some of the most respected planners in America placed a good deal of faith
in automobiles' ability to contribute to the healthy spreading out of the nation's metropolitan regions. They believed that 'automobility' would lead to
decentralization of housing and the amelioration of social disorders" (Foster
1981: 42).

However, New York is unique because it had the most sophisticated
rapid transit system in the country, and belief in the car's superiority led to
its decline. As was the case elsewhere, this privileging of the automobile
benefited some groups more than others. Whites moved into suburban developments only accessible by car, but blacks were denied access to these
same developments. Levittown, for instance, provided affordable homes to

many in the New York region by applying mass production techniques to homebuilding but "publicly and officially refused to sell to blacks for two decades after the war" (Jackson 1985: 241).

Within the city, transportation policy had a twofold discriminatory impact. First, the favoring of highways over transit harmed those who could not afford a car, since all taxpayers funded the construction of these new roads while only car owners could use them. Second, the displacement caused by highway construction had a disproportionate impact on the poor and people of color. According to Robert Caro (1975), "Although the 1950 census had found that only 12 percent of the city's population was nonwhite, at least 37 percent of the evictees and probably more were nonwhite" (968–969). Further, "only one out of every four of the evicted families earned $4,083 per year;[7] 20 percent earned less than $2,000 a year." Equally tragic, despite claims that low-income housing was being constructed for those displaced by highways and "slum clearance," the number of new units constructed was well below what was needed. A large proportion of the residents who were displaced received no assistance in finding new homes, and in the rare instances when assistance was provided, the housing was often of a lower quality and/or more expensive than the housing that was destroyed (963–969).

Again, Moses and New York City's discrimination against the poor in expressway construction was part of a larger national trend. John Mollenkopf (1983) points out that during the New Deal, the construction of expressways and roads was part of urban renewal projects that included low-income housing, but after World War II, interstate expressways were built primarily to serve the interests of private industries such as construction and trucking. The Eisenhower administration, under the influence of highway engineers, promoted better access to downtown businesses with widened streets and limited-access highways. Freeway construction tore through poor neighborhoods because residents had little political influence. The structure of urban freeways embodied the political desire of Republicans and conservative Democrats to use urban renewal programs to benefit their suburban constituencies (121).

Federally funded freeway construction also encouraged industry to leave the cities for cheaper land in the suburbs. Manufacturing jobs began leaving New York City during World War II when defense production required that new factories be located outside urban centers, making them less vulnerable to attack (Abu-Lughod 1999: 191). On Long Island these jobs were accessible via the parkways constructed in the 1920s and 1930s, but, under Moses's influence, Long Island was closed off to mass transit. In 1956 New York's outer boroughs still had a significant portion of the manufacturing in the region, but by 1980 the suburbs had come to dominate this sector of the economy (Harris 1991: 132). The influence of federal policies also became evident after World War II when manufacturing increased in southwestern cities while declining in northeastern cities, a decline that was especially pronounced in the New York City area. Federal investments that supported defense-industry growth in the Southwest corresponded to the growth of political clout in this region, while New York's influence was on the wane (Abu-Lughod 1999: 291; Mollenkopf 1983: 235–253).

Not only did the loss of manufacturing jobs cause a decline in tax revenues, it also left many more people dependent on public services ranging from housing to health care. The squeeze between declining revenues and rising expenses culminated in the fiscal crisis of 1975, which had devastating consequences for the city's infrastructure. While the causes of the crisis were complex, it is important to consider the impact of racist policies at the federal level.

First, it must be emphasized that the movement of jobs to the suburbs was not race-neutral. As Janet Abu-Lughod (1999: 294–297) shows, between 1950 and 1980, high-income households rose in the New York suburbs and declined in the city. At the same time, the suburbs remained almost exclusively white, while the city became more racially diverse. High-paying professional and managerial jobs remained in the city, but these were mostly outside the reach of Puerto Ricans and African Americans. Although people of color found success in the public sector, they remained primarily in lower-paying job categories (Brecher and Horton 1991: 111).

While the Federal Housing Administration collaborated in the exclusion of African Americans and Puerto Ricans from New York suburbs, other aspects of federal housing policy had a more mixed impact on these communities. As in most cities, a large number of tenements were torn down in the mid-twentieth century for the purpose of eliminating blight, and the public housing built for displaced tenants was inadequate. The number of units built did not match the number torn down, and new units were often unaffordable (Fogelson 2001: 344–345). On the other hand, New York City had a longer history of providing public housing than most cities; having nearly completed the construction of 2,200 units by the time the Housing Act of 1937 was passed (Abu-Lughod 1999: 180). Once the federal government made funds available for housing construction with the acts of 1937 and 1949, New York took full advantage. The city built 75,000 units in the 1950s alone, far more than Chicago or Los Angeles (ibid.: 208). Because communities of color were more likely to be displaced by urban redevelopment and more likely to face discrimination in the private housing market, it was often families from these communities who moved into public housing (Judd 1988: 274). Thus, "the projects" came to mean places of concentrated black and Latino poverty.

New York's construction of proportionally more public housing units than other cities reflected a greater support for social welfare spending in general. At the time of its fiscal crisis, New York was caricatured as a city plagued by overspending, especially on public employees and services for the poor (Tabb 1982: 56–65). However, criticisms of New York's high level of spending compared to other cities often do not take into account the smaller amount of state and county funding New York City receives for municipal services. Moreover, besides its greater commitment to public housing, New York has traditionally been more generous than other cities in supplying health care, higher education, and financial aid for the poor (Abu-Lughod 1999: 312). Historically, the city relied heavily on federal aid to fund these services, but this aid had declined dramatically by the time of the crisis in 1975. Precisely at the time New York was suffering from an economic recession, the Nixon administration's policy of New Federalism called for less dependence on Washington. Federal assistance for public housing was practically cut off in 1974 when the Housing Act was replaced by the Community Development Block Grant Program. Overall the federal portion of new revenue fell from 55 percent in 1973 to 8 percent in 1975 (Judd 1988: 275, 215).

It is no coincidence that these cutbacks had a disproportionate impact on New York blacks and Latinos. By the 1970s, problems of the city—deteriorating housing, unemployment, crime—had come to be identified with the ghettos where people of color were concentrated (Beauregard 2003: 175). Antipoverty programs appeared to be ineffective at solving these problems, and it had become increasingly popular to blame crime and poverty on the pathologies of poor families. In the eyes of politicians like Richard Nixon, not only were welfare programs not working, they were actually making urban conditions worse by encouraging degeneracy: "We have been deluged by governmental programs for the unemployed, programs for the poor, and we have reaped from these programs an ugly harvest of frustrations, violence and failure across the land" (Nixon quoted in Cronin, Cronin, and Milakovich 1981: 76). In this context, many believed cities like New York required fiscal "discipline."

Thus, when the Ford administration eventually did come to the city's aid in 1975, it required strict austerity measures imposed by an Emergency Financial Control Board. The seven members of this board, three of whom were corporate leaders, forced tremendous reductions in city services, including recreation, education, police, and of course the subway system (Tabb

1982: 30, 44). In 1974 the MTA employed a policy of "deferred maintenance" in order to meet the impending cuts in the city's contribution to its budget; this policy was to have a devastating impact. Joe Austin (2001: 135) argues, correctly, that given the history of funding problems, "it remains an open question as to whether a subway crisis of some sort was inevitable, come New York City's municipal bankruptcy or not." No doubt poor policy decisions by local officials contributed to the decline of the subways. However, the point here is that this decline also reflected federal decreases in assistance that were justified by labeling urban communities of color as dysfunctional.[8]

RESHAPING SUBWAY SPACE

In [1981], when I rode the trains, there were 600 "red tag" areas, requiring a speed limit of 16 km/h because the track was unsafe; derailments were frequent. The signaling was several generations old. Trains were dilapidated and blanketed with graffiti. Stations were urban caves carpeted with gum. Crime was increasing. Track fires were an everyday hazard. It was nothing short of a major crisis. (Kiepper 1994: 37)

We've had people say that they haven't ridden the subway for five years, but now they're going to. (Wendy Feuer,[9] quoted in Scheier 1994)

By the late 1970s the legacy of New York's disregard for public transit and the disregard throughout the United States for central cities was marked upon the New York subway. Popular films from this era depict underground New York as a place of pathological criminality (Austin 2001: 140). The subways were plagued by frequent breakdowns and delays caused by track fires. "Aging and poorly maintained subway cars clanked and lurched and then just quit, often in mid trip" (Seaton 1994: 32). Subway stations and cars were filthy and smelled bad. "All but a hundred or so of the 932 subway toilet facilities were closed in 1981 because the [Transit] Authority could not keep up with the vandals. The mouth of the tunnel has been used by thousands as the facility of choice, so that the wind of arriving trains turns certain platforms into mandatory no-breathing zones" (Dwyer 1991: 15). In 1982, with the first of a series of capital improvement programs, the MTA went about trying to remake the subways into a public monument that would serve the city and reaffirm its world-class status, much as the original builders of the IRT had hoped at its origin.

While the investment in renovation dramatically improved the performance of the trains, the MTA recognized that improved reliability was not enough to revive the system; it also needed to transform the subway's image. People avoided the subway for the same reasons that people avoided the city. According to David Gunn (1988: 7), former president of the Transit Authority, "The subway had become a symbol for uncontrolled filth and squalor in a city never renowned for its cleanliness." And despite the capital improvements, these perceptions continued. Charles Seaton (1993), deputy director of public affairs of the New York City Transit Authority (NYCTA), noted in an interview, "People that have ridden the subways in the past that have abandoned us for things like illegal vans, express buses, or private automobiles, they still have a perception that the system is the same way it was ten years ago." A writer for *Passenger Train Journal* similarly points out that despite dramatic improvements in the system, "The [NYC]TA's reputation with the riding public has not significantly improved. Too many people see the New York subway as a last-choice transportation decision" (Reid 1993: 27).

Introducing art into the tunnels was one attempt to reshape this image. Incorporating art into subway reconstruction originated in 1982, when New York City began requiring all new city-owned construction projects to dedicate 1 percent of their capital budgets to artwork. The same year, MTA incorporated a similar policy into the capital program to rebuild the infrastructure of the transit system. In 1985 MTA formed the Arts for Transit department to manage and expand the arts programs within the transportation systems under MTA jurisdiction (MTA Arts for Transit 1990a: 3).

The heart of Arts for Transit is its permanent art program. These are works selected for the newly rebuilt or renovated stations. By 2005, 152 projects were in place in the subways and 40 more were being installed (Dollar 2005). Just as the original subway art was designed to make people more comfortable with going underground, the new art was intended to make people comfortable and attract them back after ridership had been on a steady decline. The 1990 Arts for Transit catalogue explains that "Arts for Transit seeks to encourage the use of public transportation by creating visual and performing arts programs to enhance the hundreds of transit spaces in the MTA network" (1).

While Arts for Transit tried to enhance the underground space of the subways, the MTA dedicated considerably more resources to controlling the signs of "disorder" within this space, the most prominent of which was graffiti. According to former Transit Authority president Gunn (1988: 7), removing graffiti was important to restore a sense of order to the subways:

"Symbols and perceptions are important. One of our first publicly an-
nounced goals, in February 1984, was to clean the graffiti off our rolling
stock. Graffiti and filth gave passengers the impression that anarchy ruled
and no-one was in charge." A writer for *Modern Railroads* describes the
"forbidding environment of cars covered inside and out with graffiti" (Roberts 1988: 31). *Passenger Train Journal* reported that graffiti "lent an air of
danger" to the subways (Reid 1993: 26).

Gunn, who became Transit Authority president in 1984, is largely cred-
ited with eliminating graffiti. In addition to increasing the number of employees dedicated to cleaning the cars, he instituted a strictly enforced policy that prevented any subway car from being used if it contained the
slightest amount of graffiti. Cars were not allowed to leave the rail yard
without being completely cleaned of graffiti and were immediately taken
out of service if they had any graffiti because "[graffiti] writers felt greatest
pleasure seeing a fresh tag or piece moving through the city" (Dwyer 1991:
238). ("Masterpieces" or "pieces" are the more sophisticated graffiti paintings found on subway cars, while "tags" and "throw-ups" are used to cover
large areas quickly and easily.) This also meant that erasing graffiti took
precedence over on-time performance, but Gunn was unapologetic: "The
need for a concerted antigraffiti program is obvious. . . . Graffiti has a debil-
itating psychological effect on passengers. It says to them, 'the system is out
of control and no one cares'" (quoted in Austin 2001: 220).

As is indicated by the association of graffiti with a sense of "danger" and
a "forbidding environment," the appearance of graffiti was linked to a fear of
crime. The MTA's 1992 annual report contains a 1989 survey indicating fear
of crime as the top concern of subway riders. Cutting down on crime was
listed as the primary achievement in the 1992 report: "Since [1989], criminal activity *has dropped 28 percent,* with December 1992 the 27th consec-
utive month in which subway crime has decreased" (MTA 1993: 16–17).
The report credits the decline largely to new policing practices: "The Transit Police patrol strategy focused with greater intensity than ever before on
three related problems: robbery, farebeating, and disorder" (17). In this strategy, cracking down on small crimes like "farebeating" would reduce the
danger of more serious crimes: "Transit Police 'sweeps' nab farebeaters at
the gates of the system. Some have guns, lots of cash, even tokens in pocket.
Quick checks find dangerous criminals wanted for arrest. The message is
spreading: the cops are everywhere down there; if your business is crime,
don't do business on the subway" (18). By 1996, "the felony rate on the subways, dropping for 75 of the past 76 months, was 71 percent lower than in
1990" (MTA 1997: 21).

The Transit Authority also implemented design measures intended to increase security. New turnstiles for automated fare collection were designed to prevent farebeating. With the older turnstiles it was easy and not uncommon to press one's hands on both sides of a turnstile and vault over. The new turnstiles were designed like the starting gates at a horse race with a bar on the top to prevent vaulting. Security gates were also installed at various stations to limit access to particular entrances, exits, or underground passageways. These gates "effectively channel the flow of passengers in a controlled fashion, limit access of unauthorized persons to certain areas, and reduce the spaces necessary to be patrolled by police" (Jacobs 1992: 46). Cul-de-sac closures were also installed using concrete blocks or ceramic tiles to "permanently seal off areas which allow persons to hide" (ibid.).

Closed-circuit television and "talk-back communications"—a device allowing passengers to press an emergency assistance button—permit token booth clerks to monitor "remote and desolate areas within the stations." The ability to monitor remote locations from a distance was extended to passengers by placing security mirrors near the corners of passageways. These allow passengers to "see around corners to alert them of the presence of suspicious persons" (ibid.: 45), encouraging the monitoring of others as well as self-monitoring. MTA advertisements have further encouraged monitoring by emphasizing the efforts to cut down on various types of crime in the subways, for example, describing the consequences of jumping the turnstile.

One of the behaviors regularly condemned by ad campaigns is giving money to panhandlers. An ad from 1994 used comic-strip-style dialogue balloons to indicate an internal dialogue when a subway rider is confronted by a panhandler and reflects on whether to give the person money, ultimately deciding against it. At the top of the sign in bold is printed: "Panhandling on the subway is illegal. No matter what you think." Just beneath this in smaller print it says, "Give to the charity of your choice, but not on the subway."

These ads were part of a larger campaign instituted in January 1994 to cut down on panhandling and homelessness in the subways. The campaign got a boost with a 1990 ruling in the U.S. Court of Appeals for the Second Circuit that panhandling on the subways was not free speech, thereby overturning a 1990 federal district court decision. According to one analysis, the appeals court ruling was based less on the argument that begging is not a form of speech and more on the "common sense" idea that "the subway is already a somewhat scary and confining place" and that the presence of beggars made it more so (Horwitz 1993: 234).

The homeless are a strong symbol of disorder in the subways. A 1992 citywide survey found that 17 percent of respondents avoided the subway because of beggars and homeless people. "Public confidence is reduced by visible signs of public disorder such as the homeless, panhandlers, and fare evaders" (Harris 1992: 13). Homeless people have roamed the subways since the Great Depression, but their numbers increased significantly in the 1980s. In 1989, the Transit Authority instituted an outreach program: Transit Police, previously instructed to simply remove the homeless without regard for what happened to them, were directed to help find them shelter or medical assistance. However, the primary concern of police was still homeless removal. People who slept in subway cars were a particular target, and in 1996 a rule against occupying more than one seat began to be enforced "fanatically," at a rate of three tickets an hour (*New York Daily News* 1996).

The same designs instituted to cut down on crime also worked to discourage transients from living in the subways. Blocking entrances and passageways eliminates spaces to sleep undisturbed. Barriers to fare evasion make it difficult for those who have limited resources to enter and exit subway tunnels. Benches with seat divisions discourage lying down (see Figure 13). The goal of reducing sleeping space is made clearest in Grand Central and Penn Station, where special sections are marked by signs that say "For Passengers Only."

DISPLACING RESISTANCE WITH THE BUFF OF CORPORATE CAPITAL

The permanent art that graces our stations and public spaces adds a sense of comfort and security and reinforces the identity of individual stations. It brings a vitality to travel that makes the experience inviting as well as convenient and quick. (Virgil Conway,[10] quoted in MTA Arts for Transit 1996)

There was once a time when the Lexington was a beautiful line when children of the ghetto expressed with art, not with crime. But then as evolution past, the transits buffing did its blast. And now the trains look like rusted trash. Now we wonder if graffiti will ever last???????? (LEE,[11] quoted in Cooper and Chalfant 1984: 104)

A consequence of the MTA's strategy to erase signs of disorder from the subway is that signs of resistance to the sociospatial inequalities that led to the trains' deterioration are also erased. The most straightforward form of resistance is the vandalism directed at subway cars. In the 1960s, before plastic

Figure 13. Wooden benches with divisions discourage the homeless from sleeping on New York subway platforms. Photo by P. M. Fotsch.

seats were installed, wicker seats were slashed with pocketknives. In the 1970s destination signs were torn out of cars, making it difficult for riders to know which train to board. And until windows were made of fiberglass in the 1980s, they were routinely shattered by feet busting through them (Dwyer 1991: 129).

It is important to recognize that the problem of vandalism emerged not when the subway was healthy but rather when it was already collapsing.

Thus, vandalism cannot be separated from the corresponding barbarism of disinvestment and industrial decline in the city. Indeed, it can be read as a response to it: an attack precisely on the failure to maintain and invest in the infrastructure. This interpretation does not require that the vandals intended to criticize urban inequality. By bringing attention to the horrible state of the subways and making visible what was taking place beneath the surface—both in terms of the poor state of the subways and the social disparity between cities and suburbs—vandals highlight the legacy of urban neglect.

According to Stanley Cohen (1973), while the motivations for the destruction of property vary widely, vandalism is primarily directed at structures that are poorly maintained in areas of concentrated poverty. Equally interesting, Colin Ward (1973: 309) argues that vandalism is a response to the lack of control youth have over the built environment: "Above all we want to comprehend our environment. It is known that if this urge for possession has no other means of expression it would rather become destructive than look on passively." In New York the lack of power young people have over the condition of the subways is signaled not just by their inability to vote but also by the general political weakness of the urban poor.[12]

This is not to condone the vandalism that took place on the trains. Replacing windows and seats cost thousands of dollars that could have been spent on necessary repairs. The point is that vandalism exaggerated the problems of the subway; much like when buildings are burned in urban riots, the neglect of broader urban problems is magnified. Of course, these methods of protest are not necessarily effective in improving conditions, but as statements they do call for a response.[13]

A more explicit critique of urban neglect came from the graffiti found in the subways. Joe Austin (2001) shows that many graffiti writers were quite conscious of the connection between the condition of the subways and the more general impoverishment of U.S. cities. In the 1970s, graffiti masterpieces often referred to the urban landscape: "Social problems like child abuse, addiction, and poverty were themes that some writers could reference from experience as well as a sense of concern and commitment to justice in their city" (Austin 2001: 183).

Yet the power of graffiti went beyond commenting on the systemic poverty of central cities—it also asserted the potential for productivity and creativity from the city despite its conditions. Far from simply being "the rage for today's youth" (Reid 1993: 26), the significance of graffiti on trains has deep roots in the culture of urban communities. Ivor Miller (1991) finds that subway painters were part of an African American tradition that incorporated the train into art and daily life. Tracing the concept back to the West African spiritualization of iron, Miller argues that the train and subway became a form of inspiration that is spread concretely as subway (master)pieces travel throughout the city. At the same time, the use of discarded elements of urban infrastructure to produce something that resonates culturally also marks a tradition of creolization. Most simply, a creole is a mix of two or more cultures, but Miller (1994: 159) refers to a more expansive sense of the term: "Throughout the African Diaspora creole cultures have been created as a response to the imposition of the European masters' culture upon African slaves."

The materials with which slaves were permitted to work were often the cheapest or simply those discarded by others, as graffiti writer Phase 2 notes: "They gave us the guts of the pig, and we made it into some type of gourmet dinner. It's always been that way; we get the seconds all the time. Even with the second hand education we receive, we have created a new form of painting" (quoted in Miller 1994: 160). The subway exemplified something that had been discarded, and graffiti writers wished to transform this abandoned infrastructure into a work of beauty. DAZE, another writer, likewise questions the authorities' aesthetic sensibilities: "If the MTA really understood graffiti, they'd know that it's one of the best things the subways have going for them. If the city would back us up and treat us as artists instead of vandals, we could contribute a lot to the beauty of New York" (quoted in Castleman 1982: 177).

Perhaps subway graffiti's most profound role was its ability to bring youth of diverse backgrounds together. This was possible in part because trains brought the work of writers to neighborhoods throughout the city. As a creole culture, it incorporated many elements of American popular culture that youth of diverse social backgrounds understood. LEE recalls a time when the power of this mixing helped break down racial stereotypes and crossed gang barriers:

> The gangs kept neighborhoods apart, the city was a jigsaw puzzle of gangs keeping turf and territorial rights. So this movement brought people together, blacks, Puerto Ricans, whites, Orientals, Polish, from the richest to the poorest, we were equals. We took the same energy that was there to stand by your block with bats or guns and flying colors all night long, and used it to go painting, to create. (Quoted in Miller 1994: 158)

In fact, racial diversity was part of a profile police used to identify graffiti crews, as graffiti writer LADY PINK explains: "Writers came from all ethnic backgrounds, all classes, and the police knew to look for a group of kids who were racially diverse—those were the writers. If a gang was all black or white the police wouldn't bother them" (quoted in Miller 1994: 157). The attack on racial mixing in youth culture echoes the crackdown on L.A. dance clubs in the 1950s. Although graffiti writing may be a more "criminal" activity than listening to music, the zealous pursuit of writing crews still implies a degree of paranoia about the spread of "ghetto" culture.

Strangely enough, graffiti writers and the MTA's Arts for Transit division share major goals. Both seek to make the subways beautiful and the experience of riding them more pleasant. The directors of the Arts for Transit program emphasize their desire to renew the spirit of the original subway contract, which "stipulated that each station be embellished with decorative elements to uplift the spirits of riders" (MTA Arts for Transit 1990a: 2). LEE expresses similar ideas about graffiti: "If the subways were painted nice, it would make a lot of people happy. Like you walk out of your house and you look at nice pieces and it eases your mind" (quoted in Castleman 1982: 177). Moreover, graffiti writers and Arts for Transit draw on the diverse cultures of the city. The diversity of works selected by Arts for Transit ranges from the mosaics of Laura Bradley and Susan Tunick, which recall the medium of the original subway art, to a spectacular glass triptych designed by Romare Bearden and fabricated by Belgian glass masters Benoit Gilsoul and Helmut Schardt. The policy for permanent arts acquisition includes a desire to "assure that artworks are commissioned and managed in accordance with sound procurement practices, and to promote the equitable distribution of commissions among artists of both genders as well as among artists of diverse cultural heritage" (MTA Arts for Transit 1990b).

Despite those similarities, the policy of Arts for Transit and the methods of graffiti writers conflict directly. First, Arts for Transit supports the official position of the MTA, labeling graffiti vandalism rather than art. More fundamentally, graffiti is a challenge to precisely the institutions that underpin Arts for Transit. The permanent art is selected by a panel that includes "an MTA representative, who will chair the panel, and, whenever possible, a member of the Arts for Transit Advisory Committee; a representative of the operating agency and arts professionals, including artists, art critics and/or arts administrators" (ibid.: 2). This process tends to exclude those who have less access to formal art training and lack the endorsement of art schools, galleries, or museums—thus by definition graffiti writers, whose work is in many ways a response to their exclusion from traditional art institutions. Susan Stewart (1991: 227) notes, "Part of the threat of graffiti is [the writers'] claim that anyone can be an artist." Moreover, graffiti is evaluated along different criteria than the more formal art sought by Arts for Transit. For graffiti, the look of the work is often less important than the writer's skill and effort in "getting up," having one's name painted on cars as frequently as possible.[14]

The value writers place on labor over appearance points to one way that they affront not only art institutions but also institutions of capitalism. Within capitalism, what Marx called the "mysterious character of the commodity form" works to hide the labor behind a product, enabling a relation between objects to act like a relation between humans (Marx 1867/1977: 164–165). Graffiti contests the "fetishism of the commodity" that underlies market relations by emphasizing and reflecting on the work behind the surface. For example, writers frequently comment on the conditions under which they worked within their pieces, by writing "My hands were cold" or "Too Late Too Tired" or that they were "chased" by cops (Cooper and Chalfant 1984: 38). Furthermore, by bringing the signature to the forefront of their work they emphasize the presence of individual bodies behind the surface of the piece. Writers also challenge capitalism by defying the notion that expression in public space is available only to those who have money to pay for it. While they appropriate many of the methods of advertising in their attempt to gain as much exposure as possible for their names, in doing this they are also competing with advertisers' commercial use of the space.[15]

The importance of controlling challenges to the commercial dominance of public space is linked to the urban economy's increasing reliance on images. Sharon Zukin (1995: 8) argues that cities with declining industrial bases are becoming more dependent on the sale of their popular representations: "In the 1970s and 1980s, the symbolic economy rose to prominence against a background of industrial decline and financial speculation." Tourism and consumer-related businesses have become a central part of the urban economy. Consequently, notes Meethan (1996: 323), "the urban environment itself becomes a commodity to be bought and sold not only to corporate interests but also to individual consumers." Local governments now collaborate with private companies to make urban space more attractive to middle-class consumers (Hannigan 1998). The strategies the MTA uses to attract more riders to the subways follow those designed to attract consumers to the city.

One strategy, for example, has been to promote the city's cultural attractions. Theaters and art museums are viewed as an important component of the tourist economy, which urban developers hope will "counter the visual homogeneity of the suburbs by playing the card of aesthetic diversity" (Zukin 1995: 12). The introduction of art into the underground by Arts for

Transit follows the same logic. Furthermore, as in the subways, cities now use art to help transform the image of particular locations. Just as Arts for Transit sought to humanize the underground, a subsidiary of the New York State Urban Development Corporation (UDC) endeavored to transform the image of Times Square with art. In 1993, "The UDC subsidiary responsible for redevelopment joined Creative Team, a nonprofit arts organization, and the New 42nd Street Inc., another nonprofit organization established to renovate Times Square's theaters, to commission more than 20 artists and designers to install works on 'storefronts, facades, vitrines, marquees, billboards, and even rolldown grates'" (ibid.: 138–139). These temporary displays, along with significant subsidies, were used to persuade large companies, including MTV and Disney, to locate on Times Square (ibid.: 19).

The increased presence of major corporations in public spaces is promoted as a solution to the budget constraints cities have faced since the fiscal crises of the 1970s. With zoning variances and tax subsidies, private capital could be encouraged to build and maintain public sites that the government no longer provided.[16] Arts for Transit has used this strategy to construct some of its projects: "New York City zoning regulations have required a number of private developers to improve subway stations adjacent to their properties. Recently, with the encouragement of the New York City Planning Commission, improvements have included permanent art installations" (MTA Arts for Transit 1990a: 6). For example, in exchange for sponsoring an untitled etching at the Fiftieth Street station by Matt Mullican, the Zeckendorf Company was allowed to erect a building that exceeded zoning regulation height limits. This led one art critic to comment, "The Mullican mural and the gleaming new station were great, but I'm not sure that the price above ground—the massive building gained ten percent more air space—was worth it" (Alexander 1989).

In this case the impact was increased density; reliance on corporate sponsorship of public spaces can also mean reduced access for artists who are locally sponsored and rooted in the community. For example, Arts for Transit at one time sponsored a Creative Stations program that enabled communities to install temporary projects for their local subway stations. This program was phased out because the cost of some of the projects was more than half what it would have cost to install permanent works. Another program, Exhibition Centers, allowed smaller cultural institutions and arts groups to display art on large panels in five stations, but it was replaced by Light Boxes for the display of photographs chosen under a competitive process similar to the permanent art. The Light Boxes, unlike the other programs, received outside corporate sponsorship.

Another consequence of the reliance on corporate support for public space is the elimination of voices on the fringe of the market economy. In order to bring large corporations to Times Square, the many small convenience stores and adult theaters that had occupied the area were evicted, decreasing the diversity of businesses in the district (Delany 1999). A similar logic can be seen in the effort to increase advertising revenues on the subways by encouraging the purchase of ad space on entire cars. Previously, most ads in subway cars were from small businesses such as medical clinics or dating services. The nature of the ads, discussing health problems such as acne or hemorrhoids, had discouraged large corporate advertisers from advertising in the same space.

In 1995 the MTA restricted to 20 percent the space in subway cars available to small advertisers, but this policy was reversed in 1997 because large advertisers did not consistently fill the space, and half the revenue still came from small advertisers (Canedy 1997; Warner 1994). As ridership grew dramatically in the late 1990s, however, the cost of advertising also increased. Consequently, even without the previous restrictions, large companies soon began to dominate the advertising space—often covering entire cars with a single ad campaign (Goldstein 1998). In January 2005 the MTA approved a proposal to allow sponsorship of the subways. While the MTA's representative from the Riders Council expressed concern about "excessive commercialization," others saw it as a necessary strategy to help meet the financial demands of the system (Chan 2005a).

Linked to the corporate dominance of public expression is the greater surveillance and control of behavior within these public spaces to assure that nothing competes with the consumer-friendly image. This means preventing not only graffiti but also panhandling, peddling, or other signs of poverty. To achieve this, design techniques like the ones used in the subway system have become standard in parks and other public spaces. Not only does this limit the expression of graffiti writers and the homeless, it also discourages otherwise acceptable public expressions not officially sanctioned by the supervisory organization.

The incorporation of musicians into the Arts for Transit program under the banner Music Under New York (MUNY) has made it more difficult for those not in the program to perform in the subways. As with the Arts for Transit permanent art program, preference is given to musicians with a "professional" orientation. Perhaps even more telling, the panel that selects the musicians for the program—which administrators increasingly have dominated over time—is instructed to choose music that will not "aggravate" riders (Tanenbaum 1995: 139). This tends to favor mainstream elements of the different types of music featured, whether jazz, classical, or rock. The music under the banners often lacks some of the edge that is common to street or subway music. In fact, many performers often find paying gigs at other venues. This is ironic since street musicians are frequently on the street because they could not find work professionally for various reasons including inconsistent talent or alienation from the local community of musicians and club owners. While it is legal for anyone to play music in the subways, MUNY musicians are given prime locations, and police regularly harass those who are not part of the program. Members of MUNY must conform to rules that include "prohibiting the use of visual devices other than the MTA banner" (144). In summing up the achievements of MUNY, Susie Tanenbaum writes, "The transit executives and art 'professionals' who invented MUNY did not invent subway music. Rather, they adapted freelancing to promote the MTA, and unfortunately in the process they introduced exclusion into an activity that is ideologically based on inclusion" (146).

By listing these transformations of subway space, the idea is not simply to celebrate expressions of resistance and condemn expressions of corporate power. Furthermore, it should be emphasized that while books by Castleman (1982), Cooper and Chalfant (1984), Chalfant and Prigoff (1987), and others have helped to popularize the major pieces painted on trains in the 1970s and 1980s, defending the work of graffiti writers remains very controversial (Austin 2001: 268–271). However, whether graffiti is seen as a critique of young people's marginalization or as mere criminal vandalism, its significance for public transportation is the same. Both are signs of urban problems that many Americans wish to avoid, and to the extent these signs are associated with public transit, many will choose to stay on familiar suburban streets. By replacing voices of discontent with the more familiar and predictable voices of corporate advertisers, the MTA objective is to make the subways and by extension New York City more attractive to middle-class tourists and business travelers.[17]

THE LIMITS OF A "RENEWED IMAGE"

[In 1995] we proposed a five year financial plan that would put the MTA on a course toward greater self-sufficiency. Under the plan, expenses would be reduced by $3 billion, revenues would be increased by $1.5 billion, and . . . quality service for our customers would be maintained. Many thought the plan too ambitious, even unrealistic. In 1996 we showed we could make it work. (Virgil Conway, MTA chairman, quoted in MTA 1997)

And then every day when I ride this train something is happening to slow the trip. . . . Someone's sick. They're doing repairs. Whatever it is, it isn't worth the $1.50. (Elsa Slovak,[18] quoted in *New York Daily News* 1996)

In many ways the attempt to make New York more appealing to middle-class Americans has been a striking success. By 1999 New York City was second only to Orlando as the most popular tourist destination in the United States (Gottdiener 2001: 131). The image of New York's successful revitalization helped assure Rudolph Giuliani's reelection as mayor in 1997. Moreover, many commentators viewed New York's success as part of a larger trend of abandoned cities becoming popular again (Beauregard 2003: 212–213). However, the image of success hid significant problems: beneath the surface of wealth reflected in upscale restaurants and renovated warehouses was continuing poverty and disenfranchisement, leading some to label New York a "dual city" (Mollenkopf and Castells 1991). The subway's transformation is emblematic of New York's improved image, but it also reveals the flaws in this image. Moreover, since the subway's reconstruction employed the same methods lauded for achieving New York's renaissance, the subway's failings challenge the celebration of these methods.

The central tension underlying the story of New York's renewal can be traced to the shift from a manufacturing to a service-based economy in the 1980s. While this shift took place in many American cities, it was especially pronounced in New York (Castells 1989: 207). New York's role as the center of finance and banking meant it benefited from the expansion of global trade. This brought large numbers of highly paid business and legal professionals into the city, but these professionals also relied on a large number of low-wage workers to provide services like cleaning and catering (Sassen 1991: 279). Because demand for these services is highly variable, work is often part-time and temporary, increasing job insecurity for this predominantly immigrant workforce. While gentrification boosted the growth of upscale shops and entertainment venues—appealing to tourists—low-income residents were pushed into a few crowded Manhattan neighborhoods, to the outer boroughs, or onto the streets. Indeed, the number of homeless families increased fivefold during the 1980s and continued to increase in the 1990s (Nunez 2001). Meanwhile, service reductions implemented in the 1970s made it more difficult in general for low-income groups to live in the city.

Despite the polarizing impact of the economic changes that emerged in the 1980s, this impact was glossed over by the popular accolades surrounding New York's revival. Rudolph Giuliani expressed this congratulatory

attitude most forcefully, and his reelection indicated that many New Yorkers shared both his belief that the city had improved and his understanding
of why it had improved. According to Giuliani, the city's dramatic turn-
around came through tax cuts, which spurred economic growth, and a tough
attitude toward crime, which improved the feeling of safety on the streets
(*New York Times* 1998). Cutting taxes required further reducing city services—except of course those related to policing. However, by Giuliani's
logic, although many of the services cut were directed at the poor, this
actually helped the city by encouraging low-income residents to move elsewhere.[19]

Central to Giuliani's view of New York's transformation is a critique of
big government as inept. This critique has a long history—it can be found
within the progressive movement discussed in Chapter 1, and it gained
prominence in New York during the fiscal crisis of the 1970s. However, this
antigovernment sentiment achieved popularity at a national level during the
presidency of Ronald Reagan. Reagan and his followers blamed misguided
government intervention for the problems of urban America. Like Nixon,
they argued that welfare discouraged moral responsibility. Likewise, they argued that high taxes and overregulation harmed the economy by discouraging private investment. As Thomas Edsall and Mary Edsall (1991) show,
these critiques of liberal policy had an implicit racial component, since
people of color were often viewed as benefiting most from government aid.[20]

A parallel attitude in New York can be traced back to Ed Koch, who was
mayor during the 1980s. Koch became popular for his criticisms of people on
welfare as well as his tough attitude toward crime (Mollenkopf 1992). However, it was Giuliani who was able to take credit for the most prominent examples of New York's renewed image, such as the reduction in crime and the
redevelopment of Times Square (Barry 1998). Since mayors have little say in
the Transit Authority's management, Giuliani could not take credit for the
improvement in the subways. However, the strategies employed for this improvement came out of the same critique of past government failures found
in Giuliani's celebration of New York's transformation.

For example, the notion that leniency toward criminals promotes immorality helped legitimate new policies to control disorder in the subway.
In this view, vandals, thieves, and aggressive panhandlers had taken over
cities because of deluded attempts to defend the civil rights of these "pests."
George Kelling (1991: 21) complains, "The indigents hanging out in the
subways are the single biggest obstacle to restoring public order and public
confidence underground. . . . Yet in the name of civil rights and compassion,
advocacy groups . . . defend these people's rights to continue their disruptive

behavior." In this view, the rejection of urban liberalism explains the success in making the subway—and by extension New York—attractive again. George Will expresses this perspective in a 1994 column applauding the elimination of subway graffiti and mocking those who celebrated it: "Just a few years ago, intellectuals, who are more plentiful here than is healthy (and who rarely ride subways), were praising as folk art the graffiti that gang members and other pre-intellectual New Yorkers were spraying on subway cars. . . . Today, says [Police Commissioner William] Bratton, the city's subway cars are virtually free of graffiti" (Will 1994).

The strategies used to reduce crime in the subway were appropriated by Giuliani to reduce crime in New York as a whole. In fact, William Bratton, appointed by Giuliani as police commissioner, was the former head of the Transit Police and oversaw many of the strategies to eliminate "disorder" discussed above. Despite the popular belief in the effectiveness of these strategies, a close examination of the evidence by Bernard Harcourt (1998: 27) brings into question the "broken window" theory of policing. Harcourt argues that this theory of cracking down on small crimes to reduce violent crime actually supports criminal behavior on the part of police by encouraging them to be more aggressive. Evidence for this increased aggressiveness was sadly found in the 1997 attack on Abner Louima and the 1999 killing of Amadou Diallo.

Giuliani's treatment of the homeless is equally notorious. While cutting the funds of nonprofit agencies that provided housing assistance, he instructed police to begin arresting street people for charges ranging from "squeegee cleaning" to "public drunkenness" (Conason 1995). At the same time, city officials ordered systematic destruction of homeless encampments throughout Manhattan. Campers were pushed to the outer boroughs, where they settled under freeway ramps or empty fields adjoining Kennedy and LaGuardia airports (Smith 1998). Again, the primary goal was to eliminate the signs of disorder represented by people living on the street. Allen Feldman (2001) describes the tragic irony of tearing down homeless encampments, which created the illusion of safety but actually harmed public health by destroying the community that health workers relied upon to provide assistance.

It must be emphasized that Giuliani could not have been successful if his message appealed only to conservative Republicans. New York is an overwhelmingly Democratic city, but the deteriorating conditions of public facilities during the 1980s challenged the trust middle-class liberals had in the city's ability to help the poor. The homeless, who are the most visible representation of poverty, were blamed for contributing to urban deterioration just through their presence: they camped in parks and acted aggressively toward pedestrians, making daily life stressful for many residents.[21] The declining tolerance for the homeless is one element of what Neil Smith (1996: 212) labels the "revanchist city":

> The revanchist city represents a reaction to an urbanism defined by recurrent waves of unremitting danger and brutality fueled by venal and uncontrolled passion. It is a place, in fact, where the reproduction of social relations has gone stupefyingly wrong, but where the response is a virulent reassertion of many of the same oppressions and prescriptions that created the problem in the first place.

Rather than challenging an urban economy that leaves thousands on the streets, it was easier to view the problem as hopeless and simply have transients removed from Manhattan (Smith 1998).

The crackdowns on the destitute once again must be recognized as harming people of color disproportionately. According to a 2004 study, 49 percent of the homeless in U.S. cities are African American. Moreover, despite the stereotype of the homeless as middle-aged men, almost 40 percent are in families with children (Lowe 2004). Research on New York and Philadelphia shows that "by far the most likely person to become homeless in both cities is a poor black child younger than 5" (Bernstein 2001).

Another goal the MTA and the Giuliani administration shared was making government more efficient by cutting back on expenditures. In the 1980s some blamed the subway's decline not just on lack of funds but also on careless management of public resources. In particular, critics of the MTA attributed low worker productivity to poor supervision. In 1984, "the MTA's ability—or inability—to manage its workforce . . . was blasted by Sidney Schwartz, the agency's inspector-general . . . Soaring costs and bad service are the result of a 'management problem,' Schwartz told a New York State Senate Transportation Committee hearing" (Liff 1984: 32). The Transport Workers Union in turn charged the MTA bureaucracy was bloated (ibid.).

"Cost containment" became an ongoing concern with the MTA, and the number of employees was reduced by thousands in the 1990s, saving millions of dollars (MTA 1997). Yet, despite its improved efficiency, the MTA soon faced funding cuts from all levels of government. Both Mayor Giuliani and Governor George Pataki, who ran on promises to eliminate waste, decreased subsidies to the Transit Authority, arguing that it had not done enough to reduce expenses (Pérez-Peña 1995a, 1995b). As a consequence, in 1995 not only was the MTA forced to raise the subway fare from $1.25 to

$1.50, it also was forced to implement major reductions in service for the first time since the 1970s (Martin 1995).

In the MTA's 1996 annual report, chairman Virgil Conway asserted that despite severe cutbacks, MTA was providing "quality service" to customers. But interviews with customers by the *New York Daily News* (1996) indicated a very different story: "Nearly six of every 10 riders believe on-time service is worse and complained that trains are routinely delayed. More than five of every 10 said their subway cars are more crowded—and many say dirtier." The MTA's own survey revealed similar results: "The overall performance of subway service indicates a major decline among NYC travelers. In addition, the overall rating of subway station environment declined for the first time since measurement began in 1991" (Lieberman Research East 1996: 4).

By 1996, however, the subway was clearly improving in some areas. Ridership was steadily increasing, trains broke down less often, and crime was declining (MTA 1997). However, the biggest boost to the subway's revival came two years later. In 1998 the MTA introduced unlimited-ride Metrocards, meaning New Yorkers could ride all they wanted for a fixed price. Soon there were fewer riders commuting to and from work than there were traveling for nonbusiness purposes. By 2001 annual ridership had increased nearly 50 percent from its low point in 1991 (MTA 2002). Transportation consultant Bruce Schaller said, "The transit system has essentially been reincorporated back into people's life outside work" (quoted in Kennedy 2002a).

While the dramatic growth in ridership strongly indicates that the strategies used by the MTA to improve its image have been successful, many flaws in this image are not easily erased. In particular, media depictions of the subway do not always conform to the MTA's vision of a clean and safe system. The MTA attempts to control the portrayal of the subway in the media by restricting what can be filmed within the system, but film producers can always recreate the subway in another location. So, for example, when the producers of *Money Train* (1995) were prevented from filming a token booth fire in the system because it was too similar to an actual incident several years earlier, they avoided this and other restrictions by elaborately reconstructing a subway tunnel in an abandoned railroad yard in East Los Angeles (Lippman 1995). The MTA also will not allow graffiti to be filmed in the subway, given the significance of the successful battle to eliminate it, but an episode of the TV comedy series *Seinfeld* that takes place within the subways depicts graffiti covering the cars' interiors; because the show was shot in a studio, the MTA had no control over production.

In spring 2004 the MTA proposed a ban on photography that was rejected a year later (Robin 2005). Proponents of the ban claimed it was necessary to prevent terrorists from scouting potential locations for bombing, but it also would have prevented amateur photographers from capturing images of deteriorating conditions or graffiti. The growing number of digital camera owners facilitates the spread of images that challenge the MTA's portrayal of a revitalized subway. Images can be quickly circulated via cell phones and the Internet. So while the MTA maintains an official Web site, a search for "New York subways" on Google brings up many unofficial sites, some with stories critical of the MTA. And a search for "New York subway graffiti" calls up thousands of pages with many photos of current and past examples of graffiti art.

Portrayals of the subway in the news tend to focus on its continued problems and dangers.[22] A firebomb exploded in December 1994, seriously burning more than fifty people and suddenly making hazards like those depicted in films such as *Die Hard* real. This incident made salient the peril of being trapped underground where it is difficult to flee. Of course the tragedy of September 11, 2001, far surpassed earlier events in its traumatic impact on New Yorkers, including those riding the subway. The increased fear in going underground revealed itself in the greater number of people choosing to take the ferry across the Hudson River (Kelly 2002). Yet, by the time of the London underground bombings in July 2005, many riders seemed resigned to living with terrorism (Worth 2005).

Another type of fear emerged in 1999 when several people were shoved in front of subway trains: one was killed, and another lost both legs (Jacobs 1999). Nine pushing attempts were reported in the first half of 2000 (Lueck 2000). In 2003 a rash of subway stabbings compounded the fears of those already worried about terrorism (*Los Angeles Times* 2003). While the crime rate on subways continued to decline, random acts of violence received widespread media attention.

In its annual report for 2001, the MTA noted that felonies were at their lowest point since 1969, in part due to the crackdown on "quality of life" crimes (MTA 2002: 22); but, as noted earlier, some doubts remain about the effectiveness of these crackdowns. For individuals harassed by police, the tactics might make the space of the subway less safe. Even if the policing of subways is equitable, some of the design elements built to enhance safety can inspire riders to feel more threatened. For example, the security gates used to restrict the movements of criminals and the homeless also limit the number of escape routes in an emergency. With heightened fears of a terrorist attack, the need to know the quickest exit is especially vital, but many

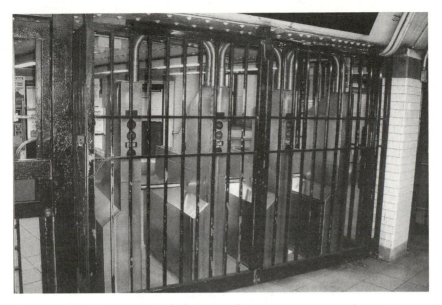

Figure 14. Gated exits are potentially dangerous when an emergency escape is necessary. Photo by P. M. Fotsch.

stations have only one exit, or additional exits are revolving gates that one must walk through slowly (see Figure 14).[23]

Surveillance through video cameras might also do more harm than good. Hille Koskela (2000) contends that these cameras make public spaces less pleasant by requiring a type of self-monitoring that Foucault linked to the panopticon. Women in particular can be made uncomfortable by becoming objects of someone's gaze. Precisely because the person looking through the camera is unknown and unseen, the feeling of vulnerability can intensify. "To be controlled by a surveillance camera—to be 'under control'—does not increase one's feeling of being 'in control'" (Koskela 2000: 259). While there is little evidence that surveillance cameras reduce violent crimes, studies do show that they reduce property crimes, such as vandalism and graffiti (ibid.: 246). Thus, the cameras may reduce symbols of resistance, but they cannot eliminate symbols of urban disorder. In fact, their mere presence reminds the rider of the potential for disorder.

Probably the greatest failure to reduce signs of disorder can be found in the continued presence of the homeless. Transients committed many of the violent acts that have brought the subways so much bad publicity over the years. The economic recession exacerbated by the 2001 World Trade Center attacks led to record numbers of homeless in New York. Some winter nights hundreds were found sleeping in the tunnels and trains of the subway (Donohue 2002b).

But the homeless make their presence known even when they are not seen. Their personal artifacts, clothing, blankets, and cardboard boxes are frequently found on the tracks, sometimes causing fires.

The continued presence of the homeless makes clear the barriers to controlling the activities and hence the expressions within the space of the subways. These barriers are found in all built environments. As noted, de Certeau outlines how despite the efforts of designers and planners, "the city is left prey to contradictory movements that counterbalance and combine themselves outside the reach of panoptic power" (1984: 95). What de Certeau does not address is the possibility that some built environments may be more successful than others in their ability to control unwanted activities. In fact, shopping malls are criticized precisely for using surveillance and extreme regulations to limit free expression and discourage activities not related to shopping (Schiller 1989: 99–100). Of course, as Rob Shields (1992) shows, even shopping malls allow for unexpected activities. However, they are still more restrictive than most New York neighborhoods. A central goal of Times Square's redevelopment has been to make it a consumer-friendly place by increasing its regulation; and although disruptive activities still occur—street performers and preachers of various kinds—that are not found in most shopping malls, in many ways this goal has been achieved.[24]

To shield visitors from less attractive neighborhoods, many cities construct what Dennis Judd (1999) calls a "tourist bubble"; however, while the MTA might like to create a more consumer-friendly space similar to that of the new Times Square, the subways are too porous to be controlled. Unlike a single business district, which can build stores and hotels with highly monitored and controlled access, the subways have multiple entrances and no center; any attempt at creating a consistent or uniform space is easily defeated. Priority was given to rebuilding the stations in Midtown and Lower Manhattan since these areas are used most by tourists and businesspeople. However, even these better-maintained and newer stations contain a layer of grime unlike that found, for example, in most airports.

Furthermore, by 2003 more than half the subway stations still had to be renovated (Kennedy 2003). In some cases, riders must negotiate around construction sites and through deteriorating tunnels filled with garbage and construction debris. Constant construction also causes frequent changes in service that confuse riders, and the signs meant to clarify service often only add to the confusion.[25] At times construction detracts from the permanent art, such as in the Times Square station, where repairs continued three years after the installation of a large mural by Roy Lichtenstein (see Figure 15).

Figure 15. Construction in the Times Square subway station mars the appearance of a Lichtenstein mural. Photo by P. M Fotsch.

Frustrations with the continued scars on the system increase each time the MTA raises fares, as it did in 2003 and 2005. In 2004 the cost of previous construction projects was catching up with the MTA; annual debt service on bonds reached $856 million (Chan 2004). Meanwhile, the continuing improvement in service seemed to reach a limit: as fires and delays increased and the cleanliness of subway cars and platforms declined, plans for a Second Avenue line appeared to be a fantasy (Donohue 2005; Schwartz 2005).

One especially repulsive element of the underground is the smell—the smell of rotten food and dead rats, but most of all the smell of urine. The smell is a powerful reminder of the subway's inability to hide urban problems. While the system has more than two hundred bathrooms, most of them were closed in 1982 because some had become a haven for sexual and drug transactions. The ones that remain open are often broken and almost unbearably foul (Kennedy 2002b; see Figure 16). At the same time, the lack of public restrooms in the city makes the tunnels a relatively private and convenient place to urinate and, where there is running water, to bathe. Since it is the homeless who most lack access to bathrooms, the smell of urine is yet another sign of their continued presence.

Figure 16. Most New York subway restrooms have been closed and locked since the early 1980s. Photo by P. M. Fotsch.

The size and openness of the subways also limits the MTA's efforts to control the voices that enter them. Despite official restrictions, people asking for money or peddling small items are ubiquitous. In addition, while the fight against graffiti on subway cars has been very successful, graffiti can still be found in other forms and many other places. The MTA has not found an effective way to eliminate "scratch graffiti," in which "taggers" use pocketknives, keys, or an acidic creme to etch their names into car windows (Donohue 2002a; see Figure 17). Tags can frequently be found on advertisements as well, since ads must remain up for a given length of time (see Figure 18). Most of all, whenever a train goes above ground, large graffiti designs can be seen everywhere on buildings and structures that border the tracks. Interestingly, one way writers have attempted to recreate the mobility of their paintings is to write on the sides of delivery trucks.

Even in the expressions that the MTA sanctions within the subway, the signs of urban disorder cannot be eliminated. On the trains, ads of various types review urban misfortunes. Public service ads discuss how to prevent child abuse and AIDS. MTA-sponsored ads that are meant to control certain behaviors, such as giving to panhandlers, remind riders that homelessness is a problem. Ads for small businesses, which used to predominate in the trains, are often directed at people with personal ills, and whether discussing

Figure 17. Scratch graffiti is frequently found on subway car windows. Photo by P. M. Fotsch.

lawsuits, addictions, or a directionless job, they serve to continually retrace urban life's challenges. Large advertisers play on the same urban sensitivities. Advertisements for nicotine patches admonish riders for their addictions; an ad campaign for a local health club encourages people to compare their bodies to others on the same train; and, perhaps most troubling of all, ads for Keri antibacterial hand lotion caution people concerning the germs one can contract simply by holding onto the poles in the cars.

One of the ads found in the summer of 1997 for Keri hand lotion deserves closer analysis because it plays on fears of urban degeneration on a more subtle level. The copy reads, "The last guy holding that pole was named Sal Monella." It is meant to humorously warn passengers of the possibility that bacteria such as salmonella can be spread among those who touch the same pole on the train. But, "Sal Monella," is also an unusual name; for many Anglo Americans it probably sounds "foreign," perhaps from Latin America or the Middle East. At a minimum, by making a pun with a fictional name, the ad reminds readers of their unfamiliarity with very diverse populations of the city.

The fear some have of these populations was expressed in a 1999 interview with Atlanta Braves pitcher John Rocker. Quoted in *Sports Illustrated*, Rocker describes his dread of riding the 7 line to Queens sitting "next to

Figure 18. Graffiti on advertisements is hard to prevent. Photo by P. M. Fotsch.

some queer with AIDS, right next to some dude who just got out of jail for the fourth time right next to some 20-year-old mom with four kids." But the thing he likes least about New York is the "foreigners": "You can walk an entire block in Times Square and not hear anybody speaking English. Asians and Koreans and Vietnamese and Indians and Russians and Spanish people and everything up there. How the hell did they get in this country?" (quoted in Pearlman 1999). Baseball officials condemned Rocker's remarks, and the interview increased Mets fans' animosity toward the pitcher, but the most interesting response came from his apologists. Several newspaper commentaries, while critical of Rocker's tone, claimed that his descriptions were basically accurate. A former resident of New York wrote in the *Tampa Tribune* that riding the subways can be scary: "however, straphangers become accustomed to rubbing shoulders with people whose appearance, in one way or another, does not invite intimacy" (Roberts 2000). Even some writers who condemned his remarks contended that his attitude was quite common outside New York: "Most Americans find New York City to be too big, too cacophonous and too gritty for their taste" (Terzian 2000).

Rocker's discomfort with the immigrant population typifies an attitude prevalent in the contemporary United States. By 2005, twenty-seven states had laws requiring that government affairs be conducted in English, and some businesses have attempted to follow suit out of concern that it may make customers uncomfortable when they cannot understand what workers are saying (Teicher 2004). One writer to the *Columbus Dispatch* expressed her discontent with the number of non-English speakers at local businesses: "Increasingly, we are feeling like strangers in our own neighborhood establishments" (Taylor 2002).

Although hostility toward immigrants is found throughout the United States, where it is estimated that one out of five speak English as a second language (Teicher 2005), it is primarily directed at cities where immigrants are concentrated. Approximately 23 percent of New York's population is foreign-born; in the United States, only Los Angeles has a higher percentage (Sabagh and Bozorgmehr 2003: 100). New York is also one of the most welcoming cities to immigrants. In 1989 an executive order declared that immigrants are to be given equal treatment regardless of legal status, and this order was reaffirmed by subsequent administrations (ibid. 2003: 116–117). Thus, while other states pass English-only legislation or attempt to restrict public benefits to newcomers, New York celebrates its status as an immigrant capital.

At the same time, it is the city's liberal attitude toward immigrants that brings scorn from elsewhere in the country. In 1999 the Washington, D.C.–based organization ProjectUSA posted billboards in New York with a message that blamed overcrowding in New York on immigrants. The reaction from local politicians was highly critical (Shulman 1999). In contrast, Iowans largely welcomed ProjectUSA when the group led a campaign condemning their governor's proposal to encourage immigration to the state (von Sternberg 2001). Clearly, places like Mason City do not want to begin looking like New York.

No better representation of New York's tolerance toward immigrants can be found than in the subway car, where one is likely to hear a dozen different languages corresponding to the neighborhoods through which the trains pass. Significantly, it was the increase in immigrant riders that gave the system a boost in the 1990s. Despite the 1995 fare increase, ridership in 1996 was the highest it had been since 1972. A study by the MTA revealed that it was mostly lines connected to neighborhoods with large immigrant populations, such as the 7 to Queens, that accounted for the increase in riders (Pierre-Pierre 1997).

The vitality that immigrant communities bring to the subways points to a vision of the city very different from that shaping Times Square; this vision embraces rather than displaces the city's diversity, including neighborhood shops, restaurants, and street festivals. This image can also be used to attract tourists. For example, *Passport's Guide to Ethnic New York* (Leeds

1996) focuses exclusively on the attractions of "ethnic" neighborhoods and includes brief histories to the neighborhood populations. By contrast, the official visitors' guide to New York is dominated by advertisements for major Broadway theaters, novelty restaurants, and golf equipment shops. Ethnic culture is not completely ignored: listings are given for the Museo del Barrio in East Harlem and events such as the Turkish American parade down Madison Avenue. Likewise, the MTA sponsors cultural events such as the Harlem Week Festival and promotes sites of diverse cultural expressions such as the Asian Society in Manhattan; but to the extent that publicity relies on large corporate capital, whether as advertisers or sponsors of art installations, the diversity of the city will receive less exposure.

REJECTING THE SUBWAYS: REJECTING NEW YORK CITY

This assessment of the subway's revival does not diminish its significant accomplishments. Certainly, the reliability and convenience of the trains has improved tremendously since the 1980s. However, signs of poverty and homelessness will continue their prevalence until they are addressed within the city as a whole. In offering his post-9/11 vision for how New York might be revitalized, historian Mike Wallace (2002) proposes a return to the ideals of the New Deal: massive funding for housing, health services, and construction projects would provide good-quality jobs. This type of return to urban liberalism seems politically unfeasible, but it is a more realistic solution to the problems that will continue to plague the subways than the current stopgap measures. The limits to these measures parallel the limits New York and other cities face as they try to improve their images for tourists and business travelers, even as they continue to be marked by profound inequalities.

In addition to reflecting the inequality within U.S. cities, the subways also reflect the growing diversity of cities. While large metropolises like New York and Chicago have consistently attracted large numbers of immigrants, it is increasingly common to encounter global populations in cities throughout the United States. David Morley (2000) finds that people's sense of home has been made problematic as formerly distant cultures become an intimate part of daily life. In this sense, experiencing the subway forces tourists from middle-class suburbs across the country to confront the often less obvious reality of immigrants in their own cities.

As a form of transportation, the subway requires contact with diverse populations in a way the automobile cannot. This is not just because riders must share the same space, but also because the subway encourages the preservation of pedestrian neighborhoods. Today, most people live in neighborhoods built after World War II that are unfriendly to pedestrians and accommodating to the automobile. Subways require no parking lots or widened streets. Furthermore, unlike a bus or trolley system, which also would reduce the need for parking lots, underground rails do not use the space of the street and so do not interfere with the flow of pedestrian traffic. Subways permit large crowds to come together quickly and conveniently. With a car, arriving to a pedestrian-friendly location is made difficult because of the need to search for parking and then walk to the desired destination; with a bus, although one may be dropped off closer to one's destination, the slowness is often inconvenient.

This superiority of subways is most evident when some event, a festival or demonstration, is taking place in a central location requiring street closures; the subway, because it does not use the street, can take one directly to the center of the event. Subways permit an intensification of street life because they permit a greater number of people with diverse backgrounds to come together than in the preindustrial city, which primarily enabled people within walking distance to gather.

If the subway signals something most of the United States has rejected, perhaps it is precisely this cultural mixing that is being rejected. It is also a rejection more generally of the marginalized populations whose problems are deemed unsolvable. In cities from Boston to Seattle, one finds complaints about the character of people riding public transportation (*Boston Globe* 2000; Hadley 2002). A bus rider in Austin declared that in one area of town bus stops are not safe "because they have become regular hangouts for alcoholic prostitutes, pimps and transients" (Dodson 1996). The racial connotations of these complaints are clear. One letter writer observed in response to criticisms of Atlanta's transit system that it was "being linked with inner-city problems such as crime and poverty. Comments like these don't have to be parsed to learn what's actually being said" (Chandler 1998).

National politics in the United States reveals a parallel disregard for public transportation and urban populations. Joyce Purnick (2000) points out that in the 2000 presidential election campaign, the only time New York's subways were mentioned was in reference to the World Series. The overall political weakness of cities was revealed in the presidential election of 2004. While many in the media emphasized the divisions between Republican "red states" and Democratic "blue states," a clearer understanding of America's political divisions recognizes a split between urban and rural voters. Even in states whose electorate voted overwhelmingly for Bush, such as Utah, the cities favored Kerry (Wilentz 2004). The swing votes are found primarily in the suburbs, so it is no surprise that neither major party shows much concern for cities.

The ability to overcome anti-urban politics may ultimately come from the growing strength of immigrants, as indicated by their role in boosting the subway, but it may also be aided by the types of social interactions visitors to New York have in the subways. Zygmunt Bauman (1998) suggests that the fear of diverse populations is produced by the homogeneity of segregated neighborhoods.[26] Overcoming this fear may simply involve sharing space with people different from oneself. When a crowd of people from very diverse backgrounds stands in the Grand Central subway station listening to a band play Latin dance music and several people begin to dance while others look on and smile, the otherwise tedious act of commuting is for a moment broken up with a shared pleasure. This type of experience might erode the fear of difference, and it is something that could not take place in an automobile.

At the same time, fear in varying forms works to assure attachment to the automobile commute. The freeways of Los Angeles are an excellent place to study this attachment. As with the subways, fear shapes the experience of many who drive on Los Angeles freeways; also as with the subways, the freeway's image is unstable and contested. The goal in the next chapter will be to uncover not only the narratives of fear that support the freeway system but also the openings these narratives provide for challenges. While the freeway's form may not allow the types of public expression that are available to those who ride a subway, it may permit other openings for oppositional voices. Edward Soja titled a chapter of his book *Postmodern Geographies* (1989) "It All Comes Together in Los Angeles," and Los Angeles brings the themes of this study together in a similar fashion. First, as the quintessential automobile-centered city, Los Angeles reveals the apogee—some may say wreckage—of the ideals that supported this now-dominant system. Second, Los Angeles reveals the ways in which forms of transportation play a role in their own depiction—by shaping the strategies people may use for public expression.

▓ ▓

CHAPTER 6

URBAN FREEWAY STORIES: RACIAL POLITICS AND THE ARMORED AUTOMOBILE

June 17, 1994, millions of people watched a white Ford Bronco bearing O. J. Simpson driven at thirty-five to forty-five miles per hour along the Los Angeles freeways followed by ten patrol cars. This event holds rich possibilities for the examination of American culture, but I wish to focus on it primarily as a moment in the cultural history of the freeway. This event, rather than being wholly bizarre as many news reports described it, in many ways embodies the freeway's evolving impact. The freeway became a site for an enormous audience and an element in a common narrative spread across the city. A central image of this narrative is the freeway's capacity for social isolation—the distancing it allows between drivers and surrounding environment. As a "victim," Simpson was protected by the ability of Al Cowlings to drive continuously without interference from crossing traffic or unfriendly pedestrians. Although pedestrians did come onto the freeway, the police shielded the Bronco in a way they could not once it left the freeway onto surface streets. On the other hand, as an "accused killer," Simpson was encircled, contained, and isolated from surrounding neighborhoods (see Figure 19). In being viewed by millions, this isolating feature of the freeway reinscribed itself into popular discourses found elsewhere in American society. These discourses legitimate social and racial hierarchies that divide contemporary metropolitan regions of the United States.

The freeway is part of dominant narratives that view African American and Latino/a residents of the central city as largely responsible for the conditions of poverty and violence amid which they live. The freeway takes on these narratives when it is embedded in contemporary media technologies such as the television, radio, and mobile phone, an embeddedness

Figure 19. The freeway allows police to isolate Simpson from surrounding neighborhoods. Photo from CNN, June 17, 1994.

exemplified by the O. J. Simpson chase. But a dramatically different reading of the automobile-freeway transportation system can be given, one that depicts the construction of this system actually helping to create the ghettos that, as part of media-constructed narratives, it now helps to legitimate. At the same time, the dramatic gathering on the freeway during the Simpson chase reveals how the freeway is part of a highly mediated, public forum that, while on the surface appears limiting and unidirectional, leaves unexpected openings—potholes—for dissenting voices.

THE FREEWAY AS URBAN SHIELD

The narrative of isolation surrounding the urban freeway begins with its connection to the suburban goal of escaping urban populations. As noted, the movement to exclusive suburbs has historically come from a desire to escape not just the crowding and industrial pollution of the central city but also the types of people who were increasingly moving into the city. At the turn of the twentieth century, advocates of the suburbs linked both the poor living conditions and the radicalism that led to strikes and anarchist bombings to the culture of new immigrants (Marsh 1990: 69–71). Today, suburbs are both racially and economically diverse and include, for example, African

Americans who live in Oceanside north of San Diego, Chinese immigrants in Monterey Park just west of downtown Los Angeles, and Latinos/as who are a significant part of several cities in Orange County. But more importantly, between and within suburbs and cities, tremendous racial and economic segregation continues.[1] For William Sharpe and Leonard Wallock (1994: 9), a reason for this segregation remains "the wish to escape racial and class intermingling."

In Chapter 1 I discussed how the escape from immigrant populations to the suburbs was first enabled by rail transportation, but taking the rail still required contact with residents of the city. The automobile allowed suburban residents to avoid contact with urban residents, but suburbanites who went to the central city for work, shopping, or entertainment still frequently had to drive through inner-city neighborhoods. The freeway took drivers downtown while shielding them from the residents of these neighborhoods.[2] Thus, the freeway distances the suburb from urban populations and embodies this distancing in its design.

The Simpson chase made clear that not only can the freeway shield the driver from urban populations; it can also help shield "dangerous drivers" from others. During the chase the freeway was closed in front of and behind the Ford Bronco, and tension noticeably increased when the Bronco left the freeway for the "surface streets." In contrast, on public transportation, if one person makes trouble, all the passengers have to deal with it, whether the "troublemaker" is simply playing a radio loudly or hassling the bus driver. A dramatic example took place in December 1993 when Colin Ferguson shot twenty-four people, killing five of them, on the Long Island Rail Road (Faison 1993). This example shows how "the violence of the city" cannot be contained as readily on public transportation as on the freeway, where an automobile can be more easily isolated.

The image of the freeway as a shield is not without gaps. A concern over aggressive driving emerged in the 1990s as news reports recounted stories of violent attacks following disagreements over driving etiquette (Adler 1997; Ferguson 1998; Vest, Cohen, and Tharp 1997). This inspired a study by the American Automobile Association (AAA) and a hearing by the House Surface Transportation Subcommittee. But reports of "road rage" in many ways reaffirmed the dominant ideal of the automobile and freeway as a shield. For example, several suggested that a possible reason for the increase in violence was the dramatic increase in the ownership of trucks and sport utility vehicles that make drivers feel safer.

"A lot of anecdotal evidence about aggressive driving incidents tends to involve people driving sport utility vehicles," says Julie Rochman of the Insurance Institute for Highway Safety. "When people get these larger, heavier vehicles, they feel more invulnerable." While Chrysler spokesman Chris Peuss discounts the notion of suburban assault vehicles being behind the aggressive-driving phenomenon, he does say women feel more secure in jumbo-size vehicles. (Vest, Cohen, and Tharp 1997)

Louis Mizell (1996), author of the AAA Foundation for Traffic Safety study, concludes his report by listing several recommendations for avoiding confrontations: "Encased in metal armor, many motorists who are normally passive become enraged road warriors when they get behind the wheel. Don't become one of them. These individuals should be advised that (a) cars are not bulletproof; (b) another driver can follow you home; and (c) you've got to get out of the car some time." The implication here is that the "normally passive" motorist will anger a truly dangerous individual who will then chase the unthinking motorist and attack him or her. The report makes this more explicit by claiming that, "as might be expected, the majority of aggressive drivers are relatively young, relatively poorly educated males who have criminal records, histories of violence, and drug or alcohol problems." A racial spin is put on these dangerous drivers in a letter to the San Diego Union Tribune: "The low-rider with the limo tint, missing front plate and obnoxious stereo is way more likely to run a red light or cut you off than the four-door sedan in the next lane" (Williams 1996).

Although drunk drivers injure more people on average in two days than were injured in seven years by aggressive driving,[3] one study found that motorists in the Washington, D.C., area felt more threatened by aggressive drivers than by drunk drivers (AAA Foundation for Traffic Safety 1998). In sum, fear of road rage reaffirms the desire for the automobile and freeway to shield the driver from the violence associated with the city.

At the same time, it is important to note that some sections of the freeway are less effective in conveying the feeling of a shield. Los Angeles freeways were perhaps the first to be touched by images of violence when in the late 1980s a few incidents of drivers shooting one another received national attention. The image became a source of humor in the 1991 film *L.A. Story* when Steve Martin's character starts shooting randomly on the freeway as rush hour begins. A different danger emerged in the fall of 1996 when unknown projectiles shattered the rear windows of more than two hundred cars. The perpetrators were later identified as "gang members" on probation (Allen 1996). In the spring of 2005, local television focused on a rash of twenty-four freeway shootings in four months, some of which were considered "gang-related" (Winton and Lin 2005). In these cases, the usefulness of the freeway as shield has deteriorated; holes have been shot through the shield. The widespread publicity of these events—in comparison to fatal accidents, which are more common—reveal how people expect the freeway to be a space free of dangers characteristic of the city.[4]

The Simpson event demonstrates how the feeling of safety and isolation linked to the freeway is extended by the media technology that surrounds it. First, helicopter television is in part a creation of the freeway, since the demand for traffic monitoring requires helicopters. The helicopter is one element of a complex technological monitoring system that includes video cameras, radar that can capture traffic violators, and mechanical counters that aid in tracking delays. The helicopter's role in monitoring traffic has been extended to monitoring criminals or potential criminals, as was seen not only in the Simpson chase but also in the coverage of the Los Angeles uprising.[5] Since the Simpson chase it has become routine to compare televised freeway chases to the event. In fact, the helicopter-televised chase has become a genre in itself. Local news stations regularly devote hours to slow-speed chases as the anchors debate police techniques and speculate on why the drivers are fleeing. Episodes of *Cops* often use chases tracked from helicopters, while *World's Scariest Police Chases* focuses exclusively on often dangerous high-speed pursuits.

These programs along with the Simpson chase make clear the ideal manner in which the helicopter can isolate and follow the chase of a dangerous driver. This is done in a way that could not take place on a commuter rail system. The helicopter provides an enhanced vision of what takes place by providing a perspective of what is immediately surrounding the driver on all sides, and this adds to a distancing that television already provides. Viewers need not fear for their safety nor for that of the camera operator.

The distancing role of the media can be traced back to the newspaper. Walter Benjamin (1955/1969: 158) saw the newspaper's goal as precisely to distance the reader from the shock of modern life: "If it were the intention of the press to have the reader assimilate the information it supplies as part of his own experience, it would not achieve its purpose. But its intention is just the opposite, and it is achieved: *to isolate what happens from the realm in which it could affect the experience of the reader*" [my emphasis]. Another illustration of this can be found in the traffic report. Here, the broadcaster announces accidents on the freeway not so drivers may share in concern for those who have been injured, but only so they may avoid the accident and take another route.

Margaret Morse (1990: 201) expands on Benjamin's argument to include the television, freeway, and shopping mall together in creating a distancing effect and allowing the "postmodern development of what Benjamin called the 'phantasmagoria of the interior,' a mixture of levels of consciousness and objects of attention." Rather than the largely distractive character of this distancing experience described by Morse, I suggest that the distancing has an important narrative content: the freeway, television, and mall provide distance from the dangerous character of the city.[6] To the extent that Simpson was seen as a black man with a gun, he symbolized a danger of the inner city, which needed to be isolated and contained.

The claim that Simpson represents urban danger may appear problematic, since he was a popular sports celebrity, but writer Toni Morrison (1997) and legal scholar Kimberlé Crenshaw (1997), among others, have explored the omnipresence of race throughout the story of Simpson's ordeal. While pundits attacked Simpson's defense team for "playing the race card," in particular through their questioning of racist detective Mark Fuhrman, race typically framed the media's portrayal of Simpson. This was most clear with the "darkening" of Simpson's photo in *Time Magazine* and the discussion of Simpson's gang membership as a youth (Crenshaw 1997: 112–113).

Like the Simpson chase, the film *Speed* (1994, Jan De Bont) demonstrates how the freeway and its surrounding communication technologies isolate and contain danger while simultaneously aiding its construction into a television format. In the film, a bus carries a bomb that will explode if it goes below fifty-five miles per hour, so it is directed onto the freeway, where a high speed can be maintained and it can be isolated from other traffic (see Figure 20). A helicopter initially plays a crucial role in directing the bus off and back onto the freeway, where it can avoid traffic. However, the helicopter's monitoring is no longer an asset when media coverage prevents the police from making a rescue attempt.

The technology of mobile phones also has an impact on the space of the freeway. In the Simpson chase a phone was used to maintain contact with Al Cowlings, the driver of the Bronco. The mobile phone plays a similar role in the film *Speed*. When the hero, a policeman played by Keanu Reeves, realizes the bus has a bomb on it, he hijacks a car and tells the driver to dial 911.[7] Here, the ability to call for help from one's car on the freeway demonstrates the sense of safety created by mobile phones, which were initially marketed for their ability to help drivers in distress.[8] Mobile phone owners derive a feeling of safety for themselves and can also help others by calling 911. Thus the mobile phone adds to the monitoring potential of the freeway.

The danger to be monitored in the film *Speed* is coded as urban primarily through the types of passengers on the bus; the film demonstrates that one time the freeway cannot shield commuters from urban problems is when they use an express bus. Passengers must deal with the poor and disen-

Figure 20. The bus is shielded by patrol cars on the freeway. *Speed* (1994, Jan De Bont).

franchised who are part of diverse neighborhoods the freeway bypasses. Many residents of Los Angeles dread association with the marginalized groups who ride the bus. This sentiment is expressed by a character in the film *Crash* (2005, Paul Haggis) who claims that the purpose of large bus windows is to "humiliate the people of color who are reduced to riding [the bus]." The scorn for bus riders was also reflected in the appalling state of service in the early 1990s, when Los Angeles buses were regularly crowded, late, and in disrepair. This led to the formation of the Bus Riders Union and a 1994 lawsuit demanding equitable treatment for central city passengers. Despite multiple court settlements in the bus riders' favor, Los Angeles's Metropolitan Transportation Authority continues to resist change, and improvements have been slow in coming (Mann 2004).

In *Speed*, the scorn for bus riders is justified by depicting them as crazy. They must confront first a man with a gun—perhaps a Latino/a gang member—but more centrally, the threat of being exploded by a man not even on the bus.[9] In short, while the freeway signals a sense of safety and distance in the film, mass transit signals danger. The danger of riding transit in Los Angeles is reaffirmed in the media in stories of gang violence taking place on buses or trains—most often as they pass through South L.A. neighborhoods that the freeway avoids (Schoch 2005).

Figure 21. Ferguson abandons his car on the freeway. *Falling Down* (1993, Joel Schumacher).

The freeway's place amid urban danger is also made clear in the film *Falling Down* (1993, Joel Schumacher). The film begins with the protagonist, Bill Ferguson, getting stuck in a freeway traffic jam, abandoning his car, and climbing over a hill (see Figure 21). This hill isolates the freeway from a neighborhood referred to in the movie simply as "gangland." One police officer in the film calls the neighborhood a "shit hole." We know immediately he is in a "bad part of town" by the graffiti-covered walls (see Figure 22). After an altercation with two Mexican American youths, Ferguson becomes the target of a drive-by shooting.

The film follows Ferguson's violent rampage across Los Angeles as he walks "home" to see his ex-wife and daughter in Venice Beach. The rampage is apparently provoked by the loss of his job and his inability to see his daughter, but it is his frustration with the freeway traffic jam that is the immediate trigger. In this initial scene, the freeway once again fails to perform its function of isolation. Ferguson is caught amid disturbing and foreign elements of the city—from the immigrants listening to a Spanish language radio station to the wealthy businessmen screaming into their car phones. But it is in the city off the freeway—the Asian merchant who "can't speak English" and the gang members who demand that he respect their territory— that his vexation escalates to violence.

The narratives about the inner city found in the Simpson chase and the films *Speed* and *Falling Down* are made even clearer if we consider how they fit within the larger genre of film and television chase scenes. Shows like *Cops* portray directly the parallel between the distancing safety of the camera and that of the automobile. As one cruises along in the patrol car, the feeling of safety is fortified by the rifle in the front seat and the knowledge that the driver is well armed. When the police car moves off the freeway and into the danger of inner city neighborhoods, it reaffirms the contrast between the safety of the freeway and the danger of the "surface streets" where the criminals are to be found and chased down.

Cops legitimates the need for freeways by portraying the residents of urban neighborhoods as dangerous, irresponsible people. The majority of both victims and suspects on shows like *Cops* are black and Latino/a residents of the city (Beckett and Sasson 2000: 113). Crime is something identified with these residents, and the poverty that engulfs their neighborhoods is depicted as their responsibility. *Cops* sets up a simplistic dichotomy between "good guys" and "bad guys" not just in the theme song of the show—"Bad Boys" by Inner Circle—but in frequent statements made by the officer-narrators who refer to the "bad guys." In this portrayal criminals are beyond reform; they are depraved.

The negative characterization of poor urban residents comes through most when the officers are called to scenes of domestic disturbances or child neglect. The police peruse the run-down homes of the poor finding evidence of drug abuse, very little food in the refrigerator, and generally unhealthy living conditions. It is not uncommon to hear an officer comment, with obvious disdain in the voice, about the suspects being on welfare. In other words, the show affirms the discourse of Reaganism, linking the degeneracy of the urban poor to government aid.

While the audience for shows like *Cops* may be limited, the same basic message about the "inner city" can be found in local television news, which is dominated by stories of violent crime. Approximately 20 percent of local

Figure 22. With the freeway in the background, Ferguson begins his journey through the "inner city." *Falling Down* (1993, Joel Schumacher).

television news stories focus on crime. While only a small percentage of the crime committed in the United States is violent crime and most violent crime is committed by persons known to the victims, most TV news stories describe crimes committed by strangers. Research also shows that blacks more than whites are depicted as violent criminals, and black suspects are portrayed in a more menacing fashion. The news further fosters white suburban fears by mostly choosing stories with white women as victims rather than black men, who are statistically far more likely to be victims (Beckett and Sasson 2000: 77–79).

In the 1990s the obsession with urban crime led to legislation at the national and local level. Opinion polls showed crime to be the top concern among Americans before the local and state elections of 1994 (Hull 1994). That year Congress passed the Violent Crime Control and Law Enforcement Act. Only $7 billion of the $30 billion crime bill was dedicated to crime prevention programs, and, as noted in the *New York Times*, the legislation did "not guarantee that Congress will actually approve the outlays [for social programs]" (Johnston and Holmes 1994). The predominant concern with law enforcement rather than, at a minimum, with job and recreation programs for youth reflects the assumption that criminals are incorrigible.[10] This viewpoint was echoed especially in the crime bill's expansion of the death penalty. The belief that someone should be put to death for a crime is the ultimate statement that this person is a monster.

The expansion of the death penalty is also interesting because two of the new crimes included in this expansion were connected to the narrative of isolation linked to the automobile. First, killings associated with "carjackings" became punishable by death. By creating the image that criminals will be deterred from attacking individuals in cars, the feeling of safety linked to being within a car is preserved. Second, murders resulting from drive-by shootings may also lead to execution. This directly paralleled a California initiative requiring increased sentencing for "second degree drive-by murder" that passed by an overwhelming majority in 1996 (Lempinen and Martin 1996). While the death penalty for carjacking serves the desire to be protected within a car, the death penalty for drive-by shooting supports a view of the automobile as enclosing and isolating potentially dangerous persons from surrounding neighborhoods.

Both new applications of the death penalty imply a desire to be isolated and shielded from particular populations. The association of carjacking with people of color was made clear in November 1994 when Susan Smith falsely accused a "black man" of carjacking her and kidnapping her children, assuming people would be more likely to believe her story if the accused was black.

Since gang members are most associated with "drive-by killings," the creation of a crime for shooting from a vehicle was in part a measure to assure voters that new steps were being taken to control gangs and to protect people who live outside urban ghettos from the danger of these ghettos spreading.[11]

The racial coding in these laws is clear. Furthermore, research shows that race plays a large role in determining whether a murder conviction leads to the death penalty. "In 22 percent of the cases involving a Black offender and a White victim, the defendant was sentenced to death. In stark contrast, only 1 percent of the cases involving a Black offender and a Black victim resulted in a death sentence" (Russell 1998: 134). Add to this the fact that support for the death penalty indicates a belief that criminals are irredeemable, the implication is that blacks are congenitally prone toward wickedness. In fact, a study conducted by Adalberto Aguirre and David V. Baker (1994) shows a link between support for the death penalty and racial prejudice. Their research indicates that "white persons who choose to discriminate against Black persons are more likely to support the death penalty" (152).

THE FREEWAY AS RACIST INSTITUTION

As a symbol the freeway is embedded in narratives that legitimate the socially segregated metropolis, but as a physical formation the freeway's construction helped create the spatial divisions now regarded as natural. Part of the freeway's strangeness is that despite frequent complaints about its crowded conditions, it is difficult to imagine U.S. cities without it. However, urban infrastructure is not inevitable; it is a product of political decisions serving the interests of some more than others. The following discussion is meant to undermine the naturalness of our built environment by filling these ubiquitous structures with an image of their sordid history.

Although federal aid for a national system of roads can be traced back to 1916, the construction of the current system is largely a product of the 1956 Interstate Highway Act. The outcome of this act came from the struggle between, on the one hand, engineers and trucking companies who wanted the highways to circumvent cities and, on the other, urban politicians who wanted highways to enter downtown. Mark Rose (1990: 59) shows that the compromise was to provide funding for both. Yet, while highway access to the city center appears normal in the United States, it would be considered strange in Europe, where highways mostly avoid the urban center (Flink 1988: 374). So what accounts for the appeal of urban freeways in the United States?

To understand this appeal, it must be recognized that the congressional coalition supporting highway financing in the 1950s was the same group that opposed aid to the inner city in the form of public housing. While the 1956 Highway Act provided federal funds to build the largest public project in history, the 1954 Housing Act provided comparatively little funding for construction of low-income housing. Equally important, the Housing Act allowed a significant amount of federal aid to be used for projects other than housing (Mollenkopf 1983: 116–122). Aid was often used to make deteriorating downtowns more attractive to corporate office builders by demolishing older housing and replacing it with luxury condominiums, hotels, and shopping malls (Kleniewski: 1984). According to John R. Logan and Harvey L. Molotch (1987: 168), "less than 20 percent of all urban renewal land went to housing: over 80 percent went for developing commercial, industrial, and public infrastructure." These renewal projects disproportionately affected African American and Latino/a neighborhoods; the authors cite an estimate that "90 percent of low income housing destroyed by urban renewal was not replaced" (169). Thus "urban renewal" became a euphemism for "Negro removal."

Freeways were an important component of urban renewal because the federal government contributed 90 percent of the funds, significantly more aid than the Housing Act could provide. These funds could be used to purchase and then demolish large stretches of housing considered "blighted." In addition, local authorities planned freeways so they would create a barrier between the downtown of corporate headquarters and nearby racially mixed neighborhoods. Mike Davis (1988: 86) writes, "It is not surprising that Los Angeles's Portman-built new downtown (like that of Detroit, or Houston) reproduces more or less exactly the besieged landscape of Peachtree Center [in Atlanta]: the new Figueroa and Bunker Hill complexes are formed in the same protective maze of freeways, moats, concrete parapets, and asphalt no-man's lands."

What made freeways especially damaging was not just their destruction of housing but also their creation of enormous concrete barriers within formerly close-knit neighborhoods. This had consequences for small businesses, since the local store that one might have been able to walk to in the past now required a trip by automobile, making a shopping center more convenient.[12] Moreover, freeways could damage the sense of community visually by blocking the view of large parts of a neighborhood. In St. Paul, Minnesota, the African American community of Rondo was destroyed in 1956 as Interstate 94 construction forced the removal of 650 families. A resident of the neighborhood powerfully describes the impact:

> As a community we had a geographical bond. Rondo was the thoroughfare, the main drag, the main contributory, the focal point, the center, the

epic center, the nexus. . . . When you walked down that street you walked past people you knew, places you ate, places you partied at, and everybody knew you. A common thread ran through everyone and when they tore that street up, it was like ripping your arm off. People were floundering. We were castaways. Where was our Rondo? (Anderson 1995: 26)

As noted, freeways were also key to enabling residential and industrial flight to whites-only suburbs. Industries were attracted to the urban periphery by the ability to acquire large sections of land at low cost. Suburban development facilitated industrial flight by setting aside land near projected or existing interstate highways. Because of a stronger tax base and less need to support services for the poor, these suburban areas were better able to compete for new industries (Gottdiener 1994: 250–254).

In the 1980s the economic renewal that came to New York spread to other central cities, but, as in New York, it had an unequal impact. Jobs for those with at least some college education increased, but for those with a high school education or less jobs decreased (Kasarda 1992: 622). Although some blacks and Latinos/as were able to take advantage of the economic growth, many more were hurt by the decline in manufacturing and blue-collar jobs. State economic development policy has encouraged new industry to locate on the urban periphery with easy access to automobiles. Consequently, people of color, who are more likely to depend on public transit and live near the city center, are deterred from applying to these jobs (Jakowitsch and Ernst 2004: 170).

In Los Angeles this spatial inequality is especially evident. In the post–World War II period, the Los Angeles region was the locus of tremendous industrial expansion. Most of these industries located in the suburbs amid the newly constructed freeway networks. African Americans and Latinos/as were largely excluded from this postwar boom. "West of the Alameda 'White Curtain' was the compacted Black ghetto, the third largest in the country, tantalizingly close to but increasingly distanced from the large pool of jobs to the east" (Soja 1989: 197). This inequality only increased in the 1970s and 1980s as employment in heavy industry near the central city dramatically declined while jobs in the high-tech industries expanded in the suburbs, especially Orange County (ibid.: 197–217). The persistence of spatial/racial inequalities is often considered a natural phenomenon, much like the structure of the interstates. However, the troublesome politics that have sustained the inequalities are linked to the very desire for segregation that is embodied in the interstates.

While the 1950s saw the emergence of a powerful civil rights movement and growing opposition to racial discrimination, Stephen Meyer (2000) notes that northern whites were more willing to oppose discrimination in education and voting than in housing. Consequently, although fair housing laws were passed in several states, including California, they had weak enforcement provisions. Moreover, in the early 1960s the push for stronger laws led to a backlash. Realtors and their white supporters claimed that fair housing laws violated homeowner property rights. Thus, in 1964 California residents voted 2 to 1 in favor of Proposition 14, giving property owners the right to refuse to rent or sell their property to anyone at their "absolute discretion" (Meyer 2000: 179). The proposition was eventually declared a violation of the Fourteenth Amendment, but the support it received revealed the strong resistance of whites to integrated housing.

Passage of Proposition 14 contributed to the African American resentment that boiled over in the 1965 Watts riots. The Watts uprising was the first of many to hit U.S. cities in the 1960s, and it helped transform the image of the civil rights movement in the eyes of many whites. White people had difficulty understanding why blacks would revolt after the passage of the 1964 Civil Rights Act and 1965 Voting Rights Act. The urban riots of the 1960s also paralleled a growing militancy among black leaders, some of whom were calling for self-defense rather than nonviolence in the face of white aggression. Consequently, the claim made by civil rights opponents— that the movement encouraged lawbreaking—appeared feasible to many whites. Barry Goldwater had made this claim in the 1964 presidential election, but it was not until a year after Watts that this rhetoric appeared to succeed politically. That year Ronald Reagan was elected as California's governor by calling for "law and order" in the streets (Horne 1995: 281).

Despite the riots' negative impact on the image of the civil rights movement, they may also have helped convince enough members of Congress to finally pass fair housing legislation. The National Advisory Commission on Civil Disorders linked housing discrimination to urban violence in its 1968 report, which helped build support for the Civil Rights Act of 1968, better known as the Fair Housing Act (Meyer 2000: 208–209). However, rather than marking a dramatic change in attitude and behavior, the weakness of the act actually marked a reaffirmation of the desire for segregation. The law made housing discrimination illegal, but because the Department of Housing and Urban Development was given little investigatory power, proving discrimination was difficult. Thus, real estate companies and banks continued to routinely discriminate against blacks who tried to buy homes in white neighborhoods (Massey and Denton 1993: 195–200).

The year Congress passed fair housing legislation was also the year Richard Nixon was elected using Reagan's rhetoric of law and order at the national level. As the unrest in Watts was repeated in cities throughout the country, Nixon capitalized on the same backlash that brought Reagan to power in California. His campaign thrived on white people's fear that problems of the ghetto might spread to the suburbs. In his speech to the Republican convention, "Nixon stressed that the right to be free of violence had become 'the forgotten civil right' and lumped together the problems of racial riots, crime in the streets, and student demonstrations" (Cronin, Cronin, and Milakovich 1981: 64). In other words, the same year whites were being told that they could no longer keep their neighborhoods segregated, the need for segregation was affirmed to them by the image of growing urban crime.

The "tough on crime" language that now dominates politics comes out of this crucial period when crime both became a national issue and was framed as a problem of liberalism. Liberalism meant not just government programs to reduce poverty and prevent racial discrimination but also increasing limits on police and prosecutors. Several Supreme Court decisions in the 1950s and 1960s increased the protections of defendants against forced confessions and illegally obtained evidence while assuring them the right to counsel and a speedy trial. As the crime rate rose in the 1960s, leniency by the criminal justice system became the most popular explanation, with the implication that the increased rights of the defendant were to blame (Edsall and Edsall 1991: 110–111).

The call for stricter laws became popular in part because liberal Democrats lacked easy solutions to the crime problem. For example, in its 1967 report, the Presidential Commission on Law Enforcement and Administration of Justice refused to blame the problem of crime on "declining morals" or a "lenient justice system." Instead Nicholas Katzenbach, the commission's director, reported that inequality, unemployment, and a lack of job training all contributed to the increase in crime (Krajicek 1998: 149). This more complex explanation for crime and disorder did not have the straightforward appeal of simply condemning criminals as amoral. As Gerald Ford, then House Republican leader, put it, "How long are we going to abdicate law and order—the backbone of any civilization—in favor of a soft social theory that the man who heaves a brick through your window or tosses a firebomb into your car is simply the misunderstood and underprivileged product of a broken home?" (quoted in Edsall and Edsall 1991: 51).

Blaming urban residents for the degraded conditions of the city provided cover for those who fled to the suburbs. The belief that blacks would bring these conditions with them meant suburban residents could legitimate keeping their neighborhoods white. In 1980, 60 percent of whites still opposed laws banning discrimination in housing—twelve years after the Fair Housing Act was passed at a national level (Massey and Denton 1993: 92).

In the 1980s Ronald Reagan confirmed the white logic of segregation whenever he addressed the issue of poverty:

> By nearly every measure, the position of poor Americans worsened under the leadership of our opponents. Teenage drug use, out-of-wedlock births, and crime increased dramatically. Urban neighborhoods and schools deteriorated. Those whom the government intended to help discovered a cycle of dependency that could not be broken. (Quoted in Beckett and Sasson 2000: 62)

By this logic, racism has nothing to do with entrenched urban poverty. Indeed, people of color had benefited from more than a decade of special treatment ranging from Head Start to affirmative action, and they still failed to succeed. The depravity of such thinking is evident in its simultaneous attack on "big government" benefits for the poor and disregard of much greater benefits that have accrued to whites through government-backed discrimination. The enormous wealth gained through racist housing policy had its origins in New Deal legislation, and this was not the only element of the New Deal that privileged whites over people of color. Blacks were often the last hired for government work projects, and in the case of unemployment insurance, a large number of blacks and Latinos/as were ineligible because domestic and farm labor were excluded from coverage. The Wagner Act of 1935, which solidified union bargaining rights, excluded farm and domestic labor. If blacks or Latinos/as were given union jobs, institutional bias often made sure they were paid less than whites.

Discrimination in education was also widespread and not limited to the South, and Mexican Americans as well as African Americans were confined to schools with overcrowded classrooms and inadequate supplies. The 1954 Supreme Court decision ending legal segregation had a very limited impact on educational inequality, in part because whites could simply move to segregated suburbs. Moreover, because school funding often comes from property taxes, predominantly suburban schools typically have more resources than racially diverse urban schools. These are just some of the components of what George Lipsitz (1998) has called a "possessive investment in whiteness," meaning that for those who could fit into the socially constructed category "white," there were social benefits in maintaining a racial hierarchy.

An unwillingness to acknowledge this legacy of white privilege has meant declining support for job programs and other forms of aid meant to redress this legacy; at the same time support for tougher penalties on criminals has increased. This is as true among Democrats as it is among Republicans. Bill Clinton supported the reactionary 1994 crime law mentioned above. Two years after the law passed, the Personal Responsibility and Work Opportunity Reconciliation Act was passed. The title of the act reveals the belief that women with children who are living in poverty have simply not tried hard enough to find work to support their families, so their benefits must be cut to force them to find a job. Thus the law perpetuates the view that irresponsibility, not structural racism, is at the root of poverty.

California voters have shown their attachment to this discourse surrounding the urban poor by voting for several measures targeting immigrants and criminal defendants. In 1994 both Proposition 187—designed primarily to cut medical and educational benefits to undocumented immigrants—and Proposition 184—a "three strikes" law increasing penalties for repeat offenders—passed with a large majority of votes. Proposition 187 revealed a view of working class Latinos/as similar to the stereotype of inner-city blacks. Supporters depicted Mexican and Central American immigrants coming to the United States primarily to take advantage of welfare benefits rather than to work in low-wage jobs central to the California economy (Lipsitz 1998: 149). Proposition 184 played on the fear that convicts were given lenient sentences and continued to commit violent crimes, but after two years the vast majority of cases prosecuted under the law were for nonviolent offenses (Beckett and Sasson 2000: 181).

In March 2000 Proposition 21, the Juvenile Crime Initiative Statute, passed with 62 percent of the vote. Backers of the proposition used the same rhetoric as for other "tough on crime" measures—blaming judicial leniency for declining morals: "Ask yourself, if a violent gang member believes the worst punishment he might receive for a gang-ordered murder is incarceration at the California Youth Authority until age 25, will that stop him from taking a life? Of course not" (Elvey, Trask, and Tefank 2000).

The proposition's focus on youth indicated another dimension to the desire for segregation. In the 1980s and 1990s police used surveillance technology to segregate youth of color. Within black and Latino/a neighborhoods, youths were monitored with random checkpoints, and if they ventured outside their neighborhoods they faced harassment and searches (Davis 1992: 286). Some cities tried to preempt police harassment of outsiders or legitimate the harassment by passing laws restricting use of public parks and other public spaces to those who reside in the city. However, the strongest method of keeping out unwanted visitors is simply to build walls around a neighborhood. This medieval strategy has become very popular in the past two decades (Blakely and Snyder 1997). Yet, all these strategies of shielding urban space from dangerous-looking youths are ultimately limited because rarely can one live completely in a gated environment. At some point residents of segregated neighborhoods must venture into spaces that are less restrictive. Therefore, the only sure way of avoiding contact with inner-city youths is to send them to prison.

Proposition 21 betrays the desire for a type of residential segregation that is not typically labeled as such: incarceration. By targeting youth of color, the effect of this initiative will likely be an increase in the already overrepresented population of blacks and Latinos/as in prison. While blacks make up only 13 percent of the nation's population, they comprise 46 percent of the prison population (De Lollis: 2001). In California, 1 in 33 African Americans is in prison: this compares to 1 in 122 Hispanics and only 1 in 205 whites (McCormick: 2001).

The consequences of this segregation can be devastating for communities of color. Large numbers lose the right to vote—in some states permanently—and when they return from prison they often face difficulty finding work. As Katherine Beckett and Theodore Sasson (2000: 196) put it, "The logical consequence of the war on crime—the incarceration of huge and growing numbers of people, especially young minorities—is at least in political and moral terms a crime of the state, the significance of which is far greater than the petty crimes committed by many of today's offenders."

FREEWAY PUBLICS

In part what made the O. J. Simpson chase so fascinating was the apparent harkening back to older forms of public interaction. The *Los Angeles Times* reported, "They cheered honked horns and lined the roadway waving—a scene more reminiscent of a parade or victory procession than a police pursuit of a murder suspect" (Berman and Goldman 1994). The description of the event as a parade articulates the freeway into a discourse about traditional urban space as a place of face-to-face contact. The space of the street has been and continues to be, in cities like New York and Paris, a place for political manifestations. The street is a place where those who historically have not had access to the exclusive bourgeois sphere may gather and gain a voice.[13] Groups have used the streets, squares, and parks to march and hold demonstrations, forming what Nancy Fraser (1992) calls a "counter-public" against the hegemonic elite. This type of protest was partially made possible by the social space of the street, something that the automobile helped to eliminate.

Today, the urban space of the park, plaza, or street has to some extent been replaced by the freeway, which has become a central part of the city and provides similar possibilities for access: one need only head for the nearest on-ramp to reach the space. The use of the freeway for a public gathering in the Simpson event momentarily seemed to counter the concern of scholars about the decline of urban public space and its replacement by the privately controlled "pseudo-public" space of shopping malls, hotel lobbies, and corporate parks (Davis 1992; Schiller 1989; Sorkin 1992). In another example, the freeway became a place of protest after the acquittal of the officers who beat Rodney King when some five hundred students sat in the middle of San Diego's Interstate 5 and blocked traffic for more than an hour (Heard 1992). Overwhelmingly, of course, social contact on the freeway is separated by automobiles, so conversation among motorists is difficult. Thus, the use of the freeway as a meeting place appears exceptional and very different from the everyday encounters that take place on pedestrian-dominated city streets.

In fact, the exceptional character of the Simpson chase indicates the power of the freeway to limit any type of random activity. Margaret Morse (1990) claims the everyday experience of the freeway is the antithesis of the experience of everyday life on pedestrian streets. Michel de Certeau (1984) suggests that within the formal system of the streets, space may be created through irregular disjunctive practices. According to Morse, the television, freeway, and shopping mall prohibit these disjunctive practices by forming a nonspace characterized by displacement from its surroundings, lack of location, and disengagement from face-to-face contact. Shopping malls present a controlled environment, a shelter from the hazards of the outside world, that transcends geographic location. Similarly, television has no geographical location. It is broadcast everywhere and nowhere at once, and television creates a shelter by distancing the viewer from the external world. Finally, for Morse, the freeway is not a location but merely a vector between the nonspace of television and shopping malls.

Morse argues that the television, freeway, and mall simultaneously develop a sense of greater community integration and permit greater privatization and isolation. People come together in malls but only as consumers; freeways bring massive numbers of individuals together, but they are separated by cars; and television has a mass audience, but it is watched individually. For Morse, the drabness of everyday work permits and leads to the need for a fantasy realm. This fantasy is of a timeless, enclosed world found in front of the television, on the freeway, and/or in the mall. Life is "made easier," in that it becomes easier to live in this fantasy world. Products on television are found in the malls, which are easily reached by freeway.

Television programming is adapted to a common work schedule to make viewing compatible with the daily routine. Thus, the passage of time is not consciously experienced either on the freeway or in front of the television: it is experienced as voids of either driving time or viewing time. Morse characterizes this passage of time in nonspace as "distraction."[14]

The events surrounding the O. J. chase challenge some elements of Morse's analysis while confirming others. On the one hand, her notion of distraction implies a certain passivity in the commensurate experience of shopping malls, televisions, and freeways. However, the gathering that watched Simpson pass indicates individuals' willingness to break out of the forced directionality of the freeway. In fact, smaller instances of the Simpson event take place on an everyday basis when drivers, "looky-lous," slow for an accident. Meaghan Morris (1990) argues that "distraction" as a view toward the audience can be challenged in its form as a female stereotype and in the way it collapses into the definition of consumers as "cultural dopes."[15] On the other hand, Morse's description of the strange community in isolation seems at least partially apt for the watching of the Simpson event. Furthermore, the wide broadcast of the chase enhanced this sense of community. But how does this community relate to more direct forms of public interaction?

Michael Warner (1992) finds that participation in an event such as this permits the viewer to be a part of a public in a way that is excluded by the construction of the traditional public sphere. He challenges the prototype of the public sphere established by Jürgen Habermas in his widely discussed book, *The Structural Transformation of the Public Sphere* (1991). Habermas describes aristocrats and bourgeoisie conducting intellectual discussions in the neutral space of a Paris salon, English coffeehouse, or German *Tischengesellschaft*. Warner claims that the media today bring out the contradiction between embodied and disembodied individuals, which Habermas's bourgeois public sphere would negate. The construction of the public sphere outwardly was presumed to ignore social characteristics but in reality included only those with certain social characteristics, that is, white male property owners. In contrast, Warner (1992: 397) finds that the mass media make ignoring social characteristics impossible: "The effect of disturbance in mass publicity is not a corruption introduced into the public sphere by its colonization through mass media. It is the legacy of the bourgeois public sphere's founding logic, the contradictions of which become visible whenever the public sphere can no longer turn a blind eye to its privileged bodies."

In other words, the corruption of the public sphere that Habermas contends mass culture brought on instead had its origins in the attempt to construct a public sphere that erased the privileges of certain subjects. The mass media only make these contradictions more clear. Moreover, Warner argues, the media can serve to enable a construction of subjectivity by those who have been excluded in the past. By permitting the mass identification with various cultural artifacts and personalities, mass culture permits individuals to include themselves within one of many possible mass publics. In particular, Warner points out how witnessing a disaster permits one to become a disembodied witness: "Disaster is popular because it is a way of making mass subjectivity available" (392).

In a similar way, through identification with the Simpson chase, the viewer takes on the publicity accorded the event, while at the same time distancing himself or herself from his or her own body. "Responding to an imminent contradiction in the bourgeois public sphere, mass publicity promises a reconciliation between embodiment and self abstraction" (ibid.: 396). This suggests why witnessing the O. J. Simpson chase was so popular. Furthermore, the viewer not only identifies with the Simpson event as a mass-mediated object but also appropriates and manipulates this object-event. The viewing becomes a creative moment as the viewer appropriates the text for future discussion or puts a spin on it, precisely as I have done here.

Yet, several complications surround the notion that viewers of the Simpson chase are members of a public. First, it is difficult to distinguish here between an "audience" and a "public." A public usually implies dialogue among members; in this case there does not appear to be a common forum through which the appropriation of the Simpson chase is expressed. Second, this notion of a public lacks a clear connection to political decision making. Viewing Simpson being chased on the freeway is very different from debating public policy. Looking at more details of the events surrounding the chase shows how the automobile and freeway can play a role in creating contemporary forums for public expression; it also shows the political nature of this expression.

First, the event demonstrated the vitality of radio as a public forum. People called in to radio stations asking Simpson not to kill himself and to stop running from the police. In addition to providing a space for public appeals to Simpson, radio furnished information on the location of the chase. This allowed people who wished to avoid traffic jams to choose a different route, and, of course, it also gave directions for those who wanted to wave at Simpson or otherwise participate in the chase.

Talk radio is a forum that thrives on the automobile and the freeway. The range of potential participants is much larger than in a geographical public space like a plaza or park, especially when the program is broadcast nationally and drivers can call in while they drive. However, the percentage of people whose voices may be heard is small compared to a gathering in a common physical space where many people may talk back and forth at the same time. Still, even those who are only listening are participating: just by listening they help keep a program on the air.

Although the ability of listeners to express their views on the radio may appear to create a model contemporary public sphere,[16] the model exposes difficulties with the ideal of a common forum for debate. Nancy Fraser (1992) argues that certain subjects—represented, for example, by their manner of expressing themselves—are consistently favored over others in particular public spheres, and even when one is a "disembodied voice" on the radio, cultural inequalities are revealed.[17] Equally important, the example of talk radio is a problem because rather than a single common audience, there are multiple radio stations and multiple audiences. This requires replacing the concept of a single public sphere with one of multiple public spheres. Fraser recognizes this multiplicity and argues, both historically and in the present, that alternative publics have formed in response to the exclusions of the dominant bourgeois public sphere.[18] Of course, there is not necessarily a direct parallel between different publics and different radio stations, and members likely can shift between publics just as they shift between radio stations. Still, the point is that the notion of a common forum for public dialogue is highly problematic.

Furthermore, Fraser's argument implies not only that different forums for expression have different audiences but also that some forums have greater prominence than others. For example, more people can listen to Rush Limbaugh than *Democracy Now!* with Amy Goodman. Access to public forums with the largest audiences, including network television, is the most restricted, and the voices come usually from representatives of groups with the most power in society. The Simpson chase allowed momentary access to the largest possible audience by those who gathered on the freeway. Unlike those who merely watched the event on television, these spectators were simultaneously part of a public forum where they could speak face to face with others and part of a nationally broadcast forum. The first of these was largely a creation of the second, since broadcasts helped direct people to the chase while also showing the celebratory atmosphere and offering a chance to be on television. Of course, the voice these spectators received on a national forum was highly limited—at most the momentary display of a sign saying, "We love the Juice."

This leads to another problem concerning the use of the term "public sphere" for the viewers of the Simpson chase: simply stating "We love the Juice" or just being seen on the freeway appears unrelated to public debate on state policy. However, simply making oneself visible on such a broad spectrum is significant for those whose voice is usually excluded from the mainstream media. John Fiske (1994: 471) contends, with regard to those who looted during the 1992 uprising: "Intentionally disruptive behavior in public is . . . one of the most readily available, if not the only, means of access to the media for the most deprived and repressed segments of our society." Public places such as shopping centers are readily accessible to television, making them ideal locations for gaining visibility. The freeway, given its heavily monitored status, increases the potential for this visibility. At the same time, Fiske cautions, "any such access will always be on the media's own terms" (471). Thus, during the coverage of the chase and the nearly hour-long wait as Simpson stayed in the Bronco at his Brentwood estate, the networks were dominated by the voices of news reporters and anchors describing the event. However, soon after Simpson was safely in jail, spectators were interviewed, and their viewpoints became a central element of the story. In part to understand what they described as an "extraordinary spectacle" and a "bizarre chase," television and newspaper reporters gave a voice to these spectators (Berman and Goldman 1994; Pringle and Morgan 1994).

Although viewers of the Simpson chase may not have immediately related their discussions to matters of public policy, the debate surrounding the event soon had clear political implications. For example, an African American woman interviewed the night of the chase stated, "Everybody said that he killed two people. How do they know that the police and the D.A. didn't make all this evidence up to make him act the way he's acting?"[19] In other words, long before the revelations concerning the racism of Mark Fuhrman, this woman constructed Simpson's arrest and, even more specifically, the chase—"the way he's acting"—into a narrative about police harassment. Because of the "bizarre" nature of the event, residents of the city who usually are ignored by the mainstream media were given a voice, albeit a limited one. Furthermore, this viewpoint was radically different from that constructed by the dominant media, which viewed his drive as an attempt to escape arrest. Front-page headlines in the Los Angeles Times and San Diego Union Tribune read, "LAPD Criticized for Leniency in Handling Case" and "LAPD, DA take heat on actions," emphasizing what some viewed as the lenient treatment by the Los Angeles Police Department (Ferrel and Malnic 1994; Holland 1994).

Implicit in the question above—"How do they know that the police and the D.A. didn't make all this evidence up?"—is a view of the criminal justice system that can be linked to a view of the freeway as similarly unjust. That is, for people of color, the freeway can be a place of danger rather than a place of safety. The same isolation that is a refuge for drivers can be hazardous for those who are pulled over: because of their disconnection from people driving by at high speeds, they are vulnerable to harassment. The beating of Rodney King was only the most publicized example of the common harassment experienced by black men (Meeks 2000).

The multiple high-speed chases of undocumented immigrants in Southern California provide another example of how the freeway can mean something very different for people of color. For all people with a dark complexion, driving from San Diego to Los Angeles on the freeway involves at minimum a regular delay as they are stopped at checkpoints along the freeway and asked to open their trunks (Sanchez 2000). But for the undocumented, it can be a space of terror as they try to avoid the border patrol. Between 1993 and 2005, seventy-five died and more than five hundred were injured in accidents that resulted from Border Patrol agents chasing suspected undocumented immigrants (Arner and Gross 2005). Like Rodney King, these immigrants may have been motivated to flee from fear of being harassed and possibly beaten after they are pulled to the side of the road. The reality of this torment was exposed to a broad audience on April 1, 1996, when a television news crew on a helicopter recorded the attack on two immigrants alongside the Pomona Freeway in Riverside County. This incident reaffirms how the freeway can work as a public space, bringing visibility to those traditionally excluded from the dominant media. A protest following the beating drew six thousand in Los Angeles and received broad media coverage (Associated Press 1996).

The response to accidents during Border Patrol chases highlights the different meanings the freeway can hold for whites and people of color. Because Latinos/as have experienced abuse by the Border Patrol and police, they often blame overly aggressive tactics for the accidents (Vargo 2002), while whites often blame the immigrants and smugglers. In July 2003 thirty residents of San Diego's East County held a protest demanding that a barrier be constructed to prevent smugglers from driving the wrong way on Interstate 8 to avoid the border patrol checkpoint (Jackson 2003). While concerned about preventing deaths caused by wrong-way driving, these residents seemed to have little interest in the way increased militarization of the border forces immigrants to take ever-greater risks on the highway. Shamefully, since 1997 almost four hundred a year have died in remote parts of Arizona and California, but these deaths are of little concern since they have no impact on the freeway driver's safety (Broder 2005).

The freeway's connection to the media in the televised Riverside County immigrant beatings at least temporarily provided visibility to an oppositional narrative surrounding the freeway—a narrative exposing the struggles of poor people of color. However, the voices of challenge remain small among prevailing media images. Following the Riverside County incident, a *Los Angeles Times* article focused on the experience of the immigrants' flight from the police and included in-depth interviews (Boyer and Cox 1996). Likewise, the *San Diego Union Tribune* began a series following the plight of a Mexican family from the economic difficulties they faced in Mexico to their multiple attempts to cross the border (Lindquist 1996a, 1996b). Still, the dominant construction of immigrants being chased on the freeway remained one of blaming them for their problems and reiterating their "illegal" status (Callahan and Petrillo 1996; Leffert 1996; Webb 1996).[20]

Not only does the dominant discourse surrounding the freeway receive more space in the media—ultimately this viewpoint has greater influence on public policy. Despite ongoing debate over the treatment of undocumented immigrants after they arrive in the United States, few politicians challenged the increased militarization of the border instituted in late 1994 that is now responsible for more than a thousand deaths.[21]

Another element of the traditional public sphere is the ability of members to influence outcomes in the issues they debate. Undocumented immigrants' exclusion from the dominant media forums assures them little if any political influence over decisions that affect them. Although African Americans are more likely to have voting rights, their limited voice in the major media also corresponds to little political influence, especially at the national level.

THE CONTENT OF URBAN FORM

The contrasting experiences that whites and people of color have on freeways translate into different political attitudes. The experiences of whites underlie the popular support for stronger penalties to fight crime. The experiences of people of color lead to a deep belief in the continuing injustices of government institutions. These contrasting attitudes are expressed through multiple forums, from talk radio to rap music, but the expressions remain largely segregated. This segregation has a hierarchy, both in how far the forums reach and in how much economic and political power members of the forum or public have.

The segregation of these publics roughly parallels the segregation of the suburbs and cities. The mostly white, middle-class suburban residents who may hold forums for discussion among themselves rarely have the benefit of dialogue with the black and Latino/a residents of segregated urban neighborhoods. Interpretations of the Simpson event underscore the segregation of opinion: a poll taken soon after the chase found that while 77 percent of whites believed Simpson should stand trial, only one-third of blacks believed he should (Associated Press 1994).

While Morse (1990) perhaps overemphasizes the passivity of contemporary freeway drivers and the isolation of individual experience around the freeway, the social interaction that she fails to see may ultimately have passive consequences. Because it is a largely segregated interaction, white suburbanites are hindered from recognizing the need for social change. While the freeway, in conjunction with television and radio, may at moments undermine this segregation by bringing usually excluded voices to a broad audience, the freeway, television, and radio also create a mediated forum for public discussion that facilitates this segregation.

This is not to romanticize a public sphere that existed before the development of contemporary media. Older mediated technologies—journals and newspapers—were and are segregated and exclusionary in terms of who may have their voices heard. Equally important, as Fraser (1992) and Warner (1992) point out, the construction of an ideal public sphere erases the social hierarchies that exist in actual public discussions. At the same time, the face-to-face contact that takes place in older cities and is prevented by the automobile has greater potential for dialogue across publics. This is not because there is more hope of eliminating inequalities; rather it is simply because the contact that takes place in common space is more random and less selective.

While the voices that can be heard on television or radio are very limited, simply sharing a space with other people means having access to that public forum. The Internet obviously dramatically increases the number of voices to be heard as well as the opportunity to express oneself, but Cass Sunstein (2002) shows that even the Internet remains highly segregated. Within the space of a public bus, which people of diverse social backgrounds must share, there is a potential for discussion among geographically segregated groups. Obviously, this potential might not become actualized, but it is significant that it is seriously reduced by the automobile and freeway.

Finally, urban transportation forms have material consequences in the ways they shape everyday understandings of the world. Wolfgang Schivelbusch (1986) describes how rail travel worked subtly to condition the body to approach the world in multiple new ways.[22] Similarly, Morse's (1990) essay is perceptive in articulating the impact freeway driving has on everyday experience. But while Morse emphasizes the freeway's erasure of texts, I wish to assert that local stories are everywhere and are always being read into urban space. The urban landscape is continually reminding those who pass through it of personal and public narratives. A particular park or parks in general can symbolize family picnics and childhood recreation or homelessness and "perversion," and each of these symbols is an element in multiple discourses about the city, contemporary politics, race, and so forth. Thus, while the freeway may foster a distracted experience of everyday life, it is also a symbol of isolation and isolatability, images that further shape the driving experience but that also, by fitting readily into racialized stories of the city, have consequences for popular politics. The challenge for those of us who wish to struggle against dominant narratives that blame urban poverty on "declining cultural mores" is to fill the landscape with rich historical narratives undermining the innocence of urban forms.

EPILOGUE

When I began thinking about the impact of transportation on urban space, I had an ideal vision of how cities should be designed. I missed the easy accessibility of Hyde Park in Chicago, where I recall Friday nights walking down the streets listening for sounds of celebration coming from apartments usually open to strangers. I had also just returned from visiting Paris during the 1991 conflict in the Middle East. There I participated in a demonstration of more than 100,000 people: a demonstration I saw facilitated by the Paris Metro. These memories contrasted dramatically with the discomfort I felt walking across roads six lanes wide and shopping at the ubiquitous Southern California strip mall.

This study has been very critical of the automobile-centered design of American cities, and I am sympathetic to scholars who critique this design as having an adverse impact on social activism. Dolores Hayden (2002) is cited for her suggestion that the automobile and suburbanization encouraged the working class to invest their time in consumption rather than political activism. Andrew Feenberg (1980: 122) develops this argument further by pointing to the parallel impact of physical dispersion encouraged by the automobile:

In an earlier period, when Engels, for example, was writing about these matters, workers were concentrated in urban centers invested by tradition with great public, symbolic significance. Workers could mobilize rapidly to seize these centers in great political actions, and the habit of mobilization was itself acquired in frequent labor struggles. The dispersed workers of contemporary American society, scattered through endless "bedroom communities," organized by institutionalized unions that discourage mobilization in any form, find it much more difficult to imagine and engage in political action.

In a similar vein, I note how the progressivism that inspired transportation projects revealed a desire to check the power of urban immigrants.

Although those who planned new highways did not necessarily intend to facilitate social division, the construction of freeways at minimum solidified existing divisions. Added to the continuing segregation based on race is the dramatic differentiation of neighborhoods based on income. Suburban developments with requirements for large lots exclude the poor and working class (Judd 1988: 184).

Yet, despite my critique of automobile-based planning and my enthusiasm for pedestrian-friendly cities, my point has not been to advance an alternative. Rather than critique different visions of the city from the position of a more ideal model, my point has been to show how all urban plans are entangled in narratives about the modern city and its problems. Solutions to these problems involve much more than creating transportation alternatives. Despite the failings of its subway system, New York is a city where people of very diverse backgrounds intermingle when they use public transportation. Although this may offer opportunities for public interaction that the freeway-dominated city cannot, these opportunities by no means inevitably lead to a harmonizing dialogue. Moreover, neighborhoods in New York can be highly segregated, and the city does not lack its share of racially motivated violence.

The barriers to those who would try to solve the problems of urban America through design are revealed in the movement for a New Urbanism. This movement, which became popular among architects and planners in the 1990s, calls for cities to be less dependent on the automobile. Its origins can be traced to the early 1980s when architects Andres Duany and Elizabeth Plater-Zyberk designed the "neotraditional" town of Seaside, Florida, with narrow, pedestrian-friendly streets that lead to a town square. Design features such as white picket fences and a band shell evoke the image of a historic town (Fulton 1996: 11).

Later in the decade, a group of architects and designers on the West Coast began promoting similar alternatives to standard suburban developments, with the significant addition of mass transit. In his 1993 book *The Next American Metropolis*, Peter Calthorpe, a leader of this West Coast group, calls for transit-oriented developments (TODs) and pedestrian-oriented developments (PODs). The first Congress for the New Urbanism met in 1993 to debate various ways to challenge traditional suburban development and in 1996 drafted a charter to express common principles. Among the principles are that "communities should be designed for the pedestrian and transit as well as the car" and that "neighborhoods should be diverse in use and population" (Leccese and McCormick 2000: vi). This entailed mixing commercial and residential buildings, integrating apartments with single-family homes, and making parks or other places for recreation easily accessible by foot. Besides reducing the reliance on automobiles, New Urbanists hoped their plans would foster strong communities and active citizens: "We are committed to reestablishing the relationship between the art of building and the making of community, through citizen-based participatory planning and design" (ibid.).

Skeptics of New Urbanism point out that representative projects such as Laguna West, California, and Kentlands, Maryland, are on the urban periphery. Thus, they are suburban developments with merely the façade of a town, and they extend rather than reduce the problem of sprawl (Hall 2003: 44). Equally significant, many of these developments are more expensive than traditional suburban housing, so they create income-segregated neighborhoods and reduce social contact among diverse groups (Fulton 1996: 20).

Perhaps the most commonly used example of New Urbanism's failures is Celebration, Florida, a town developed by the Disney Corporation. Celebration was built on land purchased by Disney in 1965 when the commercial strip development surrounding Disneyland in Southern California inspired Walt Disney to purchase a much larger piece of land around his new theme park to prevent what he considered the ugly distractions of hotels and other ventures he could not control. Disney imagined that a city would be built in conjunction with his new theme park, but his vision was of a futuristic design similar to what became the adult-oriented amusement park EPCOT Center. EPCOT (Experimental Prototype Community of Tomorrow), not Celebration, was originally the name Disney gave to the town he planned (Findlay 1992: 110). Instead, Celebration is built according to many of the New Urbanism ideals. The town is troubling in part because, like other New Urbanist developments, only those with a high income can afford to live there (Marshall 2000: 27). But perhaps as disturbing is the lack of voice residents have in the city's management. Celebration is an unincorporated town: the Disney Corporation alone determines rules and service provisions. Despite this, the town has been very successful in attracting residents who want to build a "community" (Kroloff 1997).

Critics of Celebration characterize its community as one based on a desire for an imaginary past. Dean MacCannell (1999: 111) writes, "Clearly what is being sold is not a two-hour celluloid fantasy but an entire fantasy life." The irony, according to Alex Marshall (2000), is that while these residents idealize small-town values of the past, they have abandoned the citizen engagement associated with these towns by ceding control to Disney. On the other hand, Andrew Ross (1999) emphasizes, this is not solely an attribute of a Disney-built town. Most new developments are managed by homeowners associations that restrict certain rights, so collective property values are maintained.

What makes Celebration most like a theme park is its downtown, which is more like Disneyworld's Main Street than a functioning business district. According to Marshall (2000), the stores survive not on residents but on visitors to Disneyworld. In fact, because the shops cater more to tourists, residents do much of their shopping on the highway outside of town. Strangely enough, Disney had the opportunity to locate its offices downtown, but instead it built two large buildings along the highway entering the town (16). If Disney wanted to recreate a traditional urban neighborhood, rather than building a suburban development, it could have located its offices in central Orlando and supported renovation or new construction within the city. Marshall writes, "Orlando has dozens of gridded-street, urban and semiurban neighborhoods. Many have shopping streets within walking distance. Many are closer to where at least some of Celebration's residents work, in downtown Orlando. Why buy a thin, tepid version of what one supposedly desires at a far greater cost than the real thing?" (39).

The decision not to locate in Orlando reflects development ideals that can be traced to Disney's original shift from California to Florida. John Findlay (1992: 110) points out that the choice of Disney to "start from scratch" in planning his new city of EPCOT shows a desire to avoid the problems faced by U.S. cities. Although Celebration does not resemble Walt Disney's plan for EPCOT, the limits of the Disney Corporation's goals are consistent. Anaheim, California—where Disneyland is located—is a declining city increasingly marked by the problems of Los Angeles just to the north. The *San Diego Union-Tribune* reports that "gangs have staked out turf about one mile east and west of the park, and at least one sign pointing to Disneyland is marred with graffiti" (Rofe 1997). Significantly, not only did Disney avoid constructing a "new town" within an older city and thus avoid confronting the complex problems that plague urban America, its late-1990s expansion of Disneyland used highways to distance drivers from these problems. The state widened nine miles of freeway, doubling the number of lanes from six to twelve, and built an off-ramp that leads directly to the theme park, bypassing neighborhoods where Anaheim's urban poor live (Sloan 2001). Many of these urban poor are full-time employees of Disney (Schou 2001).

Neil Smith (1999: 202) describes New Urbanism as the other side to urban revanchism: "The revenge of the new urbanism is not the visceral revenge of New York streets and politics. It is a revenge hardwired into the institutional control of the landscape and it spatial location. Precisely in its escapism, the new urbanism posits geography as the means of revenge." By choosing a landscape designed like an older city, residents feel they are strengthening civic life, but by avoiding the complex reality of contemporary cities, they merely reaffirm their disengagement.

However, to criticize New Urbanism by using Celebration as an example misrepresents the movement. While developments like Celebration, Seaside, and Kentlands are often used to demonstrate New Urban design, they are better described as reflecting the "neotraditionalist" origins of the movement. In many ways these towns conflict with the principles of the 1996 charter, such as encouraging a balanced transportation system and neighborhood diversity.

Implementing New Urbanism, beyond incorporating historic-looking elements into a new suburban development, has proved difficult. In San Diego, Peter Calthorpe participated in planning a project near the expanding light-rail system but was forced to make significant concessions to traffic engineers and allow a major arterial road through its center (Weisberg 1994). Calthorpe's development in Laguna West also faced problems including elimination of the light-rail system around which construction was centered. Instead residents must rely on the freeway (Hall 2003: 45). Laguna West was also meant to have a mix of housing types, but more single-family homes were built, and prices are higher than in surrounding neighborhoods (Fulton 1996: 13).

Another important principle of the New Urbanism Charter involves "the restoration of existing urban centers and towns within coherent metropolitan regions" (Leccese and McCormick 2000: v), but encouraging infill development while restricting construction on the urban periphery has also faced resistance. Despite many proposals to limit sprawl in major metropolitan areas during the 1990s,[1] putting these proposals into practice has proved difficult (Hall 2003: 42). Resistance comes in part from homebuilders who are reluctant to market untested housing styles (Hall 2003: 46), and in some ways their concerns are warranted. One survey shows that few consumers would choose the narrow streets and higher densities associated with New Urbanism (Harney 1999). The resistance to density is an important reason that plans to restrict sprawl fail (Hall 2003: 46). Moreover, when middle-class projects are built within older cities, high fences and gates often keep residents segregated from surrounding neighborhoods (Torre 1999: 41).

Edward Blakely and Mary Gail Snyder, authors of *Fortress America* (1997), cite estimates that "eight out of every ten new urban projects are gated" (7). In short, the difficulty of implementing New Urbanist ideals returns us to the continuing desire on the part of many middle-class whites to live in segregated neighborhoods.[2]

In their book *Suburban Nation* (2000), Andres Duany, Elizabeth Plater-Zyberk, and Jeff Speck maintain that this desire for segregation is self-perpetuating: "The more homogenous and 'safe' the environment, the less understanding there is of all that is different, and the less concern for the world beyond the subdivision walls" (46). However, one must question whether urban designs can undermine deep-rooted prejudices. The challenges faced by New Urbanism make clear that ideal designs are best considered in conjunction with the social and historical context from which they emerge. Designs are a response to particular narrative constructions of the world, and their uneven or inconsistent implementation arises from struggles over these constructions.

If elements of New Urbanism are implemented, their impact on political and social change cannot be understood apart from other material conditions that enable people to survive on a daily basis and participate in social justice activism. One of these material conditions may be improved transportation plans that bring convenient and affordable public transportation, but many other conditions, such as housing, medical care and financial security, are equally important. Achieving a more equitable distribution of these resources cannot come from a singular strategy or design.

This is not to dismiss the value of imagining alternatives to our current metropolitan mess. Visions are certainly important in motivating the struggle for change, but they must be kept in check by the recognition that they are necessarily incomplete and unstable. Moreover, their instability allows them to be appropriated in various ways, some of which may prove to reaffirm the same or new forms of inequality, as clearly seems to be the case in Celebration's appropriation of New Urbanism. On the other hand, effective struggle may also emerge from unexpected places. Brenda Jo Bright (1995) describes how Latino/a youth in Los Angeles subvert the legacy of police surveillance by transforming their automobiles into works of art that are meant to be looked at. In short, rather than expecting professional planners to build a city that fosters greater equity, critical expressions of resistance should be encouraged wherever they are found.

In his list of principles to follow when combating fascism in everyday life, Michel Foucault writes, "Prefer what is positive and multiple, difference over uniformity, flows over unities, mobile arrangements over systems. Believe that what is productive is not sedentary but nomadic" (1983: xiii).[3] In this sense, rather than attempting to stabilize mobility, my goal has been to desta-bilize it—not to create stasis but to fuse movement with critical reflection. I think this is what Chuck D of Public Enemy has in mind when he urges, "Move as a team. Never move alone. But welcome to the Terrordome."

NOTES

INTRODUCTION

1. Dolores Hayden (2003: 249) notes that the U.S. Census classifies residency in ways that make enumerating the suburban population difficult, and this is true for social science classifications as well. Nonetheless, based on a 2002 survey it is clear that a majority of people in the United States now live in the suburbs. With regard to transportation, a 2001 National Household Travel Survey (U.S. Department of Transportation 2003) reveals that 87 percent of daily trips take place in personal vehicles and that the average driver spends fifty-five minutes a day behind the wheel.

2. This was manifested in a slightly different way after Hurricane Katrina hit New Orleans in 2005.

3. Detailed political and social histories have been written on single elements of the transportation infrastructure in the United States: Scott Bottles (1987) on the decline of Los Angeles rail cars; Clifton Hood (1993) on New York's subway; Mark Rose (1990) on the interstate highways. Others have focused on the changing goals of professional planners and their struggles with transportation engineers and politicians: Mark Foster's (1981) classic overview shows the prevalence of early planners' enthusiasm for the automobile; Donald Clifford Ellis (1990) wrote an exemplary intellectual history of the planners and other visionaries who first imagined the urban freeway. A few have written on the cultural expressions that urban transportation has inspired. Michael Brooks (1997) for the New York subway and David Brodsly (1983) for the Los Angeles freeways have made clear the complexity of meanings the built environment can have in daily life. At least two others have gone further and put together ambitious studies of the automobile that pursue in detail the political and professional as well as the cultural aspects of transportation in the city. Clay McShane (1994) focuses on the multilayered impact of the automobile in the early twentieth century, and James Flink (1988) assembles a broad history of the automobile's role in twentieth-century American life.

4. Eric Arnesen (1996: 44) records that "in 1886 alone, a year that earned the title the 'great upheaval,' roughly seven hundred thousand workers either went out on strike or were locked out by their employers." But the most dramatic example of violence was to come in 1894 when federal troops were sent in to break a strike of Pullman Railway car workers and thirty-four people were killed.

5. This loosely parallels Stuart Hall's (1980) notion of a dominant code in television. The dominant code is a product of professional goals, much as transportation planners design roads according to professional standards. Hall argues that some members of the television audience may produce a reading that corresponds directly with the dominant reading, but most will produce either a negotiated or oppositional reading. However, the physicality of the built environment makes contesting its use more difficult. Contesting the meanings associated with this built environment, on the other hand, is easier, and this ultimately can influence future plans for this environment.

1. THE TROLLEY, THE AUTOMOBILE, AND AUTONOMY

1. According to Steven Diner, "The rise of investigative journalism in the first decade of the century, with sensational exposés of government corruption and corporate greed, both reflected and advanced the political mood" (1998: 203).

2. Henry George in *Progress and Poverty* wrote, "The general intelligence, the general comfort, the active invention, the power of adaptation and assimilation, the free independent spirit, the energy and hopefulness that have marked our people, are not causes, but results—they have sprung from unfenced land" (quoted in Fairfield 1993: 22).

3. Urban "nature lovers" in fact believed that their connection to the city enabled a better appreciation of the country's beauty, since they knew the ugliness and problems of urban life. Schmitt (1990: 4) quotes Cornell University educator Liberty Bailey from 1901: "'It is becoming more and more apparent that the ideal life is that which combines something of the social and intellectual advantages of the city with the inspiration and peaceful joys of the country.'"

4. Ruth Schwartz Cowan (1997: 176–177) describes how new farm technologies in the nineteenth century increased productivity, pushing down the price of grain, which led to a crisis in agriculture and a reduced demand for laborers.

5. Alexander Saxton notes how Indian removal was legitimized with the argument that native peoples lacked the initiative to develop the "open" land: "'What good man', President Jackson asked the Congress in 1830, 'would prefer a country covered with forests and ranged by a few thousand savages, to our extensive Republic, studded with towns and prosperous farms . . . and filled with all the blessings of liberty, civilization and religion?'" (1990: 153).

6. Herbert Gutman (1976: 19–32) details the significant resistance of "first-generation factory workers" to restrictions placed on aspects of their traditional culture. These included prohibitions on drinking, many holiday celebrations, and socializing during work.

7. This remark is often misquoted as, "It is the people who hang to the strap who pay you big dividends," which implies that transit companies were exploiting

strap-hangers for profits. Paul Barrett (1983) argues that the actual quote indicates that crowded cars allowed not "big" dividends but a minimum profit that would allow dividends to be paid. In other words, Yerkes is stating the difficulty of operating mass transit for profit, which public policy throughout the first half of the twentieth century assumed was possible.

8. One method was to simply prevent new immigrants from coming to the United States. Roger Daniels (1990: 279) lists seven new immigration restrictions passed into law between 1903 and 1917, including a literacy requirement and a ban on "anarchists."

9. For example, boulevards that excluded streetcars and widened streets greatly increased the average speed of the automobile in the 1920s, but trolleys, still competing for space with the auto, increased their speed only slightly over this same period (Barrett 1983: 161).

10. Bottles writes, "The point is that America's present urban transportation system largely reflects choices made by the public itself. . . . After all, that is what one would expect in a democratic society" (1987: 249).

11. A central claim among proponents of municipal ownership in Chicago was that it would reduce fares, and in New York the political difficulty of challenging the five-cent fare is sometimes blamed for accelerating the deterioration of the subways (Barrett 1983: 33–34; Hood 1993: 220).

12. No better example of this can be found than in cities throughout the South that required blacks to sit in the back of the bus and give up their seats for white passengers.

2. TOWNLESS HIGHWAYS AND HIGHWAYLESS TOWNS

1. Mumford is in part reflecting on an impression from the nineteenth century that the frontier encouraged innovative thinking: "To smell this, taste this, and feel and climb and walk over this landscape, once untouched, like an unopened letter or a lover unkissed—who would not rise to meet the expectation of the land?" (1926: 116). But, as Alan Trachtenberg (1980) argues, Mumford was not calling for a return to the past; instead he wished to revitalize an aesthetic creativity found in American writers of the late nineteenth century that had been displaced by a purely instrumental creativity.

2. There are troubling parallels between Mumford's position and some of the more recent slow-growth movements. Mike Davis (1992: 159) argues that during the 1980s in Southern California many of these movements used environmentalist arguments but were primarily directed by homeowners concerned about maintaining exclusive neighborhoods.

3. THE BUILDING OF A SUPERHIGHWAY FUTURE AT THE NEW YORK WORLD'S FAIR

1. Moses's popularity also came from his role in bringing public works, parks in particular, into the city. In the 1930s, as parks commissioner, Moses supervised the building of 255 neighborhood playgrounds (Caro 1975: 509).

2. Although this element may appear to be the least feasible of Geddes's visions, traffic planners have experimented with similar technology on a section of Interstate 15 north of San Diego (Vartabedian 2001).

3. Mark Rose (1990) argues that while divisions existed over the funding and location of an interstate highway system, few challenged the idea that one should be built.

4. The structure also has strong similarities to Jeremy Bentham's panopticon. The driver is being watched but has no way to know how he is being monitored and cannot observe the observer. This encourages self-monitoring and self-disciplining of behavior. This self-discipline, as Michel Foucault (1979) points out, is fostered by institutions and mechanisms throughout modern society: the factory, the hospital, and the school. The self-discipline of the highway is aided today by mechanisms, including speed radar and helicopter cameras, not unlike what Geddes had envisioned.

5. It is important to note that cars do not completely eliminate transportation-related labor. Workers are still needed to build and maintain roads, build and maintain automobiles, police the roads, and so forth.

4. *FILM NOIR* AND THE HIDDEN VIOLENCE OF TRANSPORTATION IN LOS ANGELES

1. "Enlightenment is as totalitarian as any system. Its untruth does not consist in what its romantic enemies have always reproached it for: analytic method, return to elements, dissolution through reflective thought; but instead in the fact that for enlightenment the process is always decided from the start. When in mathematical procedure the unknown becomes the unknown of an equation, this marks it as the well-known even before the value is inserted" (Horkheimer and Adorno 1944/1989: 24).

2. According to Samuel P. Black Jr. and John Paul Rossi (2001), while the growth in car ownership was lucrative for the insurance industry, insurance was also important for the growth in car ownership. "By providing a degree of compensation for carnage wrought by the car, truck and bus, automobile insurance facilitated acceptance of the motor vehicle transportation system and became an important part of it" (50).

3. Phyllis even tells Neff that her husband beat her: "Walter, I don't want to kill him . . . Not even when he gets drunk and slaps my face" (Wilder and Chandler 1943: 29). If her husband is abusive, her motivation to kill him becomes more than simple greed.

4. Neff marks the date when he begins recording his memo.

5. Many of the French critics who helped define *film noir* describe the characterization of women in films like *Double Indemnity* as misogynistic (Palmer 1996). They regard Phyllis as an especially malicious femme fatale, as depicted by Jeffrey Meyers (2000: xiv): "Phyllis, completely evil and cold blooded, has destroyed a once-decent man." Frank Krutnik (1991: 64) argues that the femme fatale in *film noir* often serves as a "scapegoat" for the deeper anxieties men faced in postwar America: questions about their masculinity after their military experience, having to replace

women in the workplace, and returning to the role of husband and father. Feminist critics were the first to provide a more complex reading of the female characters in *noir* (Kaplan 1980). While acknowledging Phyllis's sinister characterization, Sylvia Harvey (1980: 31) also sees her role as a "violent assault on the conventional values of family life."

6. Perhaps no one wrote about this disappointment better than Nathanael West:

All their lives they had slaved at some kind of dull, heavy labor, behind desks and counters, in the fields and at tedious machines of all sorts, saving their pennies and dreaming of the leisure that would be theirs when they had enough. Finally that day came. . . . Where else should they go but California, the land of sunshine and oranges?

Once there, they discover that sunshine isn't enough. They get tired of oranges, even of avocado pears and passion fruit. (1939/1983: 192)

7. More recently, Walter Mosley has detailed the lives of African Americans in post–World War II Los Angeles in a series of mysteries centered on war veteran Easy Rollins. Like *If He Hollers Let Him Go*, these novels, beginning with *Devil in a Blue Dress* (1990)—adapted for film in 1995—connect the corruption and violence typically found in Los Angeles *noir* to racism.

8. In the original script, written by Raymond Chandler, Buzz does kill Johnny's wife, but the U.S. Navy forced a revision (Maceck 1988: 36).

9. As musician Johnny Otis (1993) recounts, Los Angeles police in the 1950s cracked down on dances he helped promote because white teenagers would dance with African American and Mexican American teenagers. This forced the musicians to move to El Monte, where their license was again revoked (60–61).

10. James Naremore (1998: 234–235) notes that despite the significance of blacks in the Los Angeles landscape as depicted by writers such as Raymond Chandler, Hollywood in the 1940s limited their roles in *films noirs* to avoid controversy.

11. Ironically, it was constructed at a time when Mexican residents of Los Angeles were being encouraged and sometimes forced to repatriate to Mexico (Sánchez 1993: 225).

12. *Sunset Boulevard* was not the only *film noir* to satirize the film industry. An equally dismal presentation of scriptwriting is found in Nicolas Ray's *In a Lonely Place* (1950). Dixon Steele, played by Humphrey Bogart, is an alcoholic scriptwriter whose alienation seems linked to the trite plots he must write. It also appears linked to the isolation characteristic of Los Angeles. Dixon seems to have little social life until beginning a doomed relationship with his equally estranged neighbor Laurel Grey (Gloria Grahame). As in other *films noirs*, the automobile seems to embody the character of this isolation. In one of the film's pivotal scenes, Dixon, in a moment of rage, drives his car recklessly through the curving roads of West Los Angeles and sideswipes another car. He immediately starts to brutally punch the other driver. This episode leads Laurel to fear Dixon and is the beginning of the end of their relationship.

13. Alternatively, Wilder was reported as saying, "Go shit in your hat" (Lally 1996: 202).

14. Making repairs themselves was also difficult for renters, as materials cost more within the ghetto. These conditions were compounded by poor zoning. Watts became a center for industrial dumping, and the Los Angeles sanitation department ignored the area as it became infested with vermin (Bass 1960: 95–113; De Graf 1962: 72–91).

5. STORIES OF THE MTA

1. Bloodworth was curator of Art en Route.

2. See Chapter 1 for a discussion of the early-twentieth-century politics of municipal ownership.

3. Wilson (1996) argues that while the City Beautiful movement may not have paid enough attention to the practical needs of urban residents, its success came through its ability to inspire a vision of organic and magnificent cities open to all.

4. Besides being monuments to the history and beauty of the city, subway plaques and mosaic designs had the purpose of enabling the large foreign-born population, many of whom could not read English, to more easily negotiate the subway stations (Stookey 1992: 17).

5. "Having been elected mayor in a bitter contest centered on the loyalty of his German and Irish supporters to the federal government, and perhaps reacting to the surging nativism that ultimately culminated in the immigration restrictions of the National Origins Act of 1924, Hylan was sensitive to the centralization of power" (Hood 1993: 196).

6. For example, Moses prevented planners of the Bronx-Whitestone Bridge and the Van Wyk Expressway from including space for the future construction of rapid transit, and he had bridges on the Long Island Parkway built too low for buses to drive beneath (Caro 1974: 518, 546, 903–908).

7. In 1951 this was the standard of living for a family of four established by the Federal Bureau of Labor Statistics (Caro 1975: 968).

8. For elaboration on the link between federal policy and the use of "dysfunctional" to label urban blacks see Kelley (1997).

9. Feuer was director of Arts for Transit.

10. Conway was MTA chairman.

11. LEE is a graffiti writer who painted this epitaph on a subway car in 1980.

12. Judd and Swanstrom (2002: 246–250) link the lack of a federal urban policy to the shift in political power, especially since the 1960s, from cities to suburbs.

13. For example, Gerald Horne (1995: 350–351) notes that the 1965 civil disturbance in Watts drew government aid to Los Angeles in the form of health, education, and job services but also inspired a backlash that led to the 1966 election of Ronald Reagan as California governor. Horne writes that Reagan linked the civil disturbances to the failure of government programs, and ultimately his view became dominant at the federal level (301). In response to the 1992 disorder in Los Angeles, President

George H. W. Bush blamed antipoverty programs of the 1960s for urban decline (Omi and Winant 1993: 98). While the federal government did allocate emergency aid to Los Angeles, Bush later vetoed a bill providing long-term assistance to cities (Judd and Swanstrom 2002: 241–242).

14. Austin (2001) finds that the prestige of simply "getting up" has varied over time and among writers. In the mid-1970s a group of writers emerged who placed emphasis on the style and size of the works. But even for them, the careful planning and skills to paint under dangerous conditions were highly valued.

15. Stewart (1991) makes many of these same points.

16. Davis (1992: 227) and Schiller (1989: 102) describe how corporate plazas have frequently replaced the open spaces of parks and city squares. Hannigan (1998: 129–148) finds that entertainment companies often profit more than cities when public-private collaborations are negotiated.

17. The same strategy is found in places like the "new" Times Square, which, Hannigan (1998: 73–74) contends, appeals to tourists based on its promise to provide the excitement of urban life while maintaining the familiarity of a suburban shopping mall.

18. Slovak, a computer operator who took the F train into Manhattan every day, was interviewed as part of a survey conducted by the *Daily News* on the conditions of the subway.

19. At one point Giuliani claimed that reducing benefits would improve the city by pushing out the poor; he later said the statement was misinterpreted (Conason 1995).

20. Rush Limbaugh's rise in popularity during the 1990s came in part from his ability to articulate a myth that white people's success came without assistance and black people's failures came because of it: "America was conceived as a land of opportunity, not because it offered the best government handouts, but because it was the only country in the world where you could create your own job. . . . Free-market economics alone will not solve the problems of our inner cities. . . . We must discourage the government from substituting itself for the father as the head of the household in our inner cities. The reason most people—rich and poor—do not commit crimes is simply because they know it is wrong to do so" (Limbaugh 1993: 285).

21. Duneier and Molotch (1999) describe the uncomfortable interactions between homeless black men and middle-class white women, which could explain popular support for stricter policing of homeless activities.

22. A survey of more than 348 articles in the *New York Times, Christian Science Monitor, Los Angeles Times, Washington Post,* and *Wall Street Journal* between February 1994 and February 1997 found that more than half the articles mentioning the New York subways concerned crime, accidents, fires, floods, or other signs of "disorder."

23. A report on the response to a 2003 subway fire found many shortcomings in disaster plans. Because the only exit at the York Street station was obscured by smoke, passengers had to be led 1,000 feet through the tunnel to an emergency exit (Luo 2004).

24. Like shopping malls, Times Square and other business improvement districts hire their own security, garbage collection, information, and cleaning services. They also have the ability to regulate design and signage to create the unified appearance of a mall (Hannigan 1998: 139–140).

25. A 2002 study found that three-quarters of station platforms had some problem with their signage (Donohue 2002b).

26. "In a homogenous locality it is exceedingly difficult to acquire the qualities of character and the skills needed to cope with human difference and situations of uncertainty; and in the absence of such skills and qualities it is all too easy to fear the other, simply for reason of being an-other—bizarre and different perhaps, but first and foremost unfamiliar, not-readily-comprehensible, not-fully-fathomed, unpredictable" (Bauman 1998: 47).

6. URBAN FREEWAY STORIES

1. Douglas Massey and Nancy Denton (1993: 67–74) show how African Americans who live in the suburbs remain highly segregated. For several excellent case studies see Bullard, Grisby, and Lee (1994). A study of the 2000 Census finds that "the average white person in metropolitan America lives in a neighborhood that is almost 83 percent white and only 7 percent black. In contrast, a typical black individual lives in a neighborhood that is only 33 percent white and as much as 54 percent black" (Lewis Mumford Center 2001).

2. Evidence of the desire to avoid the problem of contact with people of color on public transportation exists not just in the Jim Crow South, where blacks were forced to sit in the back of the bus, but also in Los Angeles, where the Pacific Electric streetcars refused to serve blacks until World War II required their labor for local industry (Collins 1980: 42).

3. This is according to testimony given on July 17, 1997, to the U.S. House Surface Transportation Subcommittee by David K. Willis, president and chief executive officer of AAA Foundation for Traffic Safety, and David F. Snyder, assistant general counsel of the American Insurance Association.

4. The fear of unusual dangers on the freeways can be contrasted to a comparatively low concern for the common driving accident. This low concern is indicated by the many people still reluctant to wear seat belts despite their proven role in saving lives. Much higher standards of safety are imposed on airplanes (Wald 1997). Of course, unlike airplane passengers, drivers may feel a sense of control that diminishes their fears of crashing. Moreover, because automobile accidents are so common and do not harm large numbers of people simultaneously, they rarely get the same publicity as plane crashes or deaths on public transit.

5. Mike Davis (1992) describes the high-tech militarization of the Los Angeles Police Department including helicopters equipped with infrared cameras and high-powered spotlights. Television has brought this intense police surveillance to viewers.

6. Margaret Crawford (1992: 22) writes of the shopping mall: "Architects manipulated space and light to achieve the density and bustle of the city downtown—to

create essentially a fantasy urbanism devoid of the city's negative aspects: weather, traffic, and poor people."

7. The driver being hijacked is African American. At first annoyed by the trouble caused him by the white officer, he eventually is endeared to him since, after all, this is a police emergency. Thus, the scene blindly mocks the history of police harassment of blacks in Los Angeles.

8. In the mid-1990s, when service was less reliable than today, a woman who was shot during an attempted carjacking sued her cellular phone company when her calls failed to connect (Hiltzik 1997).

9. The fact that the bus carries many people, meaning it is "mass" transit, is crucial in enabling the character played by Dennis Hopper to make his demands: if one person is rescued, he still can hold the rest of the people on the bus for ransom.

10. Thomas Dumm (1993: 191) writes, "There is less effort than ever to engage in the discipline of an earlier era, in what was once called 'rehabilitation'. . . . Once such a fundamental theological category as wickedness is reintroduced to provide a justification for the infliction of punishment on 'abnormal others,' the normalized community has moved into an ominous zone, where lives might collectively be condemned as wicked and eventually be taken, all in the name of justice."

11. Dumm (1993) makes a similar point, that this fear among suburban whites helps to explain the acquittal of the officers who beat Rodney King.

12. James Flink notes how the automobile encouraged the decline of local general stores due to the economies of scale and the free parking shopping centers could offer (1988: 155, 164–165).

13. Susan G. Davis (1988), Mary P. Ryan (1992), and Richard Sennett (1990) are just three of the scholars who have discussed the importance of the street for political protests throughout U.S. history.

14. Distraction, for Morse, involves the interplay between seeing the external world as real and seeing it as idealized. It thus requires a screen or a window to distance the viewer from the outside. At one level, the individual experiences himself or herself in the car, watching television, or in the mall, and at another level he or she experiences the horizon passing by in the car window, the world displayed on television, or the life embodied in the ownership of the various commodities displayed in the mall. "Distraction as a dual state of mind depends on an incomplete process of spatial and temporal separation and interiorization" (1990: 202). Morse builds on the duality of distraction to say that the experience of the self is not static but involves a mobile subjectivity. "Because the interior of the automobile is disconnected and set in the midst of a new kind of theater of derealized space, the experience of self-awareness in a here and now—becomes one of unanchored mobility" (204). In the car the experience of the "here and now" is at the same time the experience of movement. The mobile subject also implies freedom in terms of changing location and of social advancement. Both of these are embodied in the suburban lifestyle: the freeway makes living in the suburbs convenient, and moving to the suburbs can imply an improved social status. The subject also experiences movement in the shopping mall through the constant

change in product lines and in the continual changing and remodeling of department store interiors.

15. In her criticism of popular culture theorists like Ian Chambers, Morris (1990: 23–24) attacks the distraction hypothesis for failing to present a more complicated discussion of pop-culture texts: "Here, I want to suggest that an image of the subject of pop epistemology as casual and 'distracted' obliquely entails a revival of the figure that Andreas Huyssen, Tania Modleski, and Patrice Petro have described in various contexts as 'mass culture as woman' . . . a stylistic enactment of the 'popular' as essentially distracted, scanning the surface, and short on attention span, performs a retrieval, at the level of *enunciative* practice, of the thesis of 'cultural dopes.'"

16. To some extent talk radio appears to match Nicholas Garnham's (1992) prescription for bringing Habermas's Enlightenment project into the realm of the media, specifically by constructing "systems of democratic accountability integrated with media systems of matching scale that occupy the same social space as that over which economic or political decisions will impact" (371). However, for Garnham the use of American talk radio as a model is made problematic by the commercial status of most talk radio programs, since he sees commercial funding of the media constraining public debate. Critics of conservative talk radio programs echo this criticism by pointing to the corporate ownership of the media: "Corporate ownership and sponsorship of American broadcasting is a major factor behind the limited political spectrum among talk show hosts and pundits—a spectrum that seems to extend from GE to GM" (Rendall, Naureckas, and Cohen 1995: 115). Furthermore, although hosts like Rush Limbaugh claim to encourage diverse views, in reality the hosts screen out callers who disagree with their politics (100).

Some have argued that the Internet comes closer to an ideal public sphere precisely because, unlike broadcast media, the spectrum for posting messages is not limited. However, it should be noted that the ability to post on the Internet is far from universal. Not everyone has Internet access, let alone the necessary computer skills.

17. "Public spheres themselves are not spaces of zero-degree culture, equally hospitable to any possible form of cultural expression" (Fraser 1992: 126).

18. "In fact, the historiography of Ryan and others demonstrates that the bourgeois public was never *the* public. On the contrary, virtually contemporaneous with the bourgeois public there arose a host of competing counterpublics, including nationalist publics, popular peasant publics, elite women's publics, and working-class publics" (Fraser 1992: 116). Rap music is an excellent example of a contemporary alternative public sphere. Tricia Rose (1994: 17) writes that "rap music is also Black American TV, a public and highly accessible place, where black meanings and perspectives—even as they are manipulated by corporate concerns—can be shared and validated among black people."

19. KABC, Los Angeles, June 17, 1994.

20. Border Patrol agents were given significant space in *Union Tribune* articles on the "border saga," and they were quick to blame the Mexican smugglers, calling them "parasites" and "villains" (Callahan and Petrillo 1996; Webb 1996).

21. While Republican former governor Pete Wilson supported Proposition 187, which denied medical aid and education to undocumented workers, and Democratic Senator Diane Feinstein opposed it (Yoachum and Sandalow 1994), both favored increasing the amount spent on stopping undocumented migrants from crossing the border (Gunnison 1995; *San Francisco Chronicle* 1993).

22. Schivelbusch (1986) writes: "To adapt to the conditions of rail travel, a process of deconcentration, or dispersal of attention, took place in reading as well as in the traveler's perception of the landscape outside" (69).

EPILOGUE

1. In the 1998 elections, 240 local measures addressed the need to preserve open space and control growth. Voters approved 173 of these measures (Hogan 1999).

2. Racial segregation in major metropolitan areas declined only slightly between 1990 and 2000, and it actually increased among children (Lewis Mumford Center 2001). Over the same period, the segregation of Latinos and Asians, the fastest-growing nonwhite populations, significantly increased (Fields and Herndon 2001).

3. Foucault's principles are listed in the preface to Gilles Deleuze and Felix Guattari's 1983 *Anti-Oedipus: Capitalism and Schizophrenia,* which Foucault calls "An Introduction to the Non-Fascist Life."

WORKS CITED

Abu-Lughod, Janet L. 1999. *New York, Chicago, Los Angeles: America's Global Cities*. Minneapolis: University of Minnesota Press.

Adler, Jerry. 1997. "'Road Rage': We're Driven to Destruction." *Newsweek*, June 2, p. 70.

Adorno, Theodor W. 1938/1988. "On The Fetish-Character. In Music and the Regression of Listening." Reproduced in *The Frankfurt School Reader*, ed. Andrew Arato and Eike Gebhart. New York: Continuum.

———. 1945. "A Social Critique of Radio Music." *Kenyon Review* 7 (2): 208–217.

———. 1951/1984. *Minima Moralia: Reflections from a Damaged Life*. Reprint, New York: Verso.

Aguirre, Adalberto, and David Baker. 1994. "Racial Prejudice and the Death Penalty: A Research Note." *Social Justice* 20 (1–2): 150–155.

Alexander, Max. 1989. "Art in the Underground." *Art in America*, December, p. 35.

Allen, Jane. 1996. "2 named in L.A. freeway attacks." *San Diego Union-Tribune*, October 11.

American Automobile Association (AAA) Foundation for Traffic Safety. 1998. *Aggressive Driving: Three Studies*. AAA Foundation for Traffic Safety.

American Public Transportation Association. 2003. "Percentage Workers Using Public Transportation in Urbanized Areas over 1,000,000 Population, 2000." At http://www.apta.com/research/stats/ridership.

Anderson, Benedict. 1991. *Imagined Communities: Reflections on the Origin and Spread of Nationalism*. Rev. ed. New York: Verso.

Anderson, Roger. 1995. "Profile of a Visionary: Interview with Roger Anderson." Interview by Vikki Sanders in *Remember Rondo: A Tradition of Excellence*, ed. Vikki Sanders. St. Paul, Minn.: Remember Rondo Committee.

Arner, Mark, and Gregory Alan Gross. 2005. "Toll at 5 in Fatal Collision on Route 94." *San Diego Union-Tribune,* July 2.

Arnesen, Eric. 1996. "American Workers and the Labor Movement in the Late Nineteenth Century." In *The Gilded Age: Essays on the Origins of Modern America,* ed. Charles W. Calhoun. Wilmington, Del.: Scholarly Resources Books.

Associated Press. 1994. "O.J. Poll—Study in Black and White." Reproduced in *San Diego Union Tribune,* July 10.

———. 1996. "6,000 in L.A. Protest Video Beatings." Reproduced in *San Diego Union Tribune,* April 7.

Austin, Joe. 2001. *Taking the Train: How Graffiti Art Became an Urban Crisis in New York City.* New York: Columbia University Press.

Avila, Eric. 2004. *Popular Culture in the Age of White Flight: Fear and Fantasy in Suburban Los Angeles.* Berkeley: University of California Press.

Barrett, Paul. 1983. *The Automobile and Urban Transit: The Formation of Public Policy in Chicago, 1900–1930.* Philadelphia: Temple University Press.

Barry, Dan. 1998. "The Inauguration of Rudolph W. Giuliani." *New York Times,* January 2.

Barth, Gunther. 1980. *City People: The Rise of Modern City Culture in Nineteenth-century America.* New York: Oxford University Press.

Bass, Charlotta A. 1960. *Forty Years: Memoirs from the Pages of a Newspaper.* Los Angeles: Charlotta Bass.

Bauman, Zygmunt. 1998. *Globalization: The Human Consequences, European Perspectives.* New York: Columbia University Press.

Beauregard, Robert A. 2003. *Voices of Decline: The Postwar Fate of U.S. Cities.* 2d ed. New York: Routledge.

Beckett, Katherine, and Theodore Sasson. 2000. *The Politics of Injustice: Crime and Punishment in America.* Thousand Oaks, Calif.: Pine Forge Press.

Bellamy, Edward. 1888/1996. *Looking Backward, 2000–1887.* New York: Signet Classic.

Benjamin, Walter. 1955/1969. *Illuminations.* New York: Schocken.

Berman, Art, and John J. Goldman. 1994. "Nation Transfixed by Extraordinary Spectacle." *Los Angeles Times,* June 18.

Bernstein, Nina. 2001. "Homeless Shelters in New York Fill to Highest Level since 80's." *New York Times,* February 8.

Black, John. 1939. "At The Fair II." In *Songs of the World's Fair.* Boston: Bruce Humphries.

Black, Samuel P., and John Paul Rossi. 2001. *Entrepreneurship and Innovation in Automobile Insurance: Samuel P. Black, Jr. and the Rise of Erie Insurance, 1923–1961.* Studies in Entrepreneurship. New York: Routledge.

Blakely, Edward James, and Mary Gail Snyder. 1997. *Fortress America: Gated Communities in the United States.* Washington, D.C.: Brookings Institution Press.

Bodnar, John, Michael Weber, and Roger Simon. 1988. "Migration, Kinship, and Urban Adjustment: Blacks and Poles in Pittsburgh, 1900–30." In *The Making of Urban America*, ed. R. A. Mohl. Wilmington, Del.: Scholarly Resources.

Boston Globe. 2000. "Calling for Help on the T." February 3.

Bottles, Scott L. 1987. *Los Angeles and the Automobile: The Making of the Modern City*. Berkeley: University of California Press.

Boyer, Edward, and John Cox. 1996. "Migrants Tell of Harrowing Flight from Authorities." *Los Angeles Times*, April 5.

Brackett, Charles, Billy Wilder, and D. M. Marshman. 1949. *Sunset Boulevard*. Script. Hollywood: Script City.

Brecher, Charles, and Raymond Horton. 1991. "The Public Sector." In *Dual City: Restructuring New York*, ed. John Mollenkopf and Manuel Castells. New York: Russell Sage Foundation.

Bright, Brenda Jo. 1995. "Remappings: Los Angeles Low Riders." In *Looking High and Low: Art and Cultural Identity*, ed. Brenda Jo Bright and Liza Bakewell. Tucson: University of Arizona Press.

Broder, John M. 2005. "With Congress's Blessing, a Border Fence May Finally Push Through to the Sea." *New York Times*, July 4.

Brodsly, David. 1983. *Los Angeles Freeway: An Appreciative Essay*. Berkeley: University of California Press.

Brooks, Michael W. 1997. *Subway City: Riding the Trains, Reading New York*. New Brunswick, N.J.: Rutgers University Press.

Bullard, Robert D., Eugene J. Grisby, and Charles Lee, eds. 1994. *Residential Apartheid: The American Legacy*. Los Angeles: CAAS Publications.

Business Week. 1939. "Motoring at 100 M.P.H." September 29, pp. 27–28.

Cain, James M. 1936/1978. *Double Indemnity*. Reprint, New York: Vintage Books.

Callahan, Bill, and Lisa Petrillo. 1996. "7 Immigrants Killed in Wreck." *San Diego Union-Tribune*, April 7.

Calthorpe, Peter. 1993. *The Next American Metropolis: Ecology, Community, and the American Dream*. New York: Princeton Architectural Press.

Canedy, Dana. 1997. "Subways Fail to Lure Many Upscale Ads." *New York Times*, January 28.

Carey, James W. 1989. *Communication as Culture: Essays on Media and Society*. Boston: Unwin Hyman.

Caro, Robert. 1975. *The Power Broker: Robert Moses and the Fall of New York*. New York: Vintage Books.

Castells, Manuel. 1989. *The Informational City: Information Technology, Economic Restructuring, and the Urban-Regional Process*. Oxford, England: Blackwell.

Castleman, Craig. 1982. *Getting Up: Subway Graffiti in New York*: Cambridge, Mass.: MIT Press.

Chalfant, Henry, and James Prigoff. 1987. *Spraycan Art*. New York: Thames and Hudson.

Chan, Sewell. 2004. "M.T.A. Raising Fares and Tolls in Early March." *New York Times*, December 17.

————. 2005. "M.T.A. Picks an Agent to Market Sponsorships." *New York Times*, January 28.

Chandler, Trevor. 1998. "It's Not Too Late to Realize: MARTA's the Only Way to Go." Letter. *Atlanta Journal-Constitution*, May 12.

Cohen, Barbara, Steven Heller, and Seymour Chwast. 1989. *Trylon and Perisphere: The 1939 New York World's Fair*. New York: Abrams.

Cohen, Lizabeth. 1990. *Making a New Deal: Industrial Workers in Chicago, 1919–1939*. New York: Cambridge University Press.

Cohen, Stanley. 1973. "Property Destruction: Motives and Meanings." In *Vandalism*, ed. Colin Ward. New York: Van Nostrand Reinhold.

Collins, Keith E. 1980. *Black Los Angeles: The Maturing of the Ghetto, 1940–1950*. Saratoga, Calif.: Century Twenty One.

Conason, Joe. 1995. "Police Mayor in FIRE City." *Nation*, December 18, p. 21.

Cooper, Martha, and Henry Chalfant. 1984. *Subway Art*. New York: Holt, Rinehart and Winston.

Cowan, Ruth Schwartz. 1983. *More Work for Mother: The Ironies of Household Technology from the Open Hearth to the Microwave*. New York: Basic Books.

————. 1997. *A Social History of American Technology*. New York: Oxford University Press.

Crawford, Margaret. 1992. "The World in a Shopping Mall." In *Variations on a Theme Park: The New American City and the End of Public Space*, ed. Michael Sorkin. New York: Noonday Press.

Crenshaw, Kimberlé Williams. 1997. "Color-Blind Dreams and Racial Nightmares: Reconfiguring Racism in the Post–Civil Rights Era." In *Birth of a Nation'hood: Gaze, Script, and Spectacle in the O. J. Simpson Case*, ed. Toni Morrison and Claudia Brodsky Lacour. New York: Pantheon Books.

Crider, John H. 1939. "Sloan Stresses Profit Incentive." *New York Times*, May 19.

Cronin, Thomas E., Tania Z. Cronin, and Michael E. Milakovich. 1981. *U.S. v. Crime in the Streets*. Bloomington: Indiana University Press.

Cusker, Joseph P. 1980. "The World of Tomorrow: Science, Culture, and Community at the New York World's Fair." In *Dawn of A New Day: The New York World's Fair, 1939/40*, Helen Harrison. New York: New York University Press.

Czitrom, Daniel. 1991. "Underworlds and Underdogs: Big Tim Sullivan and Metropolitan Politics in New York 1889–1913." *Journal of American History* 78 (September): 536–558.

Daniels, Roger. 1990. *Coming to America: A History of Immigration and Ethnicity in American Life*. New York: HarperCollins.

Davis, Mike. 1988. "Urban Renaissance and the Spirit of Postmodernism." In *Postmodernism and Its Discontents: Theories, Practices*, ed. E. Ann Kaplan. New York: Verso.

————. 1992. *City of Quartz: Excavating the Future in Los Angeles*. New York: Vintage.

Davis, Susan G. 1988. *Parades and Power: Street Theatre in Nineteenth-Century Philadelphia*. Berkeley: University of California Press.

de Certeau, Michel. 1984. *The Practice of Everyday Life*. Berkeley: University of California Press.

De Graf, Lawrence Brooks. 1962. "Negro Migration to Los Angeles, 1930 to 1950." PhD diss., University of California, Los Angeles.

Delany, Samuel. 1999. ". . . Three, Two, One, Contact: Times Square Red, 1998." In *Giving Ground: The Politics of Propinquity*, ed. Joan Copjec and Michael Sorkin. London: Verso.

De Lollis, Barbara. 2001. "Half of Prisoners Are Black." *Cincinnati Enquirer*, June 30.

Deutsch, Sarah Jane. 2000. "From Ballots to Breadlines: 1920–1940." In *No Small Courage: A History of Women in the United States*, ed. N. F. Cott. Oxford, England: Oxford University Press.

Diner, Steven J. 1998. *A Very Different Age: Americans of the Progressive Era*. New York: Hill and Wang.

Doctorow, E. L. 1985. *World's Fair*. New York: Fawcett Crest.

Dodson, Donald. 1996. "Improve Bus Service Now." Letter. *Austin American-Statesman*, September 28.

Dollar, Steve. 2005. "Art Review, Celebrating 20 Years of the City's Underground." *Newsday*, July 8.

Donohue, Pete. 2002a. "Homeless Travel Subways All Night Rather than Stay in Shelters." *New York Daily News*, October 19.

———. 2002b. "Subway Signs a Rail Pain." *New York Daily News*, September 5.

———. 2005. "Subway's a Real Grime Scene." *New York Daily News*, April 22.

Duany, Andres, Elizabeth Plater-Zyberk, and Jeff Speck. 2000. *Suburban Nation: The Rise of Sprawl and the Decline of the American Dream*. New York: North Point Press.

Duffy, Earle. 1931. "This Motor Ache: An Article on the Cure for Traffic Congestion." *Outlook and Independent*, August 19, 491–493.

Dumm, Thomas L. 1993. "The New Enclosures: Racism in the Normalized Community." In *Reading Rodney King: Reading Urban Uprising*, ed. Robert Gooding-Williams. New York: Routledge.

Duneier, Mitchell, and Harvey Molotch. 1999. "Talking City Trouble: Interactional Vandalism, Social Inequality, and the 'Urban Interaction Problem.'" *American Journal of Sociology* 104 (5): 1263–1295.

Dwyer, Jim. 1991. *Subway Lives: 24 Hours in the Life of the New York Subway*. New York: Crown.

Dykstra, Clarence A. 1940. "The Future of Los Angeles." In *Los Angeles: Preface to a Master Plan*, ed. George William Robbins and Leon Deming Tilton. Los Angeles: Pacific Southwest Academy.

East, E. E. 1940. "Streets: The Circulatory System." In *Los Angeles: Preface to a Master Plan*, ed. George William Robbins and Leon Deming Tilton. Los Angeles: Pacific Southwest Academy.

Edsall, Thomas, and Mary Edsall. 1991. *Chain Reaction: The Impact of Race, Rights, and Taxes on American Politics*. New York: W. W. Norton.

Ellis, Clifford Donald. 1990. "Visions of Urban Freeways, 1930–1970." PhD diss., University of California, Los Angeles.

Elvey, Maggie, Grover Trask, and Richard Tefank. 2000. *Argument in Favor of Proposition 21. Juvenile Crime. Initiative Statute.* Ballot pamphlet for primary election 2000. California Secretary of State.

Fairfield, John D. 1993. *The Mysteries of the Great City: The Politics of Urban Design, 1877–1937.* Columbus: Ohio University Press.

Faison, Seth. 1993. "Gunman Kills 5 on L.I.R.R. Train." *New York Times,* December 8.

Feenberg, Andrew. 1980. "The Political Economy of Social Space." In *The Myths of Information: Technology and Postindustrial Culture,* ed. Kathleen Woodward. Madison, Wisc.: Coda Press.

Feldman, Allen. 2001. "Philoctetes Revisited: White Public Space and the Political Geography of Public Safety." *Social Text* 19 (3): 57–89.

Ferguson, Andrew. 1998. "Road Rage: Aggressive Driving Becomes Social Problem." *Time,* January 12, p. 64.

Ferrel, David, and Eric Malnic. 1994. "LAPD Criticized for Leniency in Handling Case." *Los Angeles Times,* June 18.

Fields, Robin, and Ray Herndon. 2001. "Census Fuels Debate over Integration; Demographics." *Los Angeles Times,* June 24.

Findlay, John M. 1992. *Magic Lands: Western Cityscapes and American Culture After 1940.* Berkeley: University of California Press.

Fischler, Stanley I. 1979. *Moving Millions: An Inside Look at Mass Transit.* New York: Harper and Row.

Fishman, Robert. 1987. *Bourgeois Utopias: The Rise and Fall of Suburbia.* New York: Basic Books.

Fiske, John. 1994. "Radical Shopping in Los Angeles: Race, Media and the Sphere of Consumption Media." *Media, Culture and Society* 16, no. 3 (July): 469–486.

Flink, James. 1975. *The Car Culture.* Cambridge, Mass.: MIT Press.

———. 1988. *The Automobile Age.* Cambridge, Mass.: MIT Press.

Fogelson, Robert M. 1967/1993. *The Fragmented Metropolis: Los Angeles, 1850–1930.* Berkeley: University of California Press.

———. 2001. *Downtown: Its Rise and Fall: 1880–1950.* New Haven, Conn.: Yale University Press.

Ford, T. L. 1903. "Interurban Trolley as a Factor in Modern Life." *Overland Monthly,* November, 379–381.

Foster, Mark. 1981. *From Streetcar to Superhighway: American City Planners and Urban Transportation, 1900–1940.* Philadelphia: Temple University Press.

Foucault, Michel. 1979. *Discipline and Punish: The Birth of the Prison.* New York: Vintage Books.

———. 1983. Preface to *Anti-Oedipus: Capitalism and Schizophrenia,* by Gilles Deleuze and Felix Guattari. Minneapolis: University of Minnesota Press.

Fraser, Nancy. 1992. "Rethinking the Public Sphere: A Contribution to the Critique of Actually Existing Democracy." In *Habermas and the Public Sphere,* ed. Craig Calhoun. Cambridge, Mass.: MIT Press.

Fulton, William. 1996. *The New Urbanism: Hope or Hype for American Communities?.* Cambridge, Mass.: Lincoln Institute of Land Policy.

Garnham, Nicholas. 1992. "The Media and the Public Sphere." In *Habermas and the Public Sphere*, ed. Craig Calhoun. Cambridge, Mass.: MIT Press.

Garreau, Joel. 1992. *Edge City: Life on the New Frontier*. New York: Anchor Books.

Gebhard, David, and Harriete Von Breton. 1989. *Los Angeles in the Thirties: 1931–1941*. 2d ed. Los Angeles: Hennessey and Ingalls.

Geddes, Norman Bel. 1941. *Magic Motorways*. New York: Random House.

Gelernter, David. 1995. *1939: The Lost World of the Fair*. New York: Free Press.

Goddard, Stephen B. 1994. *Getting There: The Epic Struggle Between Road and Rail in the American Century*. New York: Basic Books.

Goldstein, Matthew. 1998. "Advertisers Jostle for Subway Space as Ridership Increases, Rules Loosen." *Crain's New York Business*, October 5, p. 23.

Gottdiener, Mark. 1994. *The Social Production of Urban Space*. 2d ed. Austin: University of Texas Press.

———. 2001. *The Theming of America: American Dreams, Media Fantasies, and Themed Environments*. 2d ed. Boulder, Colo.: Westview Press.

Gunn, David L. 1988. "Subway Returns to a State of Good Repair." *Developing Metros*, 7–9.

Gunnison, Robert B. 1995. "Wilson Says He'll Survive Maid Problem." *San Francisco Chronicle*, May 6.

Gutiérrez, David. 1995. *Walls and Mirrors: Mexican Americans, Mexican Immigrants, and the Politics of Ethnicity*. Berkeley: University of California Press.

Gutman, Herbert. 1976. *Work, Culture, and Society in Industrializing America: Essays in American Working-Class and Social History*. New York: Alfred A. Knopf.

Habermas, Jürgen. 1991. *The Structural Transformation of the Public Sphere: An Inquiry into a Category of Bourgeois Society*. Cambridge, Mass.: MIT Press.

———. 1992. "Further Reflections on the Public Sphere." In *Habermas and the Public Sphere*, ed. Craig Calhoun. Cambridge, Mass.: MIT Press.

Hadley, Jane. 2002. "Driver Tells County Council Security on Buses Is Too Lax." *Seattle Post-Intelligencer*, August 29.

Hall, Peter. 2003. "Smart Growth on Two Continents." In *Urban Villages and the Making of Communities*, ed. Peter Neal. London: Spon Press.

Hall, Stuart. 1980. "Encoding/Decoding." In *Culture, Media, Language*, ed. Stuart Hall, Dorothy Hobson, A. Lowe, and Paul Willis. London: Hutchinson.

Hannigan, John. 1998. *Fantasy City: Pleasure and Profit in the Postmodern Metropolis*. London: Routledge.

Harcourt, Bernard E. 1998. "Reflecting on the Subject: A Critique of the Social Influence Conception of Deterrence, the Broken Windows Theory, and Order-Maintenance Policing New York Style." *Michigan Law Review* 97 (2): 291–389.

Harding, Gardner. 1939. "World's Fair, New York." *Harper's Magazine*, July, 193–200.

Harney, Kenneth. 1999. "Buyer's Basic Preferences Often Not Those of Developer." *Washington Post*, June 5.

Harris, Peter Y. 1992. *New Yorker's Perception of Subway Service: Annual Citywide Survey*. New York: Metropolitan Transportation Authority.

Harris, Richard. 1991. "The Geography of Employment and Residence in New York Since 1950." In *Dual City: Restructuring New York*, ed. John Mollenkopf and Manuel Castells. New York: Russell Sage Foundation.

Harvey, David. 1989. *The Condition of Postmodernity: An Enquiry into the Origins of Cultural Change*. Oxford, England: Blackwell.

Harvey, Sylvia. 1980. "Woman's Place: The Absent Family of Film Noir." In *Women in Film Noir*, ed. E. Ann Kaplan. London: British Film Institute.

Hayden, Dolores. 1986. *Redesigning the American Dream: The Future of Housing Work and Family Life*. New York: W. W. Norton.

———. 2002. *Redesigning the American Dream: The Future of Housing Work and Family Life*. Rev. ed. New York: W. W. Norton.

———. 2003. *Building Suburbia: Green Fields and Urban Growth, 1820–2000*. New York: Pantheon Books.

Heard, Mary Betty. 1992. "Chancellor Complies with Two Demands After I-5 Is Occupied." *UCSD Guardian*, May 4.

Heller, Stephen. 1989. Prologue. In *Trylon and Perisphere: The 1939 New York World's Fair*, by Barbara Cohen, Steven Heller, and Seymour Chwast. New York: Harry N. Abrams.

Higham, John. 1963. *Strangers in the Land: Patterns of American Nativism, 1860–1925*. New York: Atheneum.

Hillis, Ken. 2005. "Film Noir and the American Dream: The Dark Side of Enlightenment." *Velvet Light Trap* 1 (55): 3–8.

Hiltzik, Michael A. 1997. "Cell Phones, 'Crime Fighters of the '90s,' Are Striking Out." *Los Angeles Times*, November 16.

Himes, Chester. 1945/1986. *If He Hollers Let Him Go*. New York: Thunder's Mouth Press.

Hirsch, Arnold R. 1983. *Making the Second Ghetto: Race and Housing in Chicago, 1940–1960*. Interdisciplinary Perspectives on Modern History. New York: Cambridge University Press.

Hise, Greg. 2004. "Border City: Race and Social Distance in Los Angeles." *American Quarterly* 3 (56): 545–558.

Hodgson, Godfrey. 1978. *America in Our Time*. New York: Vintage Books.

Hogan, Dave. 1999. "Oregon Democrat Pushes Livability into National Spotlight for Three Years." *Oregonian*, February 7.

Holland, Gale. 1994. "LAPD, DA Take Heat on Actions." *San Diego Union-Tribune*, June 18.

Holland, J. P. 1903. "The Future of the Automobile." *Munsey's Magazine*, May, 171–177.

Holston, James. 1989. *The Modernist City: An Anthropological Critique of Brasilia*. Chicago: University of Chicago Press.

Hood, Clifton. 1993. *722 Miles*. New York: Simon and Schuster.

Horkheimer, Max, and Theodor W. Adorno. 1944/1989. *Dialectic of Enlightenment*, trans. John Cumming. Reprint, New York: Continuum.

Horne, Gerald. 1995. *Fire This Time: The Watts Uprising and the 1960s.* Carter G. Woodson Institute Series in Black Studies. Charlottesville: University Press of Virginia.

Horwitz, Robert B. 1993. "Begging the Question: Consistency and Common Sense in the First Amendment Jurisprudence of Advertising and Begging." *Studies in Law, Politics, and Society* 13:213–247.

Howard, Ebenezer. 1898/1960. *Garden Cities of to-Morrow.* London: Faber and Faber.

Hull, Jon D. 1994. "Anger from the Grass Roots." *Time,* August 29, pp. 38–39.

Hyde, F. A. 1902. "Automobile Club of California." *Overland Monthly,* August, 97–103.

The Independent. 1901. "The Comforts of the Trolley." August 22, pp. 1995–1996.

———. 1902a. "Experiences of a Street Car Conductor." August 13, pp. 1920–1924.

———. 1902b. "Mission of the Trolley." June 5, pp. 1379–1380.

———. 1903a. "One More Revolution." May 14, pp. 1162–1163.

———. 1903b. "Steam Car to Trolley." April 30, pp. 1047–1048.

Jackson, Irene McCormack. 2003. "Barrier Takes Away Smugglers' Evasion Route." *San Diego Union-Tribune,* October 9.

Jackson, Kenneth. 1985. *Crabgrass Frontier: The Suburbanization of the United States.* New York: Oxford University Press.

Jacobs, Andrew. 1999. "Man Is Pushed in the Subway and Loses Legs." *New York Times,* April 29.

Jacobs, Bernard M. 1992. "Subway Security." *Mass Transit* 19, no. 7–8 (July/August): 45–47.

Jacobs, Jane. 1961. *The Death and Life of Great American Cities.* New York: Random House.

Jacobson, Matthew Frye. 1999. *Whiteness of a Different Color: European Immigrants and the Alchemy of Race.* Cambridge, Mass.: Harvard University Press.

Jakowitsch, Nancy, and Michelle Ernst. 2004. "Just Transportation in the 21st Century." In *Highway Robbery: Transportation Racism and New Routes to Equity,* ed. Robert D. Bullard, Glenn S. Johnson, and Angel O. Torres. Cambridge, Mass.: South End Press.

Johnson, L. H. 1902. "Anatomy of the Automobile." *Overland Monthly,* August, 163–170.

Johnston, Claire. 1980. "*Double Indemnity.*" In *Women in Film Noir,* ed. E. Ann Kaplan. London: British Film Institute.

Johnston, David, and Steven A. Holmes. 1994. "Experts Doubt Effectiveness of Crime Bill." *New York Times,* September 14.

Jones, Jacqueline. 1986. *Labor of Love, Labor of Sorrow: Black Women, Work, and the Family from Slavery to the Present.* New York: Vintage Books.

Judd, Dennis R. 1988. *The Politics of American Cities: Private Power and Public Policy.* 3d ed. New York: HarperCollins.

———. 1999. "Constructing the Tourist Bubble." In *The Tourist City*, ed. Dennis R. Judd and Susan S. Fainstein. New Haven, Conn.: Yale University Press.

Judd, Dennis R., and Susan S. Fainstein, eds. 1999. *The Tourist City*. New Haven, Conn.: Yale University Press.

Judd, Dennis R., and Todd Swanstrom. 2002. *City Politics: Private Power and Public Policy*. 3d ed. New York: Longman.

Jurca, Catherine. 2001. *White Diaspora: The Suburb and the Twentieth-Century American Novel*. Princeton, N.J.: Princeton University Press.

Kaplan, E. Ann, ed. 1980. *Women in Film Noir*. London: British Film Institute.

———. 1988. *Postmodernism and Its Discontents: Theories, Practices*. New York: Verso.

Kasarda, John D. 1992. "Urban Employment Change and Minority Skills Mismatch." In *Enduring Tensions in Urban Politics*, ed. Dennis Judd and Paul Kantor. New York: Macmillan.

Kasson, John F. 1978. *Amusing the Million: Coney Island at the Turn of the Century*. New York: Hill and Wang.

Kasun, Jacqueline Rorabeck. 1954. *Some Social Aspects of Business Cycles in the Los Angeles Area: 1920–1950*. Los Angeles: Haynes Foundation.

Kelley, Robin D. G. 1997. *Yo' Mama's Disfunktional! Fighting the Culture Wars in Urban America*. Boston: Beacon Press.

Kelling, George L. 1991. "Reclaiming the Subway." *NY: The City Journal* 1 (2): 17–28.

Kellner, Douglas. 1989. *Critical Theory, Marxism, and Modernity*. Baltimore: Johns Hopkins University Press.

Kelly, Mike. 2002. "For Commuters, a New Fear Underscores the New Reality." *Bergen County (N.J.) Record*, September 12.

Kennedy, Randy. 2002a. "Masses in Transit, to Anywhere but Work." *New York Times*, June 20.

———. 2002b. "Tunnel Vision." *New York Times*, June 11.

———. 2003. "The Transit Increase: Reaction." *New York Times*, March 6.

Kessler-Harris, Alice. 1982. *Out to Work: A History of Wage-Earning Women in the United States*. New York: Oxford University Press.

Kessner, Thomas. 1989. *Fiorello H. La Guardia and the Making of Modern New York*. New York: McGraw-Hill.

Kiepper, Alan F. 1994. "New York Restores Class to a Classic Metro." *Railway Gazette International* 150, no. 1 (January): 37–39.

Klein, Norman M. 1997. *The History of Forgetting: Los Angeles and the Erasure of Memory*. New York: Verso.

Kleniewski, Nancy. 1984. "From Industrial to Corporate City: The Role of Urban Renewal." In *Marxism and the Metropolis: New Perspectives in Urban Political Economy*, ed. William K. Tabb and Larry Sawers. 2d ed. New York: Oxford University Press.

Koskela, Hille. 2000. "'The Gaze Without Eyes': Video Surveillance and the Changing Nature of Urban Space." *Progress in Human Geography* 24 (2): 243–265.

Krajicek, David J. 1998. *Scooped! Media Miss Real Story on Crime While Chasing Sex, Sleaze, and Celebrities.* New York: Columbia University Press.

Kroloff, Reed. 1997. "Disney Builds a Town." *Architecture* 86 (8): 114.

Krutnik, Frank. 1991. *In a Lonely Street: Film Noir, Genre, Masculinity.* New York: Routledge.

Kuznick, Peter J. 1994. "Losing the World of Tomorrow: The Battle over the Presentation of Science at the 1939 New York World's Fair." *American Quarterly* 46 (3): 341–373.

La Guardia, F. H. 1939. "Principles and Policies of Administration." In *New York Advancing*, ed. Rebecca B. Rankin. World's Fair Edition. New York: Publishers Printing Co.

Laclau, Ernesto, and Chantal Mouffe. 1989. *Hegemony and Socialist Strategy: Towards a Radical Democratic Politics.* New York: Verso.

Lally, Kevin. 1996. *Wilder Times: The Life of Billy Wilder.* New York: Henry Holt.

Laslett, John H. M. 1996. "Historical Perspectives: Immigration and the Rise of a Distinctive Urban Region, 1900–1970." In *Ethnic Los Angeles*, ed. R. D. Waldinger and M. Bozorgmehr. New York: Russell Sage Foundation.

Le Corbusier. 1933/1967. *The Radiant City: Elements of a Doctrine of Urbanism to Be Used as the Basis of Our Machine-Age Civilization*, trans. Pamela Knight, Eleanor Levieux, and Derek Coltman. Reprint, New York: Orion Press.

Leccese, Michael, and Kathleen McCormick, eds. 2000. *Charter of the New Urbanism.* New York: McGraw-Hill.

Leeds, Mark. 1996. *Passport's Guide to Ethnic New York: A Complete Guide to the Many Faces and Cultures of New York.* 2d ed. Lincolnwood, Ill.: Passport Books.

Lefebvre, Henri. 1991. *The Production of Space.* Oxford, England: Blackwell.

Leffert, Dennis J. 1996. "Pursue All Criminals, Including the Illegal Border Crossers." Letter. *San Diego Union-Tribune*, May 3.

Lempinen, Edward W., and Glen Martin. 1996. "School, Bridge Bonds Coasting to Win: Mountain Lion Hunting Proposal Is Apparently Shot Down." *San Francisco Chronicle*, March 27.

Levinson, Pearl E. 1939. "World of Tomorrow." In *The Official Poem of the New York World's Fair, 1939.* New York: Browne.

Lewis Mumford Center. 2001. *Ethnic Diversity Grows, Neighborhood Integration Is at a Standstill.* Albany, N.Y.: Lewis Mumford Center.

Lieberman Research East. 1996. *Citywide Survey: New York City Transit Evaluation.* Prepared for Metropolitan Transportation Authority and New York City Transit.

Liff, Mark. 1984. "New York: Modernization Is the Key." *Mass Transit* 11, no. 4 (April): 8, 32.

Limbaugh, Rush. 1993. *See I Told You So.* New York: Pocket Books.

Lindquist, Diane. 1996a. "10 Years After Enactment of Reform Legislation, Immigrant Problems Have Mushroomed in Rural California." *San Diego Union-Tribune*, September 22.

————. 1996b. "A Struggle to Educate, Find Jobs for Flood of Newcomers." *San Diego Union-Tribune*, September 23.

Lippman, John. 1995. "Take the PG Train: New York Subways Travel to Hollywood." *Wall Street Journal*, August 9.

Lippmann, Walter. 1939. "A Day at the World's Fair." *Current History* 50 (July): 50–51.

Lipsitz, George. 1990. *Time Passages: Collective Memory and American Popular Culture*. Minneapolis: University of Minnesota Press.

————. 1994. *Rainbow At Midnight: Labor and Culture in the 1940s*. Urbana: University of Illinois Press.

————. 1998. *The Possessive Investment in Whiteness: How White People Profit from Identity Politics*. Philadelphia: Temple University Press.

Logan, John R., and Harvey L. Molotch. 1987. *Urban Fortunes: The Political Economy of Place*. Berkeley: University of California Press.

Los Angeles Times. 2003. "Third Stabbing in as Many Days on Subway." January 13.

Lowe, Eugene T. 2004. *A Status Report on Hunger and Homelessness in America's Cities*. Washington, D.C.: U.S. Conference of Mayors.

Luccarelli, Mark. 1995. *Lewis Mumford and the Ecological Region: The Politics of Planning*. New York: Guilford Press.

Lueck, Thomas J. 2000. "Giuliani Seeks Safer Stations For Subways." *New York Times*, June 7.

Luo, Michael. 2004. "Mistakes During a Subway Fire Spur New Emergency Training." *New York Times*, May 1.

MacCannell, Dean. 1999. "'New Urbanism' and Its Discontents." In *Giving Ground: The Politics of Propinquity*, ed. Joan Copjec and Michael Sorkin. London: Verso.

Maceck, Carl. 1988. "Blue Dahlia." In *Film Noir: An Encyclopedic Reference to the American Style*, ed. Alain Silver and Elizabeth Ward. Rev. ed. Woodstock, N.Y.: Overlook Press.

MacKaye, Benton. 1930. "The Townless Highway." *New Republic*, March 12, pp. 93–95.

MacKaye, Benton, and Lewis Mumford. 1931. "Townless Highways for the Motorist: A Proposal for the Motor Age." *Harper's Monthly*, August, 347–356.

Mann, Eric. 2004. "Los Angeles Bus Riders Derail the MTA." In *Highway Robbery: Transportation Racism and New Routes to Equity*, ed. Robert D. Bullard, Glenn S. Johnson, and Angel O. Torres. Cambridge, Mass.: South End Press.

Marsh, Margaret. 1990. *Suburban Lives*. New Brunswick, N.J.: Rutgers University Press.

Marshall, Alex. 2000. *How Cities Work: Suburbs, Sprawl, and the Roads Not Taken*. Austin: University of Texas Press.

Martin, Douglas. 1995. "Planned Bus and Subway Cuts Result in Protests at a Hearing." *New York Times*, April 28.

Marx, Karl. 1867/1977. *Capital: A Critique of Political Economy*, trans. B. Fowkes. New York: Vintage Books.

Massey, Douglas S., and Nancy A. Denton. 1993. *American Apartheid: Segregation and the Making of the Underclass*. Cambridge, Mass.: Harvard University Press.

Maxfield, James F. 1996. *The Fatal Woman: Sources of Male Anxiety in American Film Noir, 1941–1991*. Madison, Wisc.: Fairleigh Dickinson University Press.

Mazón, Mauricio. 1984. *The Zoot-Suit Riots: The Psychology of Symbolic Annihilation*. Austin: University of Texas Press.

McCormick, Erin. 2001. "Number of State Prisoners Soared in '90s." *San Francisco Chronicle*, August 9.

McDonagh, Eileen L. 1999. "The Metropolis and Multicultural Ethics: Direct Democracy Versus Deliberative Democracy in the Progressive Era." In *Progressivism and the New Democracy*, ed. S. M. Milkis and J. M. Mileur. Amherst: University of Massachusetts Press.

McShane, Clay. 1994. *Down the Asphalt Path: The Automobile and the American City*. New York: Columbia University Press.

McWilliams, Carey. 1946. *Southern California Country: An Island on the Land*. New York: Duel Sloan and Pearce.

———. 1948/1972. *North From Mexico: The Spanish-Speaking People of the United States*. Reprint, New York: Greenwood Press.

Meeks, Kenneth. 2000. *Driving While Black: Highways, Shopping Malls, Taxicabs, Sidewalks: How To Fight Back If You Are a Victim of Racial Profiling*. New York: Broadway Books.

Meethan, Kevin 1996. "Consuming (In) The Civilized City." *Annals of Tourism Research* 23 (2): 322–340.

Meikle, Jeffrey L. 1984. *The City of Tomorrow: Model 1937*. London: Pentagram Design.

Metropolitan Transportation Authority (MTA). 1990. *MTA Capital Needs and Opportunities: 1992–2011*. New York: MTA.

———. 1993. *1992 Annual Report*. New York: MTA.

———. 1997. *1996 Annual Report*. New York: MTA.

———. 2002. *2001 Annual Report*. New York: MTA.

Metropolitan Transportation Authority (MTA) Arts for Transit. 1990a. *Arts for Transit*. Brochure. New York: MTA.

———. 1990b. Permanent Art Policy. Instruction. New York: MTA.

———. 1994. *Art En Route: MTA Arts for Transit*. Exhibition catalogue. New York: MTA.

———. 1996. *Your Guide to Art in the MTA Network*. New York: MTA.

Meyer, Stephen Grant. 2000. *As Long as They Don't Move Next Door: Segregation and Racial Conflict in American Neighborhoods*. Lanham, Md.: Rowman and Littlefield.

Meyers, Jeffrey. 2000. Introduction to *Double Indemnity*, by Billy Wilder and Raymond Chandler. Screenplay. Berkeley: University of California Press.

Miller, Donald, ed. 1986. *The Lewis Mumford Reader*. New York: Pantheon Books.

———. 1989. *Lewis Mumford: A Life*. New York: Weidenfeld and Nicolson.

Miller, Ivor. 1991. "Night Train: The Power That Man Made." *New York Folklore* 17 (1–2): 21–43.

———. 1994. "Creolizing for Survival in the City." *Cultural Critique* (spring): 153–188.

Mizell, Louis. 1998. *Aggressive Driving*. Washington, D.C.: AAA Foundation for Traffic Safety.

Moberg, David. 1990. "Chicago: The Legacy of Harold Washington." In *Fire in the Hearth: The Radical Politics of Place in America*, ed. M. Davis. London: Verso.

Moffett, C. 1900. "Automobiles for the Average Man." *Review of Reviews* 21 (July): 704–710.

Moffett, S. E. 1903. "The War on the Locomotive: The Marvelous Development of the Trolley Car System." *McClure*, March, 451–462.

Mollenkopf, John H. 1983. *The Contested City*. Princeton, N.J.: Princeton University Press.

———. 1992. *A Phoenix in the Ashes: The Rise and Fall of the Koch Coalition in New York*. Princeton, N.J.: Princeton University Press.

Mollenkopf, John, and Manuel Castells, eds. 1991. *Dual City: Restructuring New York*. New York: Russell Sage Foundation.

Monkkonen, Eric H. 1988. *America Becomes Urban: The Development of U.S. Cities and Towns 1780–1980*. Berkeley: University of California Press.

Morley, David. 2000. *Home Territories: Media, Mobility, and Identity*. New York: Routledge.

Morris, Meaghan. 1990. "Banality in Cultural Studies." In *Logics of Television*, ed. Patricia Mellencamp. Bloomington: Indiana University Press.

Morrison, Toni. 1997. "The Official Story: Dead Man Golfing." In *Birth of a Nation'hood: Gaze, Script, and Spectacle in the O. J. Simpson Case*, ed. Toni Morrison and Claudia Brodsky Lacour. New York: Pantheon Books.

Morse, Margaret. 1990. "The Ontology of Everyday Distraction." In *Logics of Television*, ed. Patricia Mellencamp. Bloomington: Indiana University Press.

Mosley, Walter. 1990. *Devil in a Blue Dress*. New York: W. W. Norton.

Mueller, Roswitha. 2002. "The City and Its Other." *Discourse* 24 (2): 30–49.

Mumford, Lewis. 1924. *Sticks and Stones: A Study of American Architecture and Civilization*. New York: Horace Liveright.

———. 1926. *The Golden Day: A Study in American Experience and Culture*. New York: Boni and Liveright.

———. 1931. *The Brown Decades: A Study in the Arts in America 1865–1895*. New York: Harcourt, Brace.

———. 1938. *The Culture of Cities*. New York. Harcourt, Brace.

———. 1945. *City Development: Studies in Disintegration and Renewal*. New York: Harcourt, Brace.

———. 1953. *The Highway and the City*. New York: Harcourt, Brace and World.

———. 1955. *The Human Prospect*. Beacon Paperbacks, 13. Boston: Beacon Press.

———. 1960. Introduction to *Garden Cities of to-Morrow*, by Ebenezer Howard. London: Faber and Faber.

———. 1961. *The City in History: Its Origins, Its Transformations, and Its Prospects*. New York: Harcourt, Brace and World.

———. 1968. *The Urban Prospect*. New York: Harcourt, Brace and World.

———. 1986a. "The Regional Framework of Civilization." In *The Lewis Mumford Reader*, ed. Donald Miller. New York: Pantheon Books.

———. 1986b. "Technics and Human Development." In *The Lewis Mumford Reader*, ed. Donald Miller. New York: Pantheon Books.

Munsey, Frank. 1903. "Impressions by the Way." *Munsey's Magazine*, May, 181–183.

Naremore, James. 1998. *More Than Night: Film Noir in Its Contexts*. Berkeley: University of California Press.

Neutra, Richard J. 1940. "Homes and Housing." In *Los Angeles: Preface to a Master Plan*, ed. George William Robbins and Leon Deming Tilton. Los Angeles: Pacific Southwest Academy.

New York Daily News. 1996. "Wrong Way Subway." May 5.

New York Public Library. 1999. *African American Desk Reference*. New York: J. Wiley and Sons.

New York Times. 1939a. "Housing Is Termed Social Insurance." May 19.

———. 1939b. "Union Threatens to Widen Strike." May 19.

———. 1998. "The Inauguration of Rudolph W. Giuliani." January 2.

Norman, H. 1903. "Can I Afford an Automobile." *World's Work* 6 (June): 3502–3505.

Nuñez, Ralph. 2001. "Family Homelessness in New York City: A Case Study." *Political Science Quarterly* 116 (3): 367–379.

Omi, Michael, and Howard Winant. 1993. "The Los Angeles 'Race Riot' and Contemporary U.S. Politics." In *Reading Rodney King: Reading Urban Uprising*, ed. Robert Gooding-Williams. New York: Routledge.

Omi, Michael, and Howard Winant. 1994. *Racial Formation in the United States*. 2nd ed. New York: Routledge.

Otis, Johnny. 1993. *Upside Your Head!: Rhythm and Blues on Central Avenue*. Introduction by George Lipsitz. Hanover, N.H.: U.P. of New England.

Palmer, R. Barton, ed. 1996. *Perspectives on Film Noir*. New York: G. K. Hall.

Panunzio, Constantine. 1940. "Growth and Character of the Population." In *Los Angeles: Preface to a Master Plan*, ed. George William Robbins and Leon Deming Tilton. Los Angeles: Pacific Southwest Academy.

Pearlman, Jeff. 1999. "At Full Blast." *Sports Illustrated*, December 27.

Peiss, Kathy. 1986. *Cheap Amusements: Working Women and Leisure in Turn of the Century New York*. Philadelphia: Temple University Press.

Pérez-Peña, Richard. 1995a. "Mayor and Transit Officials Clash over Service Cutbacks." *New York Times*, February 23.

———. 1995b. "Last Minute Efforts Made to Avert 25¢ Fare Increase." *New York Times*, October 18.

Pierre-Pierre, Garry. 1997. "Immigration Fosters Surge in Subway Use." *New York Times*, February 11.

Piven, Frances Fox, and Richard A. Cloward. 1979. *Poor People's Movements: Why They Succeed, How They Fail*. New York: Vintage.

Pollock, Friedrich. 1941/1988. "State Capitalism: Its Possibilities and Limitations." Reproduced in *The Frankfurt School Reader*, ed. Andrew Arato and Eike Gebhart. New York: Continuum.

Pringle, Paul, and Shanté Morgan. 1994. "O.J. in Custody, at Last." *San Diego Union-Tribune*, June 18.

Purnick, Joyce. 2000. "City Is More Than Where a Subway Is." *New York Times*, October 23.

Rae, John B. 1965. *The American Automobile: A Brief History*. Chicago: University of Chicago Press.

Reed, Adolph L. 2005. "The 2004 Election in Perspective: The Myth of 'Cultural Divide' and the Triumph of Neoliberal Ideology." *American Quarterly* 57 (1): 1–15.

Reid, Torin. 1993. "The TA Is Back." *Passenger Train Journal* 24, no. 8 (August): 24–35.

Relph, Edward. 1987. *The Modern Urban Landscape*. Baltimore: Johns Hopkins University Press.

Rendall, Steven, Jim Naureckas, and Jeff Cohen. 1995. *The Way Things Aren't: Rush Limbaugh's Reign of Error*. New York: New Press.

Robbins, George William, and Leon Deming Tilton, eds. 1940. *Los Angeles: Preface to a Master Plan*. Los Angeles: Pacific Southwest Academy.

Roberts, Edwin A. 2000. "Sociological Thoughts of John Rocker." *Tampa Tribune*, January 16.

Roberts, Robert. 1988. "The Big Apple Has a Mega Transit Rehab Program." *Modern Railroads* 43, no. 10 (June): 26–30.

Robin, Joshua. 2005. "Camera Ban Undeveloped." *Newsday*, March 15.

Rofe, John. 1997. "Troubles Encroach on Fantasyland." *San Diego Union-Tribune*, September 7.

Rose, Mark H. 1990. *Interstate: Express Highway Politics, 1939–1989*. Rev. ed. Knoxville: University of Tennessee Press.

Rose, Tricia. 1994. *Black Noise: Rap Music and Black Culture in Contemporary America*. Hanover, N.H.: Wesleyan University Press.

Rosenzweig, Roy, and Elizabeth Blackmar. 1992. *The Park and the People: A History of Central Park*. Ithaca, N.Y.: Cornell University Press.

Ross, Andrew. 1999. *The Celebration Chronicles: Life, Liberty, and the Pursuit of Property Value in Disney's New Town*. New York: Ballantine Books.

Rubin, Jay. 1978. "Black Nativism: The European Immigrant in Negro Thought, 1830–1860." *Phylon* 39 (3): 193–202.

Ruiz, Vicki. 1992. "The Flapper and the Chaperone: Historical Memory Among Mexican-American Women." In *Seeking Common Ground: Multidisciplinary Studies of Immigrant Women in the United States*, ed. Donna R. Gabaccia. Westport, Conn.: Greenwood Press.

Russell, Katheryn K. 1998. *The Color of Crime: Racial Hoaxes, White Fear, Black Protectionism, Police Harassment, and Other Macroaggressions*. New York: New York University Press.

Ryan, Mary P. 1992. "Gender and Public Access: Women's Politics in Nineteenth-Century America." In *Habermas and the Public Sphere*, ed. Craig Calhoun. Cambridge, Mass.: MIT Press.

Rydell, Robert W. 1993. *World of Fairs: The Century-of-Progress Exposi-tions*. Chicago: University of Chicago Press.

Sabagh, Georges, and Mehdi Bozorgmehr. 2003. "From 'Give Me Your Poor' to 'Save Our State': New York and Los Angeles as Immigrant Cities and Regions." In *New York and Los Angeles: Politics, Society, and Culture: A Comparative View*, ed. David Halle. Chicago: University of Chicago Press.

Salmon, Lucy M. 1892. "A Statistical Inquiry Concerning Domestic Ser-vice." *Publications of the American Statistical Association* 3 (18/19): 89–118.

San Francisco Chronicle. 1993. "Feinstein Wants Border Control to Be a Top Priority in Budget." May 28.

Sánchez, George J. 1993. *Becoming Mexican American: Ethnicity, Culture, and Identity in Chicano Los Angeles, 1900–1945*. New York: Oxford University Press.

Sanchez, Leonel. 2000. "Latinos Protest Ethnic Profiling." *San Diego Union-Tribune*, July 24.

Sassen, Saskia. 1991. *The Global City: New York, London, Tokyo*. Prince-ton, N.J.: Princeton University Press.

———. 2001. *The Global City: New York, London, Tokyo*. 2d ed. Princeton, N.J.: Princeton University Press.

Saxton, Alexander. 1990. *The Rise and Fall of the White Republic: Class Politics and Mass Culture in Nineteenth-Century America*. New York: Verso.

Scarritt, W. E. 1903. "The Low Priced Automobile." *Munsey's Magazine*, May, 178–180.

Scharff, Virginia. 1991. *Taking the Wheel: Women and the Coming of the Motor Age*. New York: Free Press.

Schatz, Thomas. 1981. *Hollywood Genres: Formulas, Filmmaking, and the Studio System*. New York: Random House.

Scheier, Rachel. 1994. "Art Interrupts Grit and Grime in N.Y. Subways." *Christian Science Monitor*, September 23.

Schiller, Herbert I. 1989. *Culture Inc.: The Corporate Takeover of Public Expression*. New York: Oxford University Press.

Schivelbusch, Wolfgang. 1986. *The Railway Journey: The Industrialization of Time and Space in the 19th Century*. Berkeley: University of Califor-nia Press.

Schmitt, Peter J. 1990. *Back to Nature: The Arcadian Myth in Urban Amer-ica*. Baltimore: Johns Hopkins University Press.

Schneirov, Matthew. 1994. *The Dream of a New Social Order: Popular Mag-azines in America 1893–1914*. New York: Columbia University Press.

Schoch, Deborah. 2005. "Deputy, Suspect Wounded in Blue Line Shooting." *Los Angeles Times*, March 25.

Schou, Nick. 2001. "Mouse Chow." *OC Weekly*, December 14, p. 18.

Schrader, Paul. 1972. "Notes on Film Noir." *Film Comment* 8:1.

Schwartz, Richard. 2005. "Tracks of Our Tears." *New York Daily News*, May 9.

Scientific American. 1903. "Automobile News." May 9, p. 354.

Seaton, Charles. 1993. Deputy Director, Public Affairs, New York City Transit Authority (NYCTA). Interview by the author. Brooklyn, New York. August 23.

———. 1994. "Scheduled Maintenance Improves New York Subway's Service." *Mass Transit* 20 (2): 32.

Seldes, Gilbert. 1939. *Your World of Tomorrow.* New York: Rogers-Kellog-Stillson.

Sennett, Richard. 1990. *The Conscience of the Eye: The Design and Social Life of Cities.* New York: W. W. Norton.

Sharpe, William, and Leonard Wallock. 1994. "Bold New City or Built-Up Burb? Redefining Contemporary Suburbia." *American Quarterly* 46, no. 1 (March): 1–30.

Shields, Rob. 1992. "Spaces for the Subject of Consumption." In *Lifestyle Shopping: The Subject of Consumption,* ed. Rob Shields. London: Routledge.

Shulman, Claire. 1999. "Too Many Immigrants?" *New York Daily News,* September 14.

Silver, Alain, and Elizabeth Ward, eds. 1988. *Film Noir: An Encyclopedic Reference to the American Style.* Rev. ed. Woodstock, N.Y.: Overlook Press.

Skinner, M. 1902. "The Electric Car and the Changes It Has Brought." *Atlantic Monthly,* June, 799–808.

Sloan, Gene. 2001. "Disney Bets on New Anaheim 'Adventure.'" *USA Today,* February 2.

Smith, Neil. 1996. *The New Urban Frontier: Gentrification and the Revanchist City.* New York: Routledge.

———. 1998. "Giuliani Time: The Revanchist 1990s." *Social Text* 16 (4): 1–20.

———. 1999. "Which New Urbanism?: New York City and the Revanchist 1990s." In *The Urban Moment: Cosmopolitan Essays on the Late-20th-Century City,* ed. Robert A. Beauregard and Sophie Body-Gendrot. Thousand Oaks, Calif.: Sage.

Soja, Edward W. 1989. *Postmodern Geographies: The Reassertion of Space in Critical Social Theory.* New York: Verso.

Sorkin, Michael, ed. 1992. *Variations on a Theme Park: The New American City and the End of Public Space.* New York: Noonday Press.

Spectator. 1901. "Observations on Electric Railroads." *Outlook,* August 31, pp. 1000–1002.

———. 1903. "The Charm of Trolley Cars." *Outlook,* September 12, pp. 109–110.

Speed, G. 1900. "Modern Chariot." *Cosmopolitan,* June, 139–152.

St. Clair, David J. 1986. *The Motorization of American Cities.* New York: Praeger.

Steinberg, Stephen. 1989. *The Ethnic Myth: Race, Ethnicity, and Class in America.* Boston: Beacon Press.

Stewart, Susan. 1991. *Crimes of Writing: Problems in the Containment of Representation.* New York: Oxford University Press.

Stilgoe, John R. 1988. *Borderland: Origins of the American Suburb, 1820–1939*. New Haven, Conn.: Yale University Press.

Stookey, Lee. 1992. *Subway Ceramics: A History and Iconography*. Brooklyn, N.Y.: privately printed by Lee Stookey.

Sugrue, Thomas J. 1996. *The Origins of the Urban Crisis: Race and Inequality in Postwar Detroit*. Princeton, N.J.: Princeton University Press.

Sunstein, Cass R. 2002. *Republic.Com*. Princeton, N.J.: Princeton University Press.

Susman, Warren I. 1980. "The People's Fair: Cultural Contradictions of a Consumer Society." In *Dawn of A New Day: The New York World's Fair, 1939/40*, ed. Helen Harrison. New York: New York University Press.

Tabb, William K. 1982. *The Long Default: New York City and the Urban Fiscal Crisis*. New York: Monthly Review Press.

Takaki, Ronald T. 1998. *Strangers from a Different Shore: A History of Asian Americans*. Rev. ed. Boston: Little, Brown.

Tanenbaum, Susie J. 1995. *Underground Harmonies: Music and Politics in the Subways of New York*. Ithaca, N.Y.: Cornell University Press.

Tarr, Joel A. 1996. *The Search for the Ultimate Sink: Urban Pollution in Historical Perspective*. Akron, Ohio: University of Akron Press.

Taylor, Kathleen. 2002. "New Residents Ought to Learn to Speak English." Letter. *Columbus (Ohio) Dispatch*, June 22.

Tebbel, John. 1969. *The American Magazine: A Compact History*. New York: Hawthorne Books.

Teicher, Stacy A. 2004. "Where 'English Only' Falls Short." *Christian Science Monitor*, January 26, p. 13.

Terzian, Philip. 2000. "Crude, but Not off His Rocker." Opinion column. *Montreal Gazette*, January 12.

Torre, Susana. 1999. "Expanding the Urban Design Agenda: A Critique of the New Urbanism." In *Design and Feminism: Re-Visioning Spaces, Places, and Everyday Things*, ed. Joan Rothschild. New Brunswick, N.J.: Rutgers University Press.

Trachtenberg, Alan. 1980. "Mumford in the Twenties: The Historian as Artist." *Salmagundi* 49: 29–42.

———. 1982. *The Incorporation of America: Culture and Society in the Gilded Age*. New York: Hill and Wang.

Turner, Frederick Jackson. 1893. *The Significance of the Frontier in American History*. Irvington Reprint Series, History Reprint H-214. New York: Irvington.

U.S. Department of Transportation, Bureau of Transportation Statistics. 2003. Highlights of the 2001 National Household Travel Survey. Washington, D.C. At http://www.bts.gov/programs/national_household_travel_survey.

U.S. House of Representatives Surface Transportation Subcommittee. 1997. Testimony by David K. Willis, president and chief executive officer of AAA Foundation for Traffic Safety, and David F. Snyder, assistant general counsel of the American Insurance Association. July 17.

Van Duyne, Schulyer. 1939. "'Talking Train' Tour, World's Fair Exhibit." *Popular Science*, July, 102–105.

Vargo, J. O. E. 2002. "Unwanted Anniversary." *(Riverside, Calif.) Press-Enterprise,* June 2.

Vartabedian, Ralph. 2001. "Smart Highway Idea Advances, but at Only a Rush-Hour Pace." *Los Angeles Times,* May 30.

Vest, Jason, Warren Cohen, and Mike Tharp. 1997. "Road Rage: Tailgating, Giving the Finger, Outright Violence." *U.S. News and World Report,* June 2, p. 24.

von Sternberg, Bob. 2001. "Trouble over Immigration Brews in Mason City." *(Minneapolis) Star Tribune,* July 23.

Wald, Matthew L. 1997. "Appalled by Risk, Except in the Car." *New York Times,* June 15.

Waldinger, Roger David, and Mehdi Bozorgmehr, eds. 1996. *Ethnic Los Angeles.* New York: Russell Sage Foundation.

Wallace, Mike. 2002. *A New Deal for New York.* New York: Bell and Weiland.

Wallock, Leonard. 1991. "The Myth of the Master Builder: Robert Moses, New York, and the Dynamics of Metropolitan Development Since World War II." *Journal of Urban History* 17, no. 4 (August): 339–362.

Ward, Colin. 1973. "Notes on the Future of Vandalism." In *Vandalism,* ed. Colin Ward. New York: Van Nostrand Reinhold.

Warner, Fara. 1994. "DKNY Takes Upscale Ads Underground." *Wall Street Journal,* October 6.

Warner, Michael. 1992. "The Mass Public and the Mass Subject." In *Habermas and the Public Sphere,* ed. Craig Calhoun. Cambridge, Mass.: MIT Press.

Warner, Sam Bass. 1962. *Streetcar Suburbs: The Process of Growth in Boston, 1870–1900.* Cambridge, Mass.: Harvard University Press.

Webb, Michael. 1996. "Smugglers of Illegal Immigrants Are Villains in the Border Saga." Opinion column. *San Diego Union-Tribune,* December 21.

Weisberg, Lori. 1994. "Clusters of Urban Villages Key To New American Housing Dream." *San Diego Union-Tribune,* May 1.

West, Nathanael. 1939/1983. *The Day of the Locust.* Reprint, New York: Signet Classic.

Whalen, Grover. 1939. *Introduction to Your World of Tomorrow.* New York: Rogers-Kellog-Stillson.

Whitten, R. 1931. "Facilitating Traffic and Preventing Blight by Spacious Planning of Express Highways." *American City* 45 (August): 80.

Whyte, William Foote. 1981. *Street Corner Society: The Social Structure of an Italian Slum.* 3d ed. Chicago: University of Chicago Press.

Whyte, William H. 1988. *City: Rediscovering the Center.* New York: Doubleday.

Wilder, Billy, and Raymond Chandler. 1943. *Double Indemnity.* Script. Los Angeles: Paramount Studio.

Wilentz, Sean. 2004. "Hicks Nixed Slicks' Pick." *Los Angeles Times,* November 7.

Will, George F. 1994. "Squeegee Clean in New York City." *New York Times,* December 1.

Williams, Jeff. 1996. "Those Apt to Break Vehicle Laws Can Usually Be Spotted." Letter. *San Diego Union-Tribune*, June 6.

Williams, Rhonda. 1993. "Accumulation as Evisceration: Urban Rebellion and the New Growth Dynamics." In *Reading Rodney King: Reading Urban Uprising*, ed. Robert Gooding-Williams. New York: Routledge.

Wilson, Elizabeth. 1991. *The Sphinx in the City: Urban Life, the Control of Disorder, and Women*. Berkeley: University of California Press.

Wilson, William H. 1996. "The Glory, Destruction, and Meaning of the City Beautiful Movement." In *Readings in Planning Theory*, ed. S. Campbell and S. S. Fainstein. Cambridge, Mass.: Blackwell.

Wilson Quarterly. 1991. "Underground Disorder." Vol. 15, no. 3 (summer): 16–19.

Winton, Richard, and Rong-Gong Lin II. 2005. "Freeway Shootings Share Similar Traits but Seem to Be Unrelated." *Los Angeles Times*, June 29.

Worth, Robert F. 2005. "On Public Transportation, the Mood Is Wary but Calm." *New York Times*, July 9.

Wright, Gwendolyn. 1981. *Building the Dream: A Social History of Housing in America*. New York: Pantheon Books.

Yago, Glenn. 1984. *The Decline of Transit: Urban Transportation in German and U.S. Cities, 1900–1970*. New York: Cambridge University Press.

Yoachum, Susan, and Marc Sandalow. 1994. "Clinton Comes Out Against Prop 187." *San Francisco Chronicle*, October 22.

Zierer, Clifford M. 1940. "The Land Use Patterns." In *Los Angeles: Preface to a Master Plan*, ed. George William Robbins and Leon Deming Tilton. Los Angeles: Pacific Southwest Academy.

Zim, Larry, Mel Lerner, and Herbert Rolf. 1988. *The World of Tomorrow: The 1939 New York World's Fair*. New York: Harper and Row.

Zukin, Sharon. 1995. *The Culture of Cities*. New York: Blackwell.

INDEX

Italic page numbers refer to illustrations.